The [German] bivouac area was near a sand road which led through the forest. All the vehicles of the brigade headquarters and the artillery echelon were parked in the underbrush and were well camouflaged by the high trees. The entire area was under Russian observation and shells continually landed ... with no hits on important targets. One day a strong easterly wind came up, and artillery fire into the area ceased except toward the east, where an occasional muffled burst was heard to which no attention was paid. Suddenly the German sentries ran out of the woods with bewildered expressions shouting, "Fire! Fire!" And behind them could be seen a high, wide wall of fire, rushing and roaring toward the command post at great speed ...

Entirely new to the Germans was the Russian use of fires as a hot weather weapon in midsummer when the trees were tinder dry. Not only the physical but the psychological impact of such fires was severe. The crackling of the burning trees, the acrid gray-black smoke, the increasingly unbearable heat, and the feeling of uncertainty put troops under a severe strain. Fleeing before towering sheets of flame, men would fight through mile after mile of burning forest only to be confronted by enemy bunkers and fortified positions. Ammunition dumps blew sky high and gave the impression that fierce battles were raging to the rear.

FIGHTING IN HELL

The German Ordeal on the Eastern Front

Edited by Peter G. Tsouras

IVY BOOKS • NEW YORK

An Ivy Book
Published by The Ballantine Publishing Group
Introduction copyright © 1995 by Peter Tsouras/Lionel Leventhal Limited
The collective work copyright © 1995 by Lionel Leventhal Limited

Fighting in Hell comprises four U.S. Department of the Army publications that have been adjusted for this edition, with a new Introduction: *Russian Combat Methods in World War II*, Department of the Army pamphlet no. 20-230, Washington D.C., November 1950; *Effects of Climate on Combat in European Russia*, Department of the Army pamphlet no. 20-291, Washington D.C., February 1952; *Warfare in the Far North*, Department of the Army pamphlet no. 20-292, Washington D.C., October 1951; and *Combat in Russian Forests and Swamps*, Department of the Army pamphlet no. 20-231, Washington D.C., July 1951.

http://www.randomhouse.com

Library of Congress Catalog Card Number: 97-94185

ISBN 0-8041-1698-9

Manufactured in the United States of America

First Ballantine Books Edition: January 1998

10 9 8 7 6 5 4 3 2 1

Contents

Contents

Contents

List of Maps

Introduction

. . . the landscape up there in the tundra outside Murmansk is just as it was after the Creation. There's not a tree, not a shrub, not a human settlement. No roads and no paths. Nothing but rock and scree. There are countless torrents, lakes and fast-flowing rivers with rapids and waterfalls. In the summer there's swamp—and in winter there's ice, snow, and it's 40 to 50 degrees below. Icy gales rage throughout the eight months of Arctic night. This 100 kilometers of tundra belt surrounding Murmansk like a protective armor is one big wilderness. War has never before been waged in this tundra, since the pathless stony desert is virtually impenetrable for formations . . .

Such was the unappreciated warning of General Eduard Dietl to Adolf Hitler as he prepared to extend Operation BARBA-ROSSA to the shores of the White Sea. Dietl was one of the few officers with a sober appreciation of the absolutely unique environment of war into which the German Army was about to be hurled. And Dietl was describing only one of the terrible facets of the total enemy that was Russia. Yet the feckless attitude pervading the senior levels of the German armed forces and Hitler's entourage was summed up by General Alfred Jodl, Chief of Operations of OKW—Oberkommando der Wehrmacht—"The Russian colossus will be proved to be a pig's bladder; prick it, and it will burst." The Russian colossus proved to be something entirely different. Though the official name was the Soviet Union, to the Germans their titanic struggle in the East was simply Der Russland Krieg—The Russia War. There was a stark truth to the name, for Russia in its every harsh dimension was totally at war with the Germans—the land in its primitive distances; the climate in its brutal extremes; and above all, its

1

people in their almost inhuman ability to absorb far more punishment than Germany's western opponents and then lethally strike back. Russia was a monster the Germans could not tame—a monster that eventually devoured its attacker.

Fighting in Hell is the second book published by Greenhill presenting German experiences on the Eastern Front in World War II. The first, *The Anvil of War: German Generalship in Defense on the Eastern Front* dealt with operational problems of the defense. *Fighting in Hell* is the account of fighting in the hostile environment of Russia, an experience for which the Germans were thoroughly unprepared. For the average German soldier, this was truly fighting in hell. This volume presents four accounts by senior German officers of their experiences of fighting in Russia, this very special and appalling war environment. These accounts were written under the auspices of the U.S. Army after the war,[1] and appeared as U.S. Department of the Army pamphlets in the German Report Series published in the early 1950s. The employment of captured German general and staff officers to write the military histories of their own campaigns was the brainchild of the late Brigadier General S.L.A. Marshall, assigned at the end of the war to the Military History Division of the European theater of operations (ETO). Originally the Germans began writing their histories as prisoners of war. Many had patriotic objections or feared Communist reprisals to family members still living in the Soviet zone of occupation, but their cooperation was ensured when the former Chief of the General Staff of the German Army (from 1938 to 1942), General Franz Halder, agreed to supervise and coordinate the efforts of his fellow officers. Halder was to continue in this role until his retirement in 1962 as a civilian employee of the U.S. Army. One prominent archivist remarked that it was Halder who thought the U.S. Army worked for him! Nevertheless, it was Halder's sense of organization and his reputation that carried the program forward. By 1954, 2,175 manuscripts totalling 77,000 pages had been written by 501 German Army, Waffen-SS, and Luftwaffe generals and eleven admirals, in addition to hundreds of specialists. After 1947 most of the officers were released from captivity and formally employed by the U.S. Army to prepare manuscripts on various topics based on their own experiences, with captured archives placed at their disposal. The only lapse, and for historians a major one, was the Army's failure to require the authors to footnote their work.[2]

However, the U.S. Army military historians who oversaw the preparation of the series were adamant about not superimposing their own ideas on the Germans and were at pains to point out: "The reader is reminded that publications in the GERMAN REPORT SERIES were written by Germans from the German point of view. . . . [and] present the views of the German author without interpretation by American personnel. . . . The authors' prejudices and defects, whatever they may be, find the same expression in the following translations as they do in the original German." It was a remarkable demonstration of professional self-restraint.[3] It is necessary to repeat a caveat for the reader of this edition as for those of the original pamphlets: "any mention of 'normal methods' or standard infantry tactics refers to German combat doctrines, and applies to units organized and equipped in accordance with German regulations."[4]

General Erhard Rauss takes pride of place in this volume, as he did in *The Anvil of War*. Described by Guderian as one of the German Army's finest panzer generals, Rauss commanded the Fourth and Third Panzer Armies in succession on the Eastern Front, having risen from command of division and corps. His defense of Kharkov in 1943 with the XI Corps was a masterpiece of skill and leadership. His subsequent commands of two panzer armies when the tide had turned in the East against the Germans were virtuoso performances of stubborn, wily, and often brilliant employment of the defense. He was ultimately sacked on a whim by Hitler in the last months of the war. Rauss' contributions in this book are: *Russian Combat Methods in World War II* (DA Pamphlet No. 20-230, 1950) and *Effects of Climate on Combat in European Russia* (DA Pamphlet No. 20-291, 1952). General der Infanterie Dr. Waldemar Erfurth wrote *Warfare in the Far North* (DA Pamphlet No. 20-292, 1951). General Erfurth represented the German

Armed Forces High Command at Finnish Headquarters from June 1941 until Finland made a separate peace with the Soviet Union in September 1944. He was to write a fuller history of operations on the Finnish fronts in his book, *Der Finnische Krieg 1941–1944* (Wiesbaden, 1950), the year before the U.S. Army published his pamphlet.[5] The fourth account, *Combat in Russian Forests and Swamps* (DA Pamphlet No. 20-231, 1951) was written by General der Infanterie Hans von Greiffenberg, who as Chief of Operations Section of the German General Staff played a critical role in the planning of Operation BARBAROSSA, the attack on the Soviet Union. Von Greiffenberg served as the Chief of Staff for XII Corps in the last months before BARBAROSSA in the summer of 1941. In May 1941 he was appointed Chief of Staff of Army Group Center, in which he served until May 1942. He subsequently served as Chief of Staff for Army Group A through August 1943. General Franz Halder, who supervised the production of the series from which these accounts are taken, wrote the foreword for Greiffenberg's account, which is not surprising given their close association on the Army General Staff. Together, these four accounts cover the entire military environment of Russia and provide the reader with first-hand experiences of war at its worst.

It was not as if the Germans had no experience of fighting the Russians. The Teutonic Knights had invaded Russia when it was already decimated by the Mongol storm in the thirteenth century, and yet in a battle of Homeric dimensions on the frozen surface of Lake Chud had been broken by the Russians, the survivors falling through the breaking ice to their well-deserved deaths. Five hundred years later, Frederick the Great had gone into his first battle with the Russians, contemptuously encouraging his grenadiers to slaughter those barbarians. He recoiled from this experience with a completely different attitude, announcing respectfully that it was not enough to kill a Russian—you had to knock him down, too. The father of modern strategy, Major General Carl von Clausewitz, had abandoned the Prussian service in 1807 to serve Tsar Alexander I in the ongoing struggle against Napoleon. He had fought on

Katuzov's staff throughout the man-killing campaign of 1812 and was an eyewitness to the ferocity of Russia's distances, climate, and people. He had witnessed the collapse of the most thoroughly prepared invasion in modern history to that time, preparations that proved pitifully inadequate, just as the German campaign of 1941 did. The horrific winter extremes that scythed through the Grande Armée had left its mark on him, in the reddish broken blood vessels on cheeks and nose, the scars of frostbite that his students later foolishly ascribed to too much affection for the bottle. And World War I on the Eastern Front had given the Germans four years of extended operational experience in this theater.

All of this was inexplicably forgotten as Hitler and the Oberkommando des Heeres, the Army General Staff, blithely planned for a single summer campaign to break the back of the Soviet Union. Hitler's overconfidence was understandable, given his loosening grip on reality, but there was no such excuse for the equal optimism of the General Staff, an organization that prided itself on meticulous planning. Winter clothing was only ordered for the sixty divisions that were to be left in occupation of European Russia after the successful summer campaign.[6] General Rauss, a fighting soldier from first to last, was to write after the war:

> . . . he who steps for the first time on Russian soil is immediately conscious of the new, the strange, the primitive. The German soldier who crossed into Russian territory felt that he entered a different world, where he was opposed not only by the forces of the enemy but also by the forces of nature.

> In 1941 the Wehrmacht did not recognize this force [i.e. the climate] and was not prepared to withstand its effects. Crisis upon crisis and unnecessary suffering were the result. Only the ability of German soldiers to bear up under misfortune prevented disaster. But the German Army never recovered from the first hard blow.[7]

The Germans unfortunately were the willful prisoners of their own experience; their wars historically were to the west or south, and incredibly they took no interest in operations elsewhere, as General Erfurth admits:

> In the year 1941 Germany had no practical knowledge concerning the effects of intense cold on men, animals, weapons, and motor vehicles. The men in Berlin were not certain in their minds as to which type of military clothing would offer the best protection against arctic cold. In the past the German General Staff had taken no interest in the history of wars in the north and east of Europe. No accounts of the wars of Russia against the Swedes, Finns, and Poles had ever been published in German. Nobody had ever taken into account the possibility that some day German divisions would have to fight and to winter in northern Karelia and on the Murmansk coast. The German General Staff was inclined on the whole to limit its studies to the central European region.[8]

Three times the Germans had invaded France in less than a hundred years. Belgium, the Netherlands, Denmark, and even Norway tucked into the northwestern edge of Europe had largely been in similar environment. It was a decent theater of war for a self-respecting soldier. The transportation and communication systems were dense and well developed. Paved roads were the norm; the railroads were extensive, well maintained, and the same gauge as the Reichsbahn—all very convenient. The land itself had been tamed into well-tended contours that facilitated military operations. The forests were carefully cut back, almost cultivated, so well-kept were they. The swamps had long been drained to make wide, flat, rich fields. The climate, especially in France, was if anything better than in Germany for extended campaigning. And the theater was literally drenched in the resources that would support war, especially once again in France with all its rich plenty. Most remarkably, the peoples of those countries understood the etiquette of war and had the good manners to know when they were beaten and not to take too long at it either. The southern Balkans had been rougher and wilder, and the Serbs and Greeks tougher and more recalcitrant, yet not so much as to put the Blitzkrieg in doubt.

From the very first, Operation BARBAROSSA was different. With every kilometer advance east, the pages of relevant German military experience were blown one by one out of the book. The Germans might as well have found themselves on a different planet, so unprepared were they for this experience. Everything happened on a grander scale—at first even their victories in the east dwarfed their western ones. Great frontier battles raged over distances that would have consumed one small Western European country after another. Prisoners poured in firstly by tens of thousands, then hundreds of thousands. The advancing columns ate up the distances, but the land before them laid a constant supply of new distance. The survivors remembered the endless dusty plains of summer that never seemed to end, and the forests and swamps that swallowed up divisions. Then the rains came and turned the land into thick, sucking glue. And when the frosts came to make the roads passable, they paused only briefly before plunging the thermometer so far down that oil turned viscous, machinery broke, and weapons froze. And the men died of the cold or were crippled by frostbite outside Moscow faster than the Angel of the Lord slew Sennacherib's cohorts "all gleaming in purple and gold" arrayed in their pride before Jerusalem.[9] Then the Russians, beaten by any reasonable standard, turned in one great reverse from headlong retreat into fanatic counterattack through the snow. One is reminded of the scene of the great Soviet counterattack outside Moscow in the *World at War* television series from the 1970s narrated by Laurence Olivier. The snow is blowing through the street of a burning village, and an old women, her rags whipped by the wind, is bowing and crossing herself, in the profoundest homage to the sons of the Russian land as they march by in pursuit of the Germans.

The German soldier needed little imagination to think he was fighting in hell. Here was no etiquette of war. One German veteran who had fought as a panzergrenadier on both fronts commented that in the West (1944–45), war was still fought as an honorable game where no one went out of his way to be vicious and where fighting tended to taper off after five in the afternoon—but in the East, "The Russians were trying to kill you—all the time!" A panzer company commander transferred from the Eastern Front to Normandy was shocked to see cease-fires called to clear away the wounded from both sides. In the East both sides would simply have driven over them to get at the enemy. Perhaps the dying of the Sixth Army at Stalingrad sums it up. Of the quarter million Germans thrown into the battle, dubbed the Rattenkrieg or Rats War, barely 92,000 survived. Of these barely 5,000 survived Soviet brutality and typhus epidemics to return home in the 1950s. There were other dimensions to the Russian theater of war as well. Everything in the Russland Krieg was outsize. The majesty of the Caucasus Mountains and their crystal clear vistas found their way into the account of a German 88mm antitank battery on the slope of a mountain. They spied a T34 deep in one of the mountain valleys through their stereoscopic sights at an incredible 7,000 meters. Their first round, really a lark, blew it up—a salute equally to the famous 88 and the awesome dimensions of Russia.

In spite of being thrown unexpectedly into hell, the German Army as an institution and the German soldier as an individual responded with remarkable toughness and ingenuity. Rauss' pride in their achievement is evident in his conclusion to *Russian Combat Methods*. "Despite Russia and the Russian, despite cold and mud, despite inadequate equipment and a virtually ridiculous numerical inferiority, the German soldier actually had a victory over the Soviets within his grasp."[10] That the Germans had come so close, despite their initial abysmal lack of planning for the unique military environment of Russia, and despite the suicidal leadership of Adolf Hitler, is an eternal testament to their skill as soldiers. That they failed is a further testament to the consequences of an evil cause begun in a spirit of reckless adventure that no amount of skill could overcome.

Peter G. Tsouras
Lieutenant Colonel, USAR (ret)
Alexandria, Virginia
1995

Notes

1. These accounts, along with thousands of others by former German general and senior staff officers, were written originally while the officers were prisoners of war. An account of this fruitful program putting the experiences of the German Army on paper is provided in the Introduction to *The Anvil of War* (London, Greenhill, 1994).

2. Detmar H. Finke, "The Use of Captured German and Related Records in Official Military Histories," ed. Robert Wolfe, *Captured German and Related Records: A National Archives Conference* (Athens, OH: Ohio University Press, 1977), pp. 66–7.

3. See p. 13, *Russian Combat Methods in World War II*.

4. See p. 295, *Combat in Russian Forests and Swamps*.

5. S.L.A. Marshall, *Bringing Up the Rear* (Novato, CA: Presidio Press, 1979), p. 159. The officers employed by the Army had been distinguished and capable men in their own rights. Many of them were eagerly hired by the business sector or put back into uniform by the newly created Bundeswehr. Marshall recounted how some of the sharpest German generals were already working on their own futures while also working as POWs on military history.

> I saw none of them thereafter until 1965, when in Johannesburg, I ran into Major General F.W. von Mellenthin, the author of *Panzer Battles*. His is a distinguished book, the material for which he cribbed from our files while a prisoner. I wondered at the time why we were getting so little work from such a clever fellow.

6. George E. Blau, *The German Campaign in Russia: Planning and Operations (1940–1942)*, DA Pam No. 20-261a (Washington, D.C.: Department of the Army, 1955), p. 89.

7. See pp. 170 and 248, *Effects of Climate on Combat in European Russia*.

8. See p. 264, *Warfare in the Far North*.

9. George Gordon, Lord Byron, "The Destruction of Sennacherib"; Allen F. Chew, *Fighting the Russians in Winter: Three Case Studies,* Leavenworth Papers No. 5 (Leavenworth, KS: Combat Studies Institute, 1981), p. 34. By the end of the first winter of the war, the Germans had suffered in excess of a quarter million frostbite cases, of which more than 90 percent were second and third degree cases.

10. See p. 152, *Russian Combat Methods*.

PART ONE

Russian Combat Methods in World War II

By Generaloberst Erhard Rauss
Commander, Fourth and
Third Panzer Armies

Preface

Russian Combat Methods in World War II was prepared by a committee of former German officers at the EUCOM Historical Division Interrogation Enclosure, Neustadt, Germany, in late 1947 and early 1948. All of these officers had extensive experience on the Eastern Front during the period 1941–45. The principal author, for example, commanded in succession a panzer division, a corps, a panzer army, and an army group.

The reader is reminded that publications in the GERMAN REPORT SERIES were written by Germans from the German point of view. For instance, the "Introduction" and "Conclusions" to *Russian Combat Methods in World War II* present the views of the German author without interpretation by American personnel. Throughout this pamphlet, Russian combat methods are evaluated in terms of German combat doctrine, and Russian staff methods are compared to those of the German General Staff. Organization, equipment, and procedures of the German and Russian Armies differed considerably from those of the United States Army. Tactical examples in the text have been carefully dated, and an effort has been made to indicate the progress of the Russian Army in overcoming the weaknesses noted in the early stages of the war.

In the preparation of this revised edition, the German text has been retranslated, and certain changes in typography and chapter titles have been made to improve clarity and facilitate its use. The revised edition is considered to be just as reliable and sound as the text prepared by the German committee. The authors' prejudices and defects, whatever they may be, find the same expression in the following translation as they do in the original German.

Department of the Army
November 1950

Introduction

The only written material available for the preparation of this manuscript consisted of a few memoranda in diary form and similar notes of a personal nature. *Russian Combat Methods in World War II* is therefore based to a preponderant degree on personal recollections and on material furnished by a small group of former German commanders who had special experience in the Eastern Campaign. For that very reason, it cannot lay claim to completeness. This report is limited to a description of the characteristic traits of the Russian soldier, and their influence on the conduct of battle. The political, economic, and social conditions of the country, although influential factors, could only be touched upon. Detailed treatment of climate and terrain—indispensable to an understanding of Russian methods of warfare—has been omitted intentionally since those subjects are discussed in other manuscripts.

Russian combat methods have more and more become a topic of vital concern. Propaganda and legend already have obscured the facts. The most nearly correct appraisal will be arrived at by knowing the peculiarities of the Russian territory and its inhabitants, and by analyzing and accurately evaluating the sources from which they derive their strength. There is no better method than a study of World War II, the struggle in which the characteristics of country and people were thrown into bold relief. Although the passage of time may have diminished the validity of these experiences, they nevertheless remain the soundest basis for an evaluation. The war potential of the Soviet Union may be subject to change; no doubt it has increased during the last few years and will increase further, at least until the end of the current Five Year Plan. The very latest implements of war are known to have been further developed and produced in quantity, and new offensive and defensive weapons perfected. Technological advances will alter the external aspects of warfare, but the character and peculiarities of the Russian soldier and his particular methods of fighting remain unaffected by such innovations. Nor will the characteristics of Russian topography change during the next few years. In these decisively important aspects, therefore, the German experiences of World War II remain fully valid.

THE RUSSIAN SOLDIER AND RUSSIAN CONDUCT OF BATTLE

CHAPTER 1

Peculiarities of the Russian Soldier

It is possible to predict from experience how virtually every soldier of the Western world will behave in a given situation—but not the Russian. The characteristics of this semi-Asiatic, like those of his vast country, are strange and contradictory. During the last war there were units which one day repulsed a strong German attack with exemplary bravery, and on the next folded up completely. There were others which one day lost their nerve when the first shell exploded, and on the next allowed themselves, man by man, literally to be cut to pieces. The Russian is generally impervious to crises, but he can also be very sensitive to them. Generally, he has no fear of a threat to his flanks, but at times he can be most touchy about flanks. He disregards many of the old established rules of tactics, but clings obstinately to his own methods.

The key to this odd behavior can be found in the native character of the Russian soldier who, as a fighter, possesses neither the judgment nor the ability to think independently. He is subject to moods which to a Westerner are incomprehensible; he acts by instinct. As a soldier, the Russian is primitive and unassuming, innately brave but morosely passive when in a group. These traits make him in many respects an adversary superior to the self-confident and more demanding soldiers of other armies. Such opponents, however, can and must, by their physical and mental qualities, achieve not only equality, but also the superiority necessary to defeat the Russian soldier.

Disregard for human beings and contempt of death are other characteristics of the Russian soldier. He will climb with complete indifference and cold-bloodedness over the bodies of hundreds of fallen comrades, in order to take up the attack on the same spot. With the same apathy he will work all day burying his dead comrades after a battle. He looks toward his own death with the same resignation. Even severe wounds impress him comparatively little. For instance, a Russian, sitting upright at the side of the street, in spite of the fact that both lower legs were shot away asked with a friendly smile for a cigarette. He endures cold and heat, hunger and thirst, dampness and mud, sickness and vermin, with equanimity. Because of his simple and primitive nature, all sorts of hardships bring him but few emotional reactions. His emotions run the gamut from animal ferocity to the utmost kindliness; odious and cruel in a group, he can be friendly and ready to help as an individual.

In the attack the Russian fought unto death. Despite most thorough German defensive measures he would continue to go forward, completely disregarding losses. He was generally not subject to panic. For example, in the breakthrough of the fortifications before Bryansk in October 1941, Russian bunkers, which had long since been bypassed and which for days lay far behind the front, continued to be held when every hope of relief had vanished. Following the German crossing of the Bug in July 1941, the fortifications which had originally been cleared of the enemy by the 167th Infantry Division were reoccupied a few days later by groups of Russian stragglers, and subsequently had to be painstakingly retaken by a division which followed in the rear. An underground room in the heart of the citadel of Brest Litovsk held out for many days against a German division in spite of the employment of the heaviest fire power.

The sum of these most diverse characteristics makes the Russian a superior soldier who, under the direction of understanding leadership, becomes a dangerous opponent. It would be a serious error to underestimate the Russian soldier, even though he does not quite fit the pattern of modern warfare and the educated fighting man. The strength of the Western soldier is conscious action, controlled by his own mind. Neither this action on his own, nor the consciousness which accompanies the action, is part of the mental make-up of the Russian. But the fact must not be ignored that a change is taking place also in this respect.

The difference between the Russian units in World War I and those in World War II is considerable. Whereas in the earlier war the Russian Army was a more or less amorphous mass, immovable and without individuality, the spiritual awakening through communism showed itself clearly in the last war. In contrast to the situation at the time of World War I, the number of illiterates was small. The Russian masses had acquired individuality, or at least were well on the way to acquiring it. The Russian is beginning to become a perceptive human being, and hence a soldier who is able to stand on his own feet. The number of good noncommissioned officers was still not large in World War II and the Russian masses had not yet overcome their sluggishness. But the awakening of the Russian people cannot be far off. Whether this will work to the advantage or disadvantage of their soldierly qualities cannot yet be determined. For along with awareness flourish criticism and obstinacy. The arbitrary employment of masses resigned to their fate may become more difficult, and the basis of the typically Russian method of waging war may be lost. The force bringing about this change is communism, or more precisely, a spiritual awakening of the people directed by a rigidly centralized state. The Russian is fundamentally non-political; at least that is true for the rural population, which supplies the majority of soldiers. He is not an active Communist, not a political zealot. But he is—and here one notes a decisive change—a conscious Russian who fights only in rare instances for political ideals, but always for his Fatherland.

In judging the basic qualities of the Russian it should be added that by nature he is brave, as he has well demonstrated in his history. In 1807 it was the Russian soldier who for the first time made a stand against Napoleon after his victorious march through Europe—a stand which may be called almost epic.

In line with this awakening, another determining factor has been introduced into the Red Army by the political commissar—unqualified obedience. Carried out to utter finality, it has made a raw mass of men a first-rate fighting machine. Systematic training, drill, disregard for one's own life, the natural inclination of the Russian soldier to uncompromising compliance and, not the least of all, the real disciplinary powers available to the commissar, are the foundations of this iron obedience. In this connection, it must be remembered that Russia is an autocratically ruled state—an absolute dictatorship demanding and compelling the complete subordination of the individual. That blind obedience of the masses, the mainspring of the Red Army, is the triumph of communism and the explanation of its military successes.

In addition to the simplicity which is revealed in his limited household needs and his primitive mode of living, the Russian soldier has close kinship with nature. It is no exaggeration to say that the Russian soldier is unaffected by season and terrain. This immunity gave him a decisive advantage over the Germans, especially in Russian territory where season, temperature, and terrain play a decisive role.

The problem of providing for the individual soldier in the Russian Army is of secondary importance, because the Russian soldier requires only very few provisions for his own use. The field kitchen, a sacred institution to other troops, is to the Russian soldier a pleasant surprise when it is available, but can be dispensed with for days and weeks without undue hardship.

During the winter campaign of 1941, a Russian regiment was surrounded in the woods along the Volkhov and, because of German weakness, had to be starved out. After one week, reconnaissance patrols met with the same resistance as on the first day; after another week only a few prisoners were taken, the majority having fought their way through to their own troops in spite of close encirclement. According to the prisoners, the Russians subsisted during those weeks on a few pieces of frozen bread, leaves and pine needles which they chewed, and some cigarettes. It had never occurred to anyone to throw in the sponge because of hunger, and the cold (−30° F.) had not affected them.

The kinship with nature, which the Russians have retained to a greater degree than the other peoples of Europe, is also responsible for the ability of the Russian soldier to adapt himself to terrain features, and actually to merge with them. He is a master of camouflage, entrenchment, and defense construction. With great speed he disappears into the earth, digging in with unfailing instinct so as to utilize the terrain to make his fortifications very difficult to discover. When the Russian has dug himself into his native soil and has molded himself into the landscape, he is a doubly dangerous opponent.

The utmost caution is required when passing through unknown terrain. Even long and searching observation often does not reveal the excellently camouflaged Russian. Frequently, German reconnaissance patrols passed through the immediate vicinity of Russian positions or individual riflemen without noticing them, and were then taken under fire from behind. Caution must be doubled in wooded areas. In such areas the Russians often disappear without a trace, and must be driven out individually, Indian fashion. Here, sniping from trees was particularly favored by the Russians as a method of fighting.

The industrialization of the country, carried out in a comparatively short period of time, has made available to the Red Army a large number of industrial workers with full command of technical skills. The Russian has mastered all new weapons and fighting equipment, all the requirements of machine warfare, with amazing rapidity. Soldiers trained in technical subjects were carefully distributed through the ranks where they taught the necessary rudiments to their duller urban comrades, and to those who came from rural areas. The technical skill of the Russian was especially notable in the field of signal communications. The longer the war lasted, the better the Russians became at handling this type of equipment. Their communications improved steadily, and with noteworthy skill the Russians soon made themselves familiar also with German signal communications. Monitoring and tuning in, jamming and deception, all were arts which they understood very well. Whereas in World War I the telephone was still magic to the average Russian, in World War II he regarded the complicated radio as an amusing toy. In the field of signal communications, he also maintained his iron discipline, thereby propounding many a riddle for German signal intelligence.

In contrast to the good side of the Russian soldier there were bad military aspects of equal significance. To the Germans, it was one of the imponderables about each Russian unit whether the good or bad would predominate. There still remained an appreciable residue of dullness, inflexibility, and apathy which had not yet been overcome, and which probably will not be overcome in the near future.

The unpredictability of the mood of the Russian soldier and his pronounced herd instinct at times brought on sudden panic in individual units. As inexplicable as the fanatic resistance of some units, was the mystery of their mass flights, or sudden wholesale surrender. The reason may have been an imperceptible fluctuation in morale. Its effect could not be counteracted by any commissar.

His emotions drive the Russian into the herd, which gives him strength and courage. The individual fighter created by modern warfare is rare among the Russians. Most of the time a Russian who has to stand on his own feet does not know what to do. During the war, however, this serious weakness was compensated for by the large mass of men available.

A word about the craftiness of the Russian. He seldom employed large-scale ruses. The usual tricks, such as feigning the existence of troops by increased fire and other means, were just as common with the Russians as with all armies. They seldom carried out feint attacks. The Germans found, however, that they had to be on guard against dishonesty and attempts at deception by individual Russian soldiers and small units. One trick, a particular favorite, was to feign surrender, or come over to the enemy with raised hands, white flags, and all the rest. Anyone approaching in good faith would often be met by sudden surprise fire at close range. The Russian soldier, who can lie motionless for hours on end, often feigned death. An unguarded approach often cost a German his life.

CHAPTER 2

The Russian Command Echelons

The higher echelons of Russian command proved capable from the very beginning of the war and learned a great deal more during its course. They were flexible, full of initiative, and energetic. However, they were unable to inspire the mass of Russian soldiers. Most of the commanders had advanced in peacetime to high positions at a very early age, although there were some older men among them. All social levels were represented, from the common laborer to the university professor of Mongolian languages and cultures. Of course, merit in the Revolution played a part, but a good choice was made with respect to character, military understanding, and intelligence. Purely party generals apparently got positions carrying little more than prestige. The extraordinary industry with which the commanders went about their duties was characteristic. Every day, and far into the night, they sat together to discuss and to record in writing what they had seen and heard during the day.

During the various political purges an appreciable portion of this command strata disappeared. But it is a mistake to assume that a deterioration of the higher command levels resulted. Such great progress had been made in military education in Russia that even the higher commanders available at the beginning of the war were of a stature commensurate with their duties. In this connection it must be noted that a nation as young, energetic, and populous as Russia, was able to draw on an inexhaustible source of strength. In addition, this group of officers was held in high regard by the populace, was extolled in propaganda, and was very comfortably situated economically. Many things testified to the position which the military leaders of the Soviet Union enjoyed in the state and among the people: pictures in prewar illustrated Russian newspapers, the display in Red Army office buildings of artistically valuable portraits of senior officers and of paintings showing episodes in their military careers, and the exhibition on stairways and in government buildings of banners emblazoned with the pronouncements of high-ranking military officers.

The many developments in the sphere of strategy, which now and then gave rise to doubts about the ability of these leaders, require an examination of their background before they can be properly judged. The alleged failure during the Finnish winter campaign of 1939–40 is well known, but nevertheless the conjecture cannot be dismissed that there was some bluffing involved. The timing of the operation was correct and would produce results as soon as the will of the immeasurably superior attacker desired them.

Neither is the success of the German surprise attack at the opening of the campaign against Russia in 1941 any proof to the contrary. Along the Central Front, and also in the north, it appeared as though the actual war did not begin until the Dnepr and the Luga had been reached. One of Timoshenko's strategic war games, as well as the course of events at the beginning of the Eastern Campaign, tend to substantiate this assumption, which is supported by the following incident.

In mid-July 1941 the German LIII Infantry Corps joined the defensive battle in the Dnepr–Berezina triangle (Map 2) against Timoshenko's thrust into the flank and rear of Second Panzer Group which was advancing on Smolensk. Soon thereafter, corps found out that in February 1941, in a house on the Bobruysk–Rogachev road, Timoshenko and his field commanders had held a conference which lasted several days. Upon exhaustive search of that house a map was found indicating that

German armored units were assumed to be north of Rogachev, east of the Dnepr; a pincers operation was being launched against them from the regions of Zhlobin–Rogachev and Mogilev, with Bobruysk as the objective; one very strong group of forces was to advance to the northwest via Zhlobin–Rogachev, another of like strength to the southwest via Mogilev, to cut off the German armor; the two groups were to meet at Bobruysk; the intermediary daily objectives of the two groups were indicated by semicircles; a cavalry unit of three elements, committed on the west bank of the Berezina and striking northward from the Parichi area, was to cut the Slutsk–Bobruysk road and the Minsk–Bobruysk railroad, and complete the encirclement.

Since the German armored units had already defeated the northern enemy group near Orsha, there remained only the southern arm of the pincers. With a total of twenty divisions, Timoshenko carried through this part of the operation that apparently had been planned in February. He thus came in contact with LIII Infantry Corps which had in the meantime arrived in the Dnepr–Berezina triangle by way of Bobruysk. There developed a bitter three-week defense action between the Corps—comprising three divisions—and those Russian forces which had advanced across the Dnepr near Zhlobin and Rogachev. During the course of this battle the cavalry corps indicated on the map also appeared, and for a while actually reached its objectives. The LIII Infantry Corps was cut off from the rear for about a week.

Only customs and frontier guards were encountered on the Bug; very weak enemy forces appeared after a few days; finally, the big battle in the Dnepr–Berezina triangle: thus began the Eastern Campaign. Prisoner statements furnished the Germans a very clear picture of the preliminaries, concentrations, and groupings for the battle by the Russians. Again and again reports gave the impression that large-scale enemy movements did not get under way until after the opening of the campaign, and that they took place beyond the Dnepr. From the point of view of Russian grand strategy it was undoubtedly an expedient solution. Nevertheless, the German intelligence service believed that it had identified continuous troop movements to the Russo-German frontier, supposedly involving 130 divisions, as early as spring of 1940.

The events which led up to the battle of Uman on the Southern Front offer no damaging evidence against the ability of the Russian higher command, but show only the danger and the detrimental effect of injecting politics into current military operations.

Thus the Russian high command was, for the most part, competent. Whether Timoshenko's tenacity in carrying out his plan, as mentioned above, even though the northern part of the pincers operation was knocked out, should be regarded as inflexibility, or whether Timoshenko thought that there were possibilities for a great success just the same, must be left out of the discussion. During the subsequent course of the war, however, a flexibility in strategy was apparent in the Russian high command that in the field of tactics long remained absent in the performance of the intermediate and lower command echelons. An awareness of responsibility accompanied the willingness to accept responsibility, as is shown by the following example.

After the breakthrough by the German LIII Infantry Corps from the southwest to Bryansk at the beginning of October 1941, the opposing Russian Fiftieth Army, commanded by General Petrov, withdrew, badly shaken, to the wooded terrain northeast of Bryansk. The Bryansk pocket was the result. During the withdrawal the commander of the Fiftieth Army had been given command of Army Group Bryansk under which, in addition to the Fiftieth Army, were placed the Thirtieth and Thirty-third Armies. The diary of Major Shabalin, a State Security (GPU) officer attached to Fiftieth Army headquarters who was killed in the Bryansk pocket, contained the following on the subject:

I [Shabalin] congratulated General Petrov at breakfast upon his appointment as commander of Army Group Bryansk. General Petrov answered only: "So now they are going to shoot me too." I replied: "How can you talk of shooting? Your appointment as commander of the Group is an indication of confidence in your ability to get things organized again." General Petrov: "How can I get the situation back under control when I don't know where the Thirtieth and Thirty-third Armies are and what condition they are in?"

A few days later General Petrov was killed at the side of Major Shabalin, in a night attempt to break out of the Bryansk pocket. Another example was that of Marshal Kulik who, with a serious leg injury, supported himself on a cane and led 10,000 men, whom he had reassembled after the Minsk pocket, through the swamps near Bobruysk, and gave the German troops serious difficulties. The higher Red Army commanders did not spare themselves.

The way operations were launched and carried out revealed the influence of German methods on the Soviet high command. Operations against flank and rear, large-scale envelopments, and encirclements all played a part. Other maneuvers employed were mobile defense and, finally, breakthrough and breakout.

Timoshenko's plan for a double envelopment and isolation of the German large armored units which had advanced across the Dnepr undoubtedly was on the grand scale. This operation was carried out energetically and efficiently. The strategic concentration, assembly, and commitment of units participating in the attack were irreproachable.

The great thrust via Yefremov at the beginning of November 1941, in which the Russians aimed at the rear of the German armored units standing in front of Tula, and which later led to the Battle of Annihilation southeast of Plavskoye, was likewise well planned. From a strategic and tactical point of view it had a chance of success. The weakest point of the German armored thrust had been recognized and correctly exploited.

The Russian high commands had an eye for strategically and tactically weak points of the enemy. The Battle of Moscow in 1941–42 and its consequences are a good example of this as are, on a smaller scale the operations in March 1944 on the Kandalaksha front in northern Finland against XXXVI Mountain Corps. The Red Army high command can, of course, claim more and even greater successes, such as the various major offensives from 1943 to 1945.

However, the resources of their country and the large number of troop units that were available gave the Soviet command an advantage over the Germans. Equipment, training, and physical and spiritual character of their armed forces all corresponded to the conditions in the east. For this reason the Germans had to contend with a great number of difficulties which simply did not exist for the Russian high command. In addition, the low valuation placed on human life freed the Soviet high command from moral inhibitions. Whether, for example, several divisions were lost in an encirclement, or whether a reindeer division on the Murmansk front perished in a snowstorm, was of no particular importance. Not until later did the long duration of the war and the extensive losses force the Red high command to greater economy of manpower.

The flexibility demonstrated by the higher commands (army and army group) was not evident at lower levels. The lower command echelons (echelons below division level) of the Russian Army, and for the most part also the intermediate echelons (generally division level), remained for a long period inflexible and indecisive, avoiding all personal responsibility. The rigid pattern of training and a too strict discipline so narrowly confined the lower command within a framework of existing regulations that the result was lethargy. Spirited application to a task, born of the decision of an individual, was a rarity. Russian elements that had broken through German lines could remain for days behind the front without recognizing their favorable position and taking advantage of it. The Russian small unit commander's fear of doing something wrong and being called to account for it was greater than the urge to take advantage of a situation.

The commanders of Russian combined arms units were often well trained along tactical lines, but to some extent they had not grasped the essence of tactical doctrines and therefore often acted according to set patterns, not according to circumstances. Also, there was the pronounced spirit of blind obedience which had perhaps carried over from their regimented civilian life into the military field. Thus, for example, toward the end of September 1941 in the area southwest of Bryansk, the same sector was attacked by various Russian battalions every day for seven days running without any apparent reason and without success, but with severe losses. Finally, a captured battalion commander supplied the explanation. In looking through some old files, their new regimental commander had found a top-level order to the effect that continuous attacks were to be made along the entire front in order to ease the pressure on Leningrad. Since he had received a negative answer to his inquiry as to whether these attacks had already been made, he had ordered this sector attacked every day. In the meantime, however, two months had passed, and the pressure on Leningrad had long since been relieved.

This lethargy and reluctance to assume responsibility was a serious drawback to the Red Army, completely neutralizing a great many good points of the Russian soldier. Later on, the Soviet commanders learned a great deal along this line and became more flexible. The tactical employment of the 6th Rifle Division in the Battle of Annihilation southeast of Plavskoye may be termed perfect: advance, withdrawal in trucks in dangerous situations, another forward thrust, and then attack.

So far as care of the troops and internal administration were concerned, Russian unit commanders faced the same problems that confronted officers of other armies. There was great interest in hygienic measures. But also other matters, such as decorations, promotions, results of the war loan, and similar matters, kept the lower commanders very busy.

CHAPTER 3

The Commissar

The influence of the Communist party and of its representatives in the Army—the commissars—was tremendous. The commissar was probably the most controversial man in the Russian Army. Even in the Soviet Union opinions varied concerning his usefulness, his position, and his duties. He was the driving force of the Army, ruling with cunning and cold-bloodedness.

By means of a close-meshed network of especially chosen personalities, the commissars held the entire army machine under their control and in a tight grip. The commissars were to a preponderant degree real political fanatics. They came mostly from the working class, were almost without exception city people, brave, intelligent, and unscrupulous. But they also took care of the troops. Even though, during the course of the war, their intervention in the military conduct of the war was reduced thanks to Stalin's military instinct, their influence was not lessened.

However, it is not true that the Russian soldier fought well only because of fear of the commissars. A soldier who is motivated solely by fear can never have the qualities that the Russian soldier of this war displayed. The motive of fear may often have been the final resort in difficult situations, but basically the Russian has no less national—as distinguished from political—patriotism than the soldier of the Western armies, and with it comes the same source of strength. Unceasing propaganda has burned nationalism into his soul. And however impervious he may be to foreign propaganda, he nevertheless has been unable to escape the engulfing waves of his own.

Among the troops themselves the relationship of the soldier to the commissar apparently was endurable in spite of the commissar's uncompromising strictness and severity. The higher headquarters, on the other hand, appear to have regarded him with mistrust. Testimony to that conclusion is found not only in the episode mentioned below, but also in many remarks of General Petrov, the commander of the Fiftieth Army, to Commissar Shabalin, which the latter recorded verbatim in his diary. General Petrov once ironically asked Shabalin, who was sitting next to him in the tank: "Well, how many have you shot today?" Shabalin added the note: "Such sarcasm." The commissar was thus often considered an alien element by headquarters.

The prohibition of vodka in the Russian Army, which had been in effect until then, was rescinded in August 1941. A division commissar recommended that the prohibition be restored immediately and based his recommendation on an occurrence which took place at his division headquarters. The first liquor to arrive was not distributed to the troops by division headquarters, but used by the headquarters staff itself. The result was general drunkenness among the staff. The officers allegedly went out into the village street and killed geese with their pistols. When there were no more geese, an officer of division headquarters pounded the commissar on the shoulder and said, "Well, all the geese have been shot dead. Now it's your turn."

In the fighting east of Roslavl in August 1941, a Russian tank company that had been sent into action suddenly stopped on the battlefield. The leader of the tank company had received an order before going into action to refuel at a fuel depot somewhat to the rear of his bivouac area. He did not, however, want to take the trouble to go back as he thought that it would be possible to refuel farther forward at the divisional command post nearer the front. But there was no opportunity to refuel at that point. The tank company just reached the battlefield and then ground to a halt because of lack of fuel. Thereupon, the company commissar drew his pistol and shot the commanding officer on the spot.

The attitude of the common man toward the commissar was

conditioned not only by fear of his power, but also by his personal exemplification of the soldier and fighter. His concern for the welfare of the troops also determined to a large extent his relationship with the men. The commissars always made much of the well-being of the troops. Commissar Shabalin, for instance, reported to higher authority the insufferable conditions on the Moscow–Orel–Bryansk railroad. While reconnoitering for new division headquarters, he immediately sent a division commissar, whom he had discovered in the rear, back to the front with the observation: "You belong with your troops; go and take care of them." There were innumerable recommendations for the improvement of conditions in the Army hospitals.

The example set by the commissars is largely responsible for the tenacious resistance of the Russian soldier, even in hopeless situations. It is not wholly true that the German commissar order, directing that upon capture commissars be turned over to the SD (Security Service) for "special treatment," that is execution, was solely responsible for inciting the commissars to bitter last-ditch resistance; the impetus much rather was fanaticism together with soldierly qualities, and probably also the feeling of responsibility for the victory of the Soviet Union. The previously mentioned occupation of the bunkers on the Bug and the continued resistance in the citadel of Brest Litvosk can be traced to the influence of the commissars.

Then, too, in innumerable other cases dogged perseverance even under hopeless conditions was to be credited to the soldierly conduct of the commissars. For instance, in September 1941, long after the castle of Posyolok Taytsy (south of Leningrad) had been taken, and strong German troop units had been drawn up in the castle park, German tanks passing near the park wall with open hatches drew single rounds of rifle fire from close range. The shots were aimed at the unprotected tank commanders who were looking out of the turrets. Not until three Germans had been killed by bullets through the head did the passing tank unit realize that the shots were coming from a narrow trench close under the park wall ten yards away. The tanks then returned the fire, whereupon all thirteen occupants of the trench met death. They were the officers of a Russian regimental headquarters, grouped about their commissar who fell with his rifle cocked and aimed.

After the German divisions broke out of the Luga bridge-heads in August 1941, the commander of a task force inspected several Russian tanks which had been knocked out two hours earlier near a church. A large number of men were looking on. Suddenly, the turret of one of the knocked-out tanks began to revolve and fire. The tank had to be blown up. It turned out that among the crew, which had been assumed dead, there was a commissar who had merely been unconscious. When he revived and saw the many German soldiers around him, he opened fire.

When in April 1942 the Germans took a strong position along the Osuga (southwest of Rzhev), they continued to receive rifle fire from one lone barricaded bunker. All demands for surrender were in vain. When an attempt was made to shoot through the embrasure with a rifle, the Red soldier grabbed it and fired the last three shots. Two of the bullets wounded German soldiers. The commissar, who was defending the bunker alone in the midst of his dead comrades, then shot himself with the third.

It might appear that much of the fighting spirit and concern for the welfare of the troops which the commissars displayed should have been the responsibility of the commanding officers and not of the commissars. However, it was always a question of situations in which something had to be done. The commanding officers generally did little, while the commissars acted. The passive character of the Russian officers was responsible for the fact that it was not the commander but the commissar who discovered the road to action. Therefore, the commissar was really a necessary part in the structure of the Red Army. He was a sort of front-line conscience.

It was difficult for the Russians themselves to properly judge this matter, and much more so for anyone distantly removed. Rejecting an institution which had its good points under the prevailing conditions would have been a mistake.

The commissars found special support among the women

who served within the framework of the Soviet Army. Russian women served in all-female units with the so-called partisan bands, individually as gunners in the artillery, as spies dropped by parachute, as medical corps aides with the fighting troops, and in the rear in the auxiliary services. They were political fanatics, filled with hate for every opponent, cruel, and incorruptible. The women were enthusiastic Communists—and dangerous.

It was also not unusual for women to fight in the front lines. Thus, uniformed women took part in the final breakout struggle at Sevastopol in 1942; medical corps women in 1941 defended the last positions in front of Leningrad with pistols and hand grenades until they fell in the battle. In the fighting along the middle Donets in February 1943, a Russian tank was apparently rendered immobile by a direct hit. When German tanks approached, it suddenly reopened fire and attempted to break out. A second direct hit again brought it to a standstill, but in spite of its hopeless position it defended itself while a tank-killer team advanced on it. Finally it burst into flame from a demolition charge and only then did the turret hatch open. A woman in tanker uniform climbed out. She was the wife and cofighter of a tank company commander who, killed by the first hit, lay beside her in the turret. So far as Red soldiers were concerned, women in uniform were superiors or comrades to whom respect was paid.

The four elements which determine the nature of Russian warfare—the higher command, the troops, the commissar, and the Russian terrain—fitted together in such a way that their combination was responsible for good performance and great successes. The weakest elements were the intermediate and lower leaders. Their shortcomings, however, were made up for in part by appropriate action of the higher command and by the good will, the discipline, the undemanding nature, and the self-sacrificing devotion to duty of the enlisted men under the influence of energetic commissars who were filled with a belief in the essential necessity of victory. The Russian soldier thereby became an instrument which provided his leaders with the sort of fighter needed for the operations.

CHAPTER 4

The Combat Arms

I. Infantry

The picture of the Russian soldier presented up to this point applies primarily to the infantry. This branch supplied the bulk of the fighting men in active combat, and most clearly exemplified the peculiar characteristics of the Russian. The Red Army infantry was for a long period of time the mainstay of the Russian fighting machine, and in the Arctic this was true for the entire war period. As is apparent from the previously described characteristics of the Russian soldier, the Soviet infantry was willing, undemanding, suitably trained and equipped, and, above all, brave and endowed with a self-sacrificing devotion to duty. The communist philosophy appeared to have become firmly rooted among the great mass of the younger people and to have made them loyal soldiers, differing much in their perseverance and performance from those of World War I. Subject to rapidly changing moods, the Russian infantryman was jovial one moment, cruel the next.

The Russian infantryman was a member of the herd, preferring to fight in concert with others rather than to be left to his own devices. In the attack, this characteristic was evidenced in the massed lines, sometimes almost packs; in the defense it was shown by the stubbornly resisting bunker complements. Here, there was no individual action for one's personal advantage. The soldiers aided each other and even displayed an interest in their comrades' family affairs.

As has already been pointed out the Russian soldier was virtually immune to seasonal and terrain difficulties. Further, he was almost complete master of the terrain. There appeared to be no terrain obstacles for the infantryman. He was as much at home in dense forest as in swamp or trackless steppe. Difficult terrain features stopped him only for a limited time. Even the broad Russian streams were crossed quickly with the help of the most primitive expedients. The German could never assume that the Russian would be held back by terrain normally considered impassable. It was in just such places that his appearance, and frequently his attack, had to be expected. The Red infantryman could, if he chose, completely overcome terrain obstacles in a very short time. Miles of corduroy road were laid through marshy terrain in a few days; paths were tramped through forest covered with deep snow. Ten men abreast, with arms interlocked, and in ranks 100 deep, prepared these lanes in fifteen-minute reliefs of 1,000 men each. Teams of innumerable infantrymen moved guns and heavy weapons wherever they were needed. During the winter, snow caves which could be heated were constructed to furnish night shelter for men and horses. The Russian matériel was useful in this respect: motorization reduced to an absolute minimum; the lightest vehicles; tough horses that required little care; suitable uniforms; and, finally, again the human mass which moved all loads and performed all required tasks like a machine.

A singular kinship to nature makes the Russian infantryman an ideal fighter in forests, barren country, and swamps. In the Arctic, small units of several men stayed for weeks in the desolate area in the German rear, accompanied at times by female radio operators who were treated with particular respect.

Wounds were endured patiently and without complaint. Frostbite was a punishable offense because it was avoidable. Recovery, even from serious injuries, was rapid. Many an injury that would have been fatal to a Central European was endured and overcome.

The best weapon of the Russian infantryman was the machine pistol. It was easily handled, equal to Russian winter conditions, and one which the Germans also regarded highly. This weapon was slung around the neck and carried in front on the chest, ready for immediate action. The mortar also proved highly valuable as the ideal weapon for terrain conditions where artillery support was impossible. At the beginning of the Eastern Campaign, Russian infantry far surpassed the German in mortar equipment and its use.

The same was true for the Russian antitank gun, which at the beginning of the campaign considerably surpassed the antitank gun of the German infantry divisions in efficiency, and therefore was readily put to use whenever captured. The antitank gun was an auxiliary weapon from which the Russian soldier never separated. Wherever the Russian infantryman was, antitank defense could be expected by his enemy. At times it appeared to the Germans that each Russian infantryman had an antitank gun or antitank rifle, just as infantrymen of other armies had ordinary rifles. The Russian moved his antitank defense everywhere with great skill. It was to be found even where no German tank attacks might be expected. Emplacements were set up within a few minutes. If the small gun, always excellently camouflaged, was not needed for antitank defense, its flat trajectory and great accuracy were put to good use in infantry combat. The Germans had a rule to cope with this: Engage Russian infantry immediately following their appearance, for shortly thereafter not only the soldier but also his antitank defense will have disappeared into the ground, and every countermeasure will be twice as costly.

In World War II the Russian infantryman had a noteworthy negative characteristic: He was not inquisitive. His reconnaissance often was extremely poor. Combat patrols were for him the means of gathering information about the enemy only when he thought it necessary. Although the Russian proved himself an excellent scout, he made too little use of his abilities in this field. The higher Russian command was always well informed on the German situation by means of radio monitoring, interrogation of prisoners, captured documents, and other means. But the intermediate and lower commanders apparently were only slightly interested in their opponents. Here again the cause lay in the lack of self-reliance and in the individual Russian infantryman's inability to assemble into a useful report the observations made while on patrol.

The clothing and equipment of the Russian infantryman suited his summer as well as winter requirements. The Germans were amazed at how well the Siberian infantry was clothed in the winter of 1941–42. As might be expected, the fighters in the Arctic were likewise suitably clothed. The Russian infantryman was inferior to the German and the Finn only in skiing. Of course, attempts were made to correct this deficiency through intensified training, but all efforts were doomed to failure since there was never more than one pair of skis available for several men.

Equipment carried by all Germans was often discarded by the Russian infantryman as nonessential. Gas masks were commonly stored in division depots; steel helmets were rarely worn in the arctic wilderness.

II. Artillery

The efficiency of the Russian artillery varied greatly during the various stages of the war. In the beginning it was unable to achieve an effective concentration of fire, and furthermore was unenthusiastic about firing on targets in the depth of the battle position even when there was excellent observation. The Rogachev water tower, for example, and the railroad control towers as well as the high railroad embankment at Zhlobin, all of which were in Russian hands during the battle in the Dnepr–Berezina triangle, commanded a view over the entire area for many miles; nevertheless, they were not used for directing fire on the very important targets behind the German lines. On the Kandalaksha front, continuous German supply transport operations at the Karhu railroad station took place within sight of Russian observation posts. These operations were never taken under fire by Russian artillery. On the other hand, the Russian artillery liked to distribute its fire over the front lines, and occasionally shelled a road intersection located not too far from the front.

During the course of the war the artillery also developed to a high degree the use of mass as a particularly characteristic procedure. Infantry attacks without artillery preparation were rare. Short preparatory concentrations lasting only a few minutes, frequently employed by the Germans to preserve the element of surprise, seemed insufficient to the Russians. Thus, counting on the destructive effect of massed fire, they consciously accepted the fact that the Germans would recognize their intentions of attacking. Russian artillery fire often had no primary target, but covered the entire area with the same intensity. The Russian artillery was most vulnerable to counterbattery fire. It ceased firing or changed position after only a few rounds from the German guns. The rigidity of the fire plan, and a certain immobility of the Soviet artillery—at least during the first years of the war—was pronounced. Only in rare cases was the artillery successful in promptly following the infantry. Most of the time the artillery was unable to follow up; it remained stuck in the old positions, leaving the infantry without fire support. This practice frequently took the momentum out of the Russian attacks.

Attack tactics of Russian artillery improved constantly during the war. Eventually, however, their tactics resolved into an ever-repeated, set scheme. Heavy preparatory fire, laid down broad and deep and lasting from one to two hours, was the initial phase; it rapidly mounted to murderous intensity. Once an attack was about to get under way, the Russians would suddenly lift their fire from very narrow lanes (about 80 to 100 yards wide), along which the infantry was to advance. At all other points the fire continued with undiminished fury. Only the most careful German observation allowed recognition of those lanes. This method gave the impression that artillery preparation was still continuing in full force, though in reality the infantry attack had already begun. Here again, one notes the same concept: human lives meant nothing at all. If defensive fire forced the Russian infantry out of their narrow lanes, or if their own artillery was unable to maintain the lanes accurately—*Nichevo!*—those were operating expenses.

However, despite many shortcomings, the Russian artillery was a very good and extremely dangerous arm. Its fire was effective, rapid, and accurate. Particularly during the large-scale attacks in the summer of 1944 it became apparent that the Russians had learned well how to mass and employ large artillery units. Establishment of a definite point of main effort and the use of superior masses of artillery crushed the thin lines of German opposition at many places at the Eastern Front before the actual attack had begun. This successful procedure of establishing definite points of main effort will be used by the Russians in the future whenever they have the masses of artillery and ammunition required.

III. Armored Forces

The heart of the Russian armored force was the well-known T34 tank. Because of its wide tracks, its powerful engine, and its low silhouette, the performance of the T34 in Russian terrain was frequently superior to that of the German tanks, particularly with respect to cross-country mobility. To the surprise of all the German experts, the T34 easily negotiated terrain theoretically secure against mechanized attack. The caliber of its guns was too small, however, and forced the Russians to produce several new types of tanks (KV1 and Stalin) which, like the German models, became successively heavier. Despite all improvements the new tanks remained on the whole inferior to the T34. The Russians recognized this fact, and continued to mass produce the T34 until the end of the war.

Not until late did the Russians decide to launch concerted attacks by large tank forces. During the first years of the war, Russian tanks generally were used for local infantry support. Soviet tank attacks as such took place only after a sufficient number of the vehicles had become available. Here, too, the Russians adhered to their usual habit of employing great masses of men and machines.

Tank attacks generally were not conducted at a fast enough pace. Frequently they were not well enough adapted to the nature of the terrain. Those facts the Germans noted time and again through the entire war.

The training of the individual tank driver was inadequate; the training period apparently was too short, and losses in experienced drivers were too high. The Russian avoided driving his tank through hollows or along reverse slopes, preferring to choose a route alone the crests which would give fewer driving difficulties. This practice remained unchanged even in the face of unusually high tank losses. Thus the Germans were in most cases able to bring the Russian tanks under fire at long range, and to inflict losses even before the battle had begun. Slow and uncertain driving and numerous firing halts made the Russian tanks good targets. Premature firing on the Russian tanks, though wrong in principle, was always the German solution in those instances. If the German defense was ready and adequate, the swarms of Russian tanks began to thin out very quickly in most cases. This fault in Russian tank tactics can be corrected only by peacetime training, but it can hardly be totally eliminated.

On the whole, the Russian armored force was not as good as the Russian artillery. Limited flexibility, and the inability of the subordinate commanders to exploit favorable situations rapidly and adroitly, were evident and frequently prevented the Russians from achieving successes almost within their grasp. Toward the end of the war, however, the inadequate facilities of the Germans were no longer able to stand up against the masses of equipment of the Reds.

IV. Horse Cavalry

In the campaign the Russian cavalry, despite many changes in tactics and equipment, achieved a significance reminiscent of old times. In the German Army, all cavalry except one division had been replaced by panzer units. The Russians followed another course. The German LIII Infantry Corps quite often encountered Russian cavalry divisions, and once a cavalry corps comprising three cavalry elements—always in situations in which cavalry was a suitable arm for the purpose.

In the battle of the Dnepr–Berezina triangle, a cavalry corps comprising three elements appeared west of the Berezina near Bobruysk, out of the Pripyat Marshes, in the rear of the German corps which was engaged in hard fighting. This cavalry force cut the Slutsk–Bobruysk highway and the Minsk–Bobruysk railroad, and thereby isolated the corps for a week from its supply and contact with the rear. Bobruysk itself, together with the bridges there, was seriously threatened. Only by prompt emergency measures were the Germans able to ease the pressure. During that period the corps ammunition supply dropped to twenty rounds per 105mm gun, and that at a time when

Timoshenko's major offensive had reached its peak. Forces other than cavalry would have been unable to conduct such a raid.

In the advance out of the Bryansk pocket northward past Plavskoye to the upper Don in October–November 1941, the 112th Infantry Division of LIII Infantry Corps was met by a Russian cavalry division just as it reached the Orel–Tula road. There ensued some very unpleasant delays. The cavalry division accomplished its mission by occupying every town along the route of advance, withdrawing from each one as soon as the division advanced to attack. Thus the 112th Division was kept occupied by constant small-scale warfare.

During the battle of annihilation southeast of Plavskoye, cavalry divisions appeared on both wings of the Russian attack front. The cavalry division just mentioned was on the northern wing. The Russian command had diverted it to the battlefield as soon as the 112th Infantry Division turned in that direction. The cavalry division, with its greater speed, reached the Plavskoye area ahead of the 112th Division and blocked its advance until a Russian rifle division arrived at the front. The cavalry division mentioned earlier was on the southern wing. That division was to reach the Orel–Tula highway in a forced march so as to cut it near Chern—under prevailing circumstances, a rewarding and practicable task for a cavalry division. The corps' further advance to the upper Don was constantly accompanied and watched by a cavalry division five to ten miles off its right flank. The cavalry division would have been able to intervene at once, in any manner whatsoever, if the Russian higher command had had any occasion for ordering it to do so.

The above examples are drawn from situations in which the missions in question could have been executed only by cavalry. The German armored vehicles were out of action in October during the muddy period. Only cavalry could operate through the Pripyat Marshes.

Under conditions as characterized in Central Russia by great forest and swamp areas, muddy periods, and deep snow, cavalry is a usable arm. Where the German motor failed, the Russian horse's legs continued to move. The tactical employment of the cavalry forces was, however, not always suited to the situation and sometimes was even awkward. Leadership and training in the Russian cavalry were not up to the World War I standard.

CHAPTER 5

Russian Battle Techniques

Just as the Russian soldier had his own peculiarities in his internal make-up, so he had them in his combat methods. The most common Russian form of combat was the use of mass. Human mass and mass of matériel were generally used unintelligently and without variation, but under the conditions, they were always effective. Both had to be available before they could be used so lavishly and were therefore dependent upon limitless Russian supplies. The Russian disdain for life—always present, but infinitely heightened by communism—favored this practice. A Russian attack which had been twice repulsed with unheard-of losses would be repeated a third and a fourth time at the same place and in the same fashion. Unimpressed by previous failures and losses, new waves always came on. An unusual inflexibility of mind and unimaginative obstinacy lay in this use of masses, and was dearly paid for. It is not possible to estimate Russian casualties in World War II with any degree of accuracy; there will always be a potential error of many hundred thousands. This inflexible method of warfare, with the objective of accomplishing everything through the use of human masses, is the most inhuman and costly possible.

Characteristic of the disdain for human life was the complete elimination of military funeral rites. There was no such thing as a funeral ceremony for the ordinary citizen in communist Russia. It ran counter to the antireligious philosophy and the mass sacrifice of human beings. There were occasional burial mounds in which a thick peg, painted red, had been driven into the ground at the head end, inscribed with the heroic deeds of some commissar killed in action. The bulk of the dead millions were unceremoniously plowed under. Thus, all outward indications of the number of dead were obliterated.

Not until 1944 did the Russians start using their men more sparingly. Only after there were no new millions available did there appear in orders the first reference to consideration in the use of men and admonitions to avoid losses. Nevertheless, a thinning of the attack waves was virtually unknown to the Russians until almost the last days of the war. The herd instinct and lack of self-reliance on the part of the subordinate commanders time and again misled them into the concentrated employment of troops. It was not particularly difficult to crush the attack of the human mass so long as the opposition possessed a mass of material in trained hands.

In the winter of 1941, the Russians cleared a German mine field south of Leningrad by chasing over it tightly closed columns of unarmed Russian soldiers shoulder to shoulder. Within a few minutes, they became victims of the mines and defensive fire.

The inflexibility of Russian methods of warfare was evidenced repeatedly. Only the top Russian command during the last years of the war was an exception. This inflexibility manifested itself as high as army level; in divisions, regiments, and companies it was unquestionably the retarding factor in the way the Russians fought. A division boundary was a sacred wall, and a neighbor's interest halted at his side of that wall. The senseless repetition of attacks, the rigidity of artillery fire, the plotting of lanes of attack and movement without regard to terrain, were all additional symptoms of inflexibility. The leaders displayed a certain flexibility in their frequent shifting of units in the front lines. These units disappeared unnoticed overnight and reappeared several days later in another sector of the front. It was, however, no feat to relieve and exchange troops so long as one had the reserves that the Russians had; on the other hand, it was all the more difficult if one had none, as was the case with the Germans. The Russians have this method to thank for the fact that only a few of their units became thoroughly depleted during the course of prolonged battles; on the German side such a depletion became inevitable over the years of continuous service of units. None of the Soviet units that were thus shifted from sector to sector ever disappeared. It could be safely assumed that the unit withdrawn would be recommitted within the same army sector. The organization of an army and the assignment of divisions to it also remained fixed. It seldom happened that divisions were interchanged between the armies.

Though generally no master of improvisation, the Russian command nevertheless knew how to bring battered infantry units up to strength and how to constitute new units as replacements for destroyed ones. This procedure frequently was accomplished with startling speed, but it soon turned out to be a game played with human lives. For example, the inhabitants of a threatened city, or perhaps the entire male population of areas which the Germans had recently evacuated, were gathered up quickly by means of excellent organization. Regardless of age, nationality, deferred status, or fitness, they were used to fill out these units. With no training at all, or at most only a few days of it, and often without weapons and uniforms, these "soldiers" were thrown into battle. They were supposed to learn in combat all that was necessary, and to acquire their weapons from their dead comrades. The Russians themselves were aware of the fact that these men were no soldiers, but they filled gaps and supplemented the sinking numbers of the human mass. During the fighting in a bridgehead southeast of Kremenchug in September 1943, the Russians at nighttime used to drive ahead of their armed soldiers large numbers of civilians whom they had gathered up, so that the German infantry might expend its scant supply of ammunition.

The Russians repeated the same tactics again and again: employment of masses, and narrow division sectors held by large complements replenished time after time. Therefore also the mass attacks. In the twinkling of an eye the terrain in front of the German line teemed with Russian soldiers. They seemed to grow out of the earth, and nothing would stop their advance for a while. Gaps closed automatically, and the mass surged on until the supply of men was used up and the wave, substantially thinned, receded again. The Germans often witnessed this typical picture of a Russian attack. It is impressive and astounding, on the other hand, how frequently the mass failed to recede, but rolled on and on, nothing able to stop it. Repulsing such an attack certainly depended on the strength of the forces and means for defense; primarily, however, it was a question of nerves. Only seasoned soldiers mastered the fear which instinctively gripped everyone upon the onslaught of such masses. Only the true soldier, the experienced individual fighter, could in the long run stand up under the strain; only a multitude of them could stop those masses.

Another specifically Russian battle technique was infiltration. It was a practice which especially suited the Russian, and of which he was a master. Despite closest observation of the avenues of approach, the Russian was suddenly there; no one knew where he had come from, nor how long he had already been there. Wherever the terrain was considered impassable, but was still kept under close observation to be doubly safe— just there the Russian infiltrated. He was suddenly there in substantial numbers and had already vanished into the earth. Nobody had seen a thing. Because of the drawn-out German defense fronts, it was no particular art to steal between the widely separated strong points, but it was always a surprise when, despite all watchfulness during the night, the Germans found the next morning that strong Russian units fully equipped with weapons and ammunition had assembled and dug in far behind the front. These operations were executed with unbelievable skill, completely noiseless and almost always without a struggle. It was a very profitable technique which succeeded in hundreds of cases and gained the Russians great advantages. There was only one method of countering it: extreme watchfulness, and heavily occupied, deep positions, secured throughout at all times.

Of the same nature was the Russian's constant effort to establish bridgeheads (or advance covering positions, which are here included in the same category). These bridgeheads often served to harass the German and to sap his strength, and often were used as a base for Russian attacks. They were established by infiltration or by attack, and were a dangerous Russian tactic. It always proved wrong and absolutely fatal to do nothing about such bridgeheads or to postpone their elimination, no matter what the reasoning. It was certain that Russian bridgeheads which had existed only twenty-four hours would during that time have grown into a serious menace. Though only one Russian company might have occupied the newly formed bridgehead in the evening, by the next morning it was sure to have turned into an almost invincible fortress held by at least a regiment and bristling with heavy weapons. No matter how heavy and accurate the German fire, the flow of men into the bridgehead continued. Regardless of all countermeasures the bridgehead continued to swell until it ran over. Only by using very strong forces and planned attack could it still be contained or eliminated, provided one was lucky and not afraid of heavy losses. Therefore, the warning against these bridgeheads can never be stressed sufficiently. There was only one way of fighting them, and that had to be made a rule: Every Russian bridgehead in the process of being formed, and every advanced position, no matter how small, must be attacked *immediately*, while it is still undeveloped, and eliminated. If the Germans waited even a few hours, they were in most cases too late, and on the next day success was more remote than ever. Even if there were but one platoon of infantry and one tank available, they had to be committed at once; the Russian was not yet dug in, he was still visible and within reach, he still had no organized defensive fire and no heavy weapons in the new position. A little later he would have all of these. Every delay brought disaster; only an immediate counterattack led to success.

The Russian's kinship with nature expressed itself also in his preference for night operations. Shifts from one position to another, and concentrations, executed rapidly and silently in darkness, were more frequent than night attacks, which themselves were no rarity. However, the Russian generally avoided large-scale night attacks, since it appeared to him that the individual soldiers and subordinate commanders lacked the necessary self-reliance. A major offensive operation was conducted at night only when a victory definitely expected by the highest command had not been achieved in the course of daylight attacks. Such large-scale night attacks were mostly acts of desperation that failed to produce success. On the other hand, night attacks with a limited objective were a method which the Russians liked to employ in order to gain advantages for the next day, or to recapture lost ground. These night attacks were mostly infantry battles only, without use of artillery. The Germans found that it paid to be prepared for a Russian attempt to regain in the night a position that had been lost during the day.

The Russian's excellent utilization of railroads should be noted, even though it does not actually fall into the category of combat. The Russians accomplished strategic concentrations or shifts of large units, one or more armies, in an unbelievably short time with the help of the railroads. The imperfect rail net of European Russia did not often present opportunity for such measures, but whenever a chance offered itself, it was thoroughly utilized. Every expedient was used even though it bore the unmistakable mark of improvisation: a continuous succession of trains without any technical railroad safety measures; trains traveling one within sight of the next, or on two tracks in the same direction; reckless overcrowding and overloading of trains. The number of trains necessary per unit was less here than for any other army. The Russian neither had nor needed baggage or accessories, clerk's bulky lockers, surplus vehicles, or large food supplies. He could be packed into railroad cars like a sardine in a can. The wider gauge and the corresponding greater width of the Russian railroad car was significant in this respect. In any event, by using this type of railroad transport the Russians succeeded in surprising the German command, since such rapidity in large-scale troop movements by railroad contradicted all experience.

Fighting the Russian on his own ground necessitated orientation in a new type of combat. Fighting had to be primitive and unscrupulous, but rapid and flexible. The German could never afford to hesitate even in the face of the most surprising occurrences and unexpected turns of events. Russian reactions to the tactical rules of warfare, and to tricks of the trade such as envelopment, flanking threat, feint, surprise, etc., could never be determined beforehand. One time the Russian would react according to the rules and give up sooner than anticipated; on another occasion all efforts were to no avail, and neither encirclement nor flank attack fazed him. The struggle with the Russians was thereby placed on an entirely new basis; predictive calculation was useless, and every action was full of suspense and surprise. At times, positions which were tactically decisive according to normal concepts would be evacuated by the Russians without delay. At other times, individual terrain features of no evident importance would be held even in the face of serious losses. In those instances the Russian often relied only on his intuition, which he substituted for his practical schooling. It must be conceded that this tactical instinct often stood the Russian in better stead than the theories of many academies could have done. The soundness of many an action which at first seemed surprising, often had to be recognized at a later time.

There was just one tactical misconception which the Russians could not relinquish despite all losses: the belief that an elevation was in every case the only terrain feature of value. They tried for every elevation, fought for it with perseverance and strong forces, without estimating whether it actually dominated the terrain or whether the situation demanded its possession. If the elevation was really important, the Germans thought it well to occupy it before the Russians; otherwise, it was to be expected that the elevation could be taken only with heavy losses. In more cases than had earlier been assumed, however, the possession of level ground was sufficient; the value of the elevation was frequently overestimated.

Thus the Russian soldier voided a number of tactical principles. Still others were altered because of the nature of the country itself, a factor discussed in the following chapter.

CHAPTER 6

Russia as a Theater of Operations

In the characteristics of Russian terrain, the German Army was faced with an inordinate number of new experiences which made necessary the formulation of new doctrines of combat. The Germans had to become thoroughly familiar with Russian land and climate—new enemy weapons to them—in order to deal with them, or at least, to neutralize their restrictive effects. Their qualities altered tactical procedures formerly in common use, and forced the adoption of measures necessary for military operations in that particular area and climate.

In many instances, climate and soil conditions in the U.S.S.R. would for extended periods of time void all rules governing military movement. The German Army was not modern enough to overcome these difficulties, and therefore was forced to fight in winter and during muddy periods as best it could without the assistance of operative motor vehicles. This retrogression of about a century was a problem which could be dealt with only by improvisation.

The great forest and swamp areas of Arctic, Northern, and Central Russia often forced all movement into the narrow lanes of a few sand and swamp roads, and made it extremely difficult and time-consuming. Development of the columns was generally out of the question. The execution of any and all measures required a multiple of the usual amount of time, and the advantage of motorization was almost negligible.

Sand, mud, and snow impeded the advance of all types of troops, and put great strain on motors. Lined up and jammed along one road, the troops slowly and painfully inched forward—a long snake crawling slowly over the difficult ground.

The halt of one part of the snake stopped all parts behind it, pressing them still closer together. Weak bridges barely supported the infantry vehicles. Extensive bridge and road repairs were necessary, and many defiles had to be traversed. Previous experiences and doctrines were useless under these conditions. Time calculations, the most important factor in operations, had to be based on entirely new concepts. Frequently the time required for a movement could not be estimated even approximately. It continued to run far in excess of the expected maximum. Remedies were difficult and could be achieved only by flexibility and practice.

In by far the largest part of Southern Russia, and in most of the swampless areas of Northern and Central Russia, travel in dry weather was considerably better, and the terrain, too, was passable for vehicles of all types almost everywhere. During that time, operations on even the largest scale were possible everywhere with the exception of the swamp areas.

The principle of establishing lanes of movement rather than routes of advance proved satisfactory for the Germans as well as for the Russians; the same was true of the separation of lanes of movement for motorized and nonmotorized units. Here, the German motorized troops had to be allotted the lanes with the best roads. Engineers were always placed far up in the column so that they might quickly reinforce bridges and eliminate terrain obstacles. Only strict regulation of traffic and relentlessly severe discipline guaranteed the best possible progress. Every halt for rest had to be closely timed, passing procedure strictly regulated, and priority definitely determined. Each driver who pressed forward in unguarded moments became a traffic violator. For that reason, trained troops were needed for traffic control, and had to be used, just as every tactical unit, according to the point of main effort. Likewise, all staffs and higher headquarters had to abide by traffic discipline since exceptions only caused confusion. In particularly difficult large-scale movements, special purpose staffs under the command of senior officers were employed.

The rate of progress of motorized troops could be roughly estimated in advance only if they were traveling on hard-surfaced roads. A rule of thumb was that on average dry road-ways, motorized troops made from five to six miles per hour, and foot troops from one to less than three miles per hour. Terrain and road conditions in the east required, according to German experience, three to four times the amount of motor fuel needed under normal conditions in Europe.

The assumption that long columns can easily be stopped by the enemy appears justified. However, it developed that the Russian over-estimated the constraining effect of channeled movements. In almost every case he blocked only the roads and bridges with task forces deployed without breadth or depth. It was, therefore, not too difficult to knock out such enemy blocking attempts by attacks against the flanks and rear of the enemy groups. This maneuver required two conditions for success: reconnaissance far to the front, and incorporation of combat forces capable of cross-country movement at the head of the march groups. No matter how easy it was for vehicles with cross-country mobility to cross great, open stretches in any direction during dry seasons, on long marches they were confined mostly to the existing roads, since the Russian terrain always confronted them with terrain obstacles which they were unable to overcome (swamps, watercourses, ravines, steep rises, etc.). Furthermore, it required considerably more time and fuel to move cross-country.

In drawing any conclusions from the battles of the German armies in the east it is to be noted that the German armed forces went unprepared into the Russian winter and into the muddy periods, and for that reason they faced numerous difficulties and emergencies which could have been avoided by conscientious preparation.

PECULIARITIES OF RUSSIAN TACTICS

CHAPTER 7

General

An understanding of Russian tactics demands a clear conception of the premises on which they are based. Russian tactics have their roots in the Russian himself and in his social order; in the Russian landmass with its climate and soil conditions, its expanse, and its varied topography. These points will be described in detail in the following pages, and illustrated by numerous examples. The examples should permit insight into the practical effect of these characteristics under various conditions, and should illustrate how the German command coped with them.

While the bulk of the Red Army consisted of infantry divisions which were combined into corps and armies and supplemented by numerous GHQ troops (artillery, antitank, and engineer brigades, as well as tank and self-propelled artillery elements), there were also the large, highly mobile tank and mechanized corps—the strategic force—which in most instances were combined into tank armies. Tank corps and mechanized corps were seldom placed under infantry armies. This method of organization reveals the effort of the Russian high command to assure strategic mobility. That mobility was demonstrated in the sweeping employment of these large, fast forces. As soon as the battle fronts became static (position warfare), the Russian command withdrew its tank and mechanized forces, and did not commit them again until the infantry had breached the enemy defensive system. This mode of employment coincided with the concepts expressed in the Russian field service regulations. In fighting for a system of defensive positions, GHQ tank and self-propelled artillery regiments (that is, not the organic forces of the mobile corps) supported the infantry divisions in great numbers.

Because of the long duration of the war it was possible to observe the combat methods of the Russian in all phases. During the first winter in Russia it was evident that the German lower command would have to find new methods of fighting if it wanted to be successful. The extensive area, the mass employment of men, the peculiar characteristics of Russian fighting methods, and the different climatic conditions forced the Germans to develop a new line of tactical doctrine. In logical sequence, this doctrine was derived from close observation of all Russian habits, Russian reaction to German fighting methods, and thorough exploitation of Russian weaknesses. Only a better-led soldier, and one superior in fighting qualities, had any prospect of success. In order to make details about the characteristics of the Russian available to all concerned, it was exceedingly important to compile the information and to disseminate it, particularly to the replacement training units and to the schools. There had to be a constant flow of instructors with combat experience to these units in order to train replacements and new recruits according to the latest experiences.

These measures proved invaluable to the Germans. Divisions that had been newly formed, or transferred from other theaters, and sent to the East without enough officers and noncommissioned officers with prior experience in the East, failed in the beginning almost without exception and suffered heavy losses. On the other hand, even remnants of divisions which had long been going through the hard school of the East, made outstanding accomplishments, both in Russia and on all other fronts.

CHAPTER 8

Reconnaissance and Security

Russian march reconnaissance and security generally corresponded to German concepts. Activity was not especially intense, but very skillfully adapted to the objective and to local conditions (terrain, climate, transportation routes, and weather). In his march reconnaissance the Russian was very hesitant, groping, and cautious, and allowed himself much time. If he found no enemy resistance, he frequently plunged ahead into the unknown without further reconnaissance.

The engagement at Maloryta at the end of June 1941 grew out of the thrust of a Russian rifle division east of the Bug near Wlodawa into the flank of German armored units which were rolling from Brest Litovsk through Kobryn in the direction of Slutsk. The Russian division had sent ahead armored reconnaissance cars. These made their appearance about half a day in advance of the division itself, and encountered the German 255th Infantry Division which was advancing from Wlodawa on Maloryta. Although the terrain (Pripyat Marshes) was extremely unfavorable for reconnaissance by armored cars, they advanced until two cars had been knocked out. The others withdrew. Instead, there appeared after a few hours infantry security detachments, already deployed as a thin screen of skirmishers. Several miles behind followed the rifle division split into battle teams, which were deployed over a front of about six miles, with large gaps between the teams.

The rifle division had undoubtedly anticipated an encounter with the Germans in the vicinity of Maloryta, and had sent out motorized reconnaissance to obtain the information needed for deployment of the division. The infantry screens following later served as local security for the battle teams.

In an action southeast of Plavskoye in November 1941 the Russians intended to thrust from Yefremov along the main road to the northwest in the direction of Tula, into the rear of German armored units which were before Tula (Map 5). When the leading elements of the German 167th Infantry Division met them near Teploye, the Russians were as surprised as the Germans. It is certain that they had not counted on meeting the enemy there. On this basis, their advance can be taken as typical of a Russian march against the enemy with only one usable road available, when direct contact with the enemy is not yet expected. Again, several armored reconnaissance cars appeared at first, but they seemed to have only local reconnaissance missions. They moved ahead by bounds. Behind them, following German procedure, came infantry security detachments. Only then followed the foremost division (6th Rifle). This division possessed numerous trucks which, however, were not used until later during local shifts on the battlefield. They were not intended for the strategic forward displacement of the division at this time. On the road behind the 6th Rifle Division, further infantry divisions with fewer trucks followed. Several days later, when the battle was already in progress, a cavalry division which had come up on a bad side road running to the west appeared. A tank brigade which had been standing ready behind the long column of rifle divisions was thrown forward in a single movement only when the battle had reached its climax.

It seemed as if in an advance against the enemy, the chain of rifle divisions following one another was not to be disturbed. Accordingly, though it would have been possible to move a single division forward, this was not done. Perhaps this maneuver was also made to prevent the enemy from recognizing the movement prematurely. Had the cavalry division advanced simultaneously with the rifle divisions, the Russians would not have been able to surprise the Germans.

The following example from the Kandalaksha front shows the use of stationary security detachments for the protection of a flanking movement. About one mile in front of German strong points in the no man's land of primeval forest north of the Arctic Circle there was a small range of hills, the Ahvenvaara. It was unoccupied most of the time, but now and then either side would occupy it temporarily as an anchor point for operations. One day in March 1944 this range of hills was again occupied by weak Russian forces. Assuming that the Russians would, as they had for years, leave again after a short time, the Germans took no action. In a few days, however, a whole battalion had infiltrated, and it was too late to dislodge them. In the same way, the Russians occupied an elevation farther to the west, where they drove off weak German security detachments and immediately set up a strong point. Under the protection of these two points, the Russians moved their attack troops into the northern front. This was an instance of planned, farsighted preparation for moving attack troops into the jump-off position for a subsequent attack based on a stabilized front. The Russians were completely successful in their security measures for those movements.

The preceding three examples reveal that the Russian demonstrated great adaptability in march reconnaissance and security, and that he knew how to take proper action under diverse circumstances. In mobile warfare the use of fast-working motorized reconnaissance can be observed on approaching an expected enemy, and as its result the developed advance of battle groups under cover of local infantry security detachments. In advancing upon an enemy with whom an engagement is not anticipated in the near future, the Russian normally employs an almost schematic local march-reconnaissance pattern: armored reconnaissance cars moving ahead in rapid bounds, and behind them normal infantry march security. There also seems to be a definite effort to hold the forces together and to prevent ventures on the part of individual elements. Further, in a kind of position warfare—even in primeval forest wilderness—first there is the methodical establishment of firm strong points, under the protection of which the march movements of the units destined to attack are subsequently to be executed. Surprise attacks into the Russian march movement—in the example presented, such surprise attacks would have meant a flanking march of almost forty miles—are thereby to be eliminated.

On stabilized fronts, the Russian conducted his reconnaissance with patrols, or by reconnaissance in force. He was exceedingly adept at combat reconnaissance in offensive as well as in defensive operations. He knew how to adapt his reconnaissance patrols to the terrain and how to employ them in great numbers. Seldom could any conclusion as to the intentions of the Russian enemy be drawn from his reconnaissance-patrol activity.

For reconnaissance in force, the Russian employed forces at least in company strength, but frequently also in battalion and regimental strength. They were supported in their operations by concentrated artillery fire, and often by accompanying tanks as well. The main objective of such attacks was the taking of prisoners, and sometimes the capture of an important terrain feature.

Another frequently employed Russian method of reconnaissance was the ambush of enemy reconnaissance patrols. The Russian was a master at this procedure. Well camouflaged, he could lie in wait for hours until the opportunity presented itself. He also knew how to sneak up and surprise isolated outguards. The employment of dogs trained in tracking ambush patrols proved a satisfactory German countermeasure.

The Russians also made considerable use of the civilian population for intelligence missions, using them to obtain the desired reports on the enemy situation. A favorite practice was the employment of boys eight to fourteen years old. They were first trained for this work and then allowed to infiltrate at suitable front sectors. Before the offensive in July 1943, for example, more than a dozen such children were picked up in the Byelgorod sector alone. They gave detailed reports on the kind of training they received and on their *modus operandi*. The training of these children had been supervised by Russian officers. It had lasted four weeks, and there had been sixty participants. The youths came from communities near the front on both sides of the battle lines and therefore were thoroughly familiar with the locale. Many were staying with relatives or acquaintances in German-occupied localities, and were therefore not easy to discover and apprehend. Their talent for observation and their skill at spying were remarkable. For this reason, civilians in localities near the front (four to six miles behind the front line) had to be evacuated not only because of the danger from enemy fire, but also as a preventive measure against espionage.

CHAPTER 9

Offense

The national characteristics, which have already been described, and the peculiarities of the country were the principal factors determining the Russian conduct of battle.

I. Winter: the Preferred Season

The Russians preferred to carry out their major offensives in winter because their troops were accustomed to that season and very well equipped and trained for it. The Russians were superior to all peoples of Central and Western Europe in enduring rigors of weather and climate. Casualties from the cold were an exception in the Red Army. Soldiers with frostbite were severely punished. Even in the harsh winter of 1941–42 the Russians were able to spend many days in the snow, protected only by simple windbreaks, without detriment to their health.

For instance, in the winter of 1941–42, from 6 December 1941 to 14 April 1942, the Soviets carried out their first major offensive in the area west of Moscow. They penetrated to the Vyazma–Rzhev line. In their large-scale attack from the Stalingrad–Don area the Russians succeeded in encircling the German Sixth Army at Stalingrad, and in overrunning the front of the German allies. Between 19 November 1942 and the middle of March 1943 they succeeded in creating a fluid situation along a 1,000-mile stretch of the Eastern Front, and in penetrating up to 300 miles toward the west.

On Christmas of 1943 the Russians began an offensive from the area southwest of Kiev. It continued until the thaw started in March 1944 and led to the annihilation of German divisions in the Cherkassy pocket, the encirclement of Tarnopol and of the German First Panzer Army, and the retrograde correction of the German front to a line east of Stanislaw–Lwow–Kowel.

The Russian general offensive, begun along the entire Eastern Front in mid-January of 1945, culminated in the occupation of Hungary, Poland, Silesia, East Prussia, and Pomerania. After short local halts, the Russians stood before Vienna and Berlin, and in cooperation with the armed forces of the Western Powers brought about the end of the war.

II. The Employment of Mass

Only the use of masses of men and equipment enabled the Russians to accomplish these great feats. Even in World War I the "steamroller" was the core of the Russian system of attack. At that time the concept was limited to the employment of the human mass, which resulted in initial successes but cost myriads of human lives. Later, undermined politically from within, the system finally disintegrated sealing the doom of the Russian Imperial Army.

The surprise element of the attack on the Eastern Front by the Germans in June 1941 prevented the immediate use of Russian mass tactics and caused Soviet reverses. Relying, however, on inexhaustible reserves and the rigors of its boundless territory, the Soviet Army concentrated human masses and created anew the famous steamroller. Strengthened by a mass of equipment and welded together by the caresses and whiplashes of communism, it became invincible despite numerous setbacks. Step by step the German Army was pounded to pieces and crushed as it succumbed to what might be termed the modern "super steamroller."

As early as 1941 the Russians made repeated attempts to check the German offensive by counterattacks. To this end they opposed it with cavalry and tank forces, and sometimes with masses of infantry. They succeeded in checking the German Army locally and temporarily, but were unsuccessful in stopping the great offensive as a whole. The following examples illustrate the Russian type of attack at that time.

The battle in the Dnepr–Berezina triangle (mid-July to mid-August 1941) resulted from Timoshenko's plan to envelop in a pincers movement both flanks of the German armored units which had advanced across the Dnepr, and to cut them off from the rear. Since the northern arm of the pincers had already been destroyed near Orsha, and the German LIII Infantry Corps had almost made connection with the armored units on the Dnepr by a rapid advance via Slutsk–Bobruysk, a battle developed not between Timoshenko and the armored units, but between the Russians and LIII Infantry Corps, which was assuming the protection of the flanks and rear of the German armored unit (Map 3).

The attack was very carefully prepared. As early as February 1941, during a conference near Bobruysk, Timoshenko had discussed this operation in a kind of map exercise with his higher commanders. In order to put it into effect, three divisions located in the vicinity of Kiev were transferred to the neighborhood of Gomel immediately after the outbreak of hostilities. Here, they were excellently concealed and kept in readiness until the time for action came. The Moscow School of Artillery was called upon. By interrogation of Russian prisoners, fifty-three different rifle regiments were identified during the course of battle, some of them coming from as far away as the Caucasus. In order to take immediate advantage of the expected success, a detachment of specialists from Moscow very quickly repaired the railroad bridge over the Dnepr at Zhlobin during the course of the battle. The bridge had been blown prematurely when German armored units approached the town. Timoshenko reopened the bridge in person. Thus, all preparations seemed to have been made to ensure the success of the operation and to exploit it. The higher command had done as much as could be expected.

Tactical measures during the first stage of the battle were entirely appropriate. The German 4th Panzer Division, which had crossed the Dnepr near Rogachev, was thrown back across the river. Simultaneously with the withdrawing armored vehicles, the Russians crossed the Dnepr in close pursuit, and for the time being there was nothing to stop their advance, since the armor had turned off to the north. At Zhlobin, where there were only weak armored security forces, the Soviet Army faced practically no opposition at all. The Russians did not take advantage of this favorable situation. They moved forward very slowly, so that very small, hastily motorized forces of the German 255th and 267th Infantry Divisions could be thrown against them. These German forces held the Russians at bay until the divisions themselves arrived after a day or two. Thus it happened that the Russians pushed only six miles to the west of the Dnepr both at Zhlobin and Rogachev. One might almost think that this was the area that had been planned as the first day's objective in Timoshenko's war game. More territory could unquestionably have been taken, had the advance been conducted more energetically. Lack of follow-up, however, can be attributed to the intermediate command. By the time the high command learned of the situation, it was too late. The subsequent Russian attacks were carried out in the form of outflanking and enveloping movements while pinning down the front. They occasioned many a critical situation, but when the Germans' greatest worry had been eliminated after the commitment of the 55th Infantry Division, and the front began to be more stabilized, the Russian command exhausted itself by repeated attacks on the same points. The Russians failed to recognize that the opposing forces were now of equal strength, and that therefore nothing more was to be achieved by the battle.

It was soon evident that the strategic situation of the Russians was becoming steadily less tenable. The advance of XII Infantry Corps northeast of Rogachev, and of XLIII Infantry Corps to the lower Berezina, made the grave danger facing the Russians unmistakably clear. Nevertheless, they held firmly to the originally planned thrust, even after it was time to escape envelopment. This situation led to the formation of the Gomel pocket and the annihilation of the Russian main attack army, a catastrophe which could have been avoided, had the Russian command drawn its conclusions from the situation in time.

In the fighting in the Porechye bridgehead on the Luga (mid-July to August 1941) a strong combat element of the 6th Panzer Division succeeded in effecting a surprise capture of the two Luga bridges at Porechye (60 miles southwest of Leningrad) on 14 July 1941, and in forming a bridgehead (Map 4). The strong armored forces which were to follow remained stuck for days in swampy forests. Therefore, the 6th was for a long time entirely on its own. Three alerted proletarian divisions and armored units were dispatched from Leningrad to the Luga by rail and motor vehicles, with the mission of destroying the German force consisting of two infantry battalions, one panzer battalion, two artillery battalions, one Flak battalion, and a company of engineers.

Nevertheless, the German force was able to stand its ground against an enemy six times as strong, despite the fact that it could no longer be reached and supported by aircraft. The bridgehead was over two miles deep, but only 400 yards wide, and was completely surrounded by swampy forests which could be traversed in summer by infantry. The Russians, however, had no visibility, because the edges of the woods were in German hands. Russian artillery fired twenty times as many rounds per day as did the German batteries. It pounded the bridges and the edges of the woods. In unobserved fire the Russians sent more than 2,000 medium shells a day in the direction of the bridges without ever hitting them. Enemy aircraft roared all day above the narrow corridor of the bridgehead and inflicted serious losses. Soon, therefore, the road was lined with a long row of German soldiers' graves, marked with birchwood crosses. As often as ten times a day the enemy attacked the road fork which was enclosed by the projecting arc of the bridgehead. Each attack was headed by as many tanks, echeloned in depth, as the narrow road would accommodate. Time and again the enemy attacks were repulsed, and time and again they were renewed. Wave after wave of Russian forces assembled, concealed by many wrecked tanks and heaps of corpses, and stormed recklessly into the murderous defensive fire. The attacks did not subside until the enemy no longer had the necessary men and ammunition at his disposal. Soon, however, replacements of proletarians and new ammunition supplies arrived from Leningrad. The assaults on the road fork were stubbornly and incessantly resumed until passage through the narrow attack corridors was no longer possible because they were completely clogged by disabled enemy tanks and decaying heaps of corpses. Later, the Germans counted more than 2,000 dead Russians and seventy-eight knocked-out enemy tanks in this narrow combat zone alone.

The only variation consisted of enemy attacks, sometimes along both sides of the road leading to the fork from the north, and at other times on the road coming from the south. A simultaneous attack from both sides never took place, however, for different divisions were involved which did not coordinate their attacks. The tanks always attacked along the northern road. Their attacks, too, ceased only when it was no longer possible to pass between the seventy-eight wrecks. The swampy forests and a reservoir fifty feet deep prevented bypassing.

The next attacks were made through the woods to cut off the bridgehead. It was impossible to prevent the mass assaults since there were only a small number of forces to man the long flanks of the bridgehead. The attacks were expected and the defense arranged accordingly. Two tank units held in readiness, one at the road fork and one at the bridges, were reinforced by armored infantry companies and had orders to attack immediately from both sides and to annihilate the enemy if he broke through to the road. This flexible fighting method proved effective. With the same stubbornness he had formerly shown in attacking the road fork, the enemy made several assaults daily on the flanks, and each time succeeded in reaching the road. Within a scant half hour he would be attacked from both sides and destroyed by tank fire. Only remnants succeeded in escaping through the woods. Not until the attempt to cut off the group failed repeatedly with severe losses, did the enemy give up this procedure and attack the bridges directly. In this way a 150-man Russian battalion succeeded in reaching the southern bridge after overcoming its weak defenses. While the forces were crossing the bridge, German armored personnel carriers took them by surprise and completely destroyed them. Contrary to his usual custom, the enemy did not repeat this venture. Instead, he sent a reinforced infantry regiment from Kingisepp, and later two battalions of the 3d Proletarian Division, against the rear of the bridgehead. Both operations were caught in a pincers movement between the leading elements of the main German forces, which had been stalled but were then approaching from the southwest, and a reinforced armored unit of the bridgehead coming from the opposite direction. The regiment was scattered and the two battalions were destroyed. The bridgehead was then strengthened by German forces coming up from the rear, and became impregnable.

The foregoing example demonstrates the complete failure of the intermediate and lower Russian commands which did not understand how to coordinate the various units and weapons into a common, simultaneous attack from all sides. The weak German units, which were fighting a losing battle, would not have been able to withstand such an attack.

The Russian attacks in the battle southeast of Plavskoye (Map 5) in November 1941 developed from a pure meeting engagement. The Russian forces, which were to advance against German armored forces before Tula, suddenly faced LIII Infantry Corps coming from the west. The Russian command adapted itself skillfully to the new situation—a situation made easier on both sides because the points met first and each opponent was then able to deploy its forces from depths. It was, therefore, several days before the battle mounted to a climax once both sides had deployed their long columns.

Strategically, the Russian thrust on Tula was well planned. At this stage the Russian higher command also acted correctly from a tactical standpoint, and the Russian 6th Rifle Division, which bore the initial brunt of the battle, was tactically well commanded. Under the completely unclarified conditions, the Russian higher command apparently wanted to avoid having its foremost division repulsed, and so brought it to a halt. The division, deployed laterally, blocked the advance of the first German regiment to appear. In addition, the Russian higher command attempted to bring up for the anticipated battle all forces available in the vicinity. The Russian cavalry division, which had advanced north of the combat area, abandoned its operations against the 112th Infantry Division and appeared on the scene. A cavalry division located near Yefremov was ordered forward, over side roads past the march columns of the Russian rifle division, to cut the Orel–Plavskoye road in the neighborhood of Chern. In this connection there ensued a sharp clash between the commander of the Bryansk Army Group in Yelets, who was in command here, and the commander of the cavalry division from Yefremov.

According to captured documents the army group commander ordered the cavalry division to proceed by a forced march to the Orel–Tula road, a distance of forty miles. The cavalry division commander made a written reply stating that this was impossible because 20 percent of his horses were completely unshod and, of the remaining horses, 80 percent had no hind shoes and 20 percent no fore shoes. For that reason the division was unfit to move. Thereupon the higher commander repeated the order for the forced march. The cavalry division started out, but actually went only twenty-five miles. It could go no farther, but it had effected a connection with the front and extended it. The iron determination of the army group commander had not achieved the desired success, but it had created new difficulties for the Germans.

The Red 6th Rifle Division was very mobile in its fighting. When its western flank was threatened and the divisions following it had not yet arrived, it withdrew far enough in its numerous trucks to eliminate the threat to its flank. It did not move forward again until the next division could be turned to cover the threat to its flank. The other divisions were employed according to the prevailing situation and formed concentrated points of main effort. They attacked by deploying directly from march columns, without going into assembly positions. Not until they were all disposed along the battle front was the tank brigade, which had been far to the rear, committed in order to strike the decisive blow against whatever seemed to be the weakest spot. This was on about the fifth day of battle. Only rapid shifting of German forces prevented a Russian success.

To be sure, when LIII Infantry Corps subsequently launched its attack, the rifle division, which had become immobile to a great extent, was wiped out and the westernmost cavalry division had already been eliminated. However, the bulk of the Russian forces escaped annihilation by hasty withdrawal, sacrificing much of their equipment. This was the first instance in the corps' experience in which the Russian high command withdrew troops from a situation that was beginning to take an unfavorable turn, instead of continuing to attack. The intervention of LIII Infantry Corps upset the Russian large-scale plan of operation from the very start. The attempt to force a way to Tula in spite of this had failed. The Russian high command now actually drew the proper inferences from the situation. They adopted new methods.

III. Development of Russian Offensive Tactics

The Russians carried out their first preconceived large-scale offensive in the severe winter of 1941–42 in the Moscow area. It was well thought out, and cleverly exploited the detrimental effect which the muddy period and the onset of winter had on the striking power of the German Army, unprepared as it was for winter warfare. This offensive marked the turning point in the Eastern Campaign; it did not, however, decide it, as the Russians had expected it to do. Therefore, it did not achieve the intended purpose.

According to the Russian fighting method the mass attack was supposed to shatter the German front. Units penetrating and infiltrating through the lines were to cut off the supply lines.

The German front was not yet ready for defense when frost set in. Some sectors were still fluid. The solidly frozen ground and the exceedingly heavy snowfalls precluded the methodical construction of a defensive position. Taking advantage of the dusky weather and the blizzards, the first waves of Russians, clad in white camouflage coats, worked their way close to the German positions without being detected. Wave after wave, driven on by the commissars, surged against the German lines. At that time the Russians knew nothing about methodical preparation for an attack by concentrated fire of heavy weapons and artillery, or by the employment of massed tanks.

When the attacks continually failed and enormous losses were incurred, the Russians changed to infiltration tactics. Forces capable of rapid movement were generally used for this purpose. Tanks and ski units were preferred when the terrain permitted their use. Except for a few local reconnaissance thrusts, the Russians regularly attacked on a broad front. They always assembled far superior forces for those attacks. Cooperation between the different arms of the service improved noticeably. It was patterned after German offensive tactics. Russian methods of attack were subjected to many changes as a result of war experiences. In 1941–42 the Russians always resorted to mass attacks after bringing up strong reserves. Thus, for example, they repeated their attacks in the same place against the Fourth Army for weeks at a time during the so-called Battles of the *Rollbahn* (express motor highway, in this case the Minsk–Moscow road) near Smolensk between 21 October and 4 December. Cooperation between the various infantry weapons likewise was imperfect. Attacks on German unit boundaries, which the Russians always sought and usually detected, were dangerous. Artillery support was active, but as yet often without a definite fire plan.

The year 1943 brought a definite change in the method of attack. Concentrated artillery fires were employed more frequently and supplemented by massed mortar attacks. The Russians tried to infiltrate through known German weak points. For this purpose they preferred forest areas or hollows previously designated by the tactical command. If they succeeded in infiltrating by this system, they immediately entrenched themselves and laid mines. Subsequently, a period of vulnerability set in because the artillery and heavy weapons were brought up slowly, and cooperation with them ceased abruptly.

The employment of massed tanks brought about a revolutionary change in Russian tactics in 1944. After a drum fire of artillery, a large number of tanks led off the attack, followed by the infantry in deep wedges. While the artillery gave good support at first, communications with it frequently broke off during a further advance. To the very end of the war it was difficult for the Russians to coordinate fire and movement. The penetrations were deep, and invariably in a straight line. Then a halt was called in order to bring up the greatest possible number of infantry during the night. These masses of infantry dug in as soon as they reached the points of the attack. The assault wedges closed up in echelons behind the tanks.

Since the German counterattacks were usually launched when the enemy infantry was separated from its tanks, the Russians began in 1945 to make deep thrusts with infantry riding on tanks. These thrusts often went so deep that contact with the main forces was lost. The Russians were able to take the risk because the German front of 1945 no longer had adequate reserves available to destroy the far-advanced, strong enemy forces.

Though the Russians built field fortifications whenever they halted it did not follow that they had plans of attacking. The Russian always dug in. The time to be suspicious came only when a gradual sapping toward the German lines into a jump-off position for an assault could be noted in connection with their entrenchment activities. That usually meant preparation for attack. Recognized preparations behind a front sector did not necessarily indicate an attack at that particular point. Surprise attacks were launched by skillfully and quickly shifting attack forces to the planned assembly area during the course of one night. Numerous reconnaissance thrusts, supported by artillery and tanks, and conducted on a broad front both by day and night in strength up to a regiment, were to procure information for an attack and to confuse or deceive the Germans as to the time and place of the attack. Movement behind the front, even at night, was not necessarily followed by an attack. The Soviets were very skillful in the use of feints, sham installations, and dummy matériel of all types. Evaluation of artillery observation data, often painstakingly carried on for weeks, and constant interrogation of prisoners, whose statements were checked by German reconnaissance operations, produced reliable evidence of an impending attack. The Russians often cleverly concealed a projected assembly of their artillery by extraordinary emplacement activity and by a highly mobile employment of roving guns and batteries. They were also very cautious about fire for registration whenever it was not executed for purposes of deception.

Nor until later did the Russians make extensive use, in the attack, of artillery fire based on mathematical computation. Despite all their efforts to conceal their true intentions, however, the pattern of enemy artillery activity, carefully worked out day by day, still revealed very reliable clues as to impending enemy attacks. The Germans could often observe that a few days before an attack the enemy moved about as little as possible by day or night, and that his combat activity decreased noticeably, until suddenly the attack was launched out of a clear sky.

Secondary attacks and feints were often launched at the same time as the main attack in order to make the assault front appear as broad as possible, and at the same time cause the Germans to split up their defense forces. In the summer of 1943, the Russians used smoke on a broad front while carrying out attacks across the Donets. This concealed preparations and denied observation to the Germans. At that time the Russians incurred severe losses. The German XXX Infantry Corps repulsed all attacks and attempts to cross the Donets by immediately concentrating the fire of all heavy weapons straight into the smoke. At that time the Russians still were very inexperienced in the use of smoke and did not use dummy smoke screens. Likewise, they failed to understand the principle of laying a smoke screen over German observers in order to blind them. At that time, too, the Russians did not necessarily carry out their attacks with artillery preparation. When they did, their artillery, massed into points of main effort, laid a rigid concentration on infantry positions, battery positions, towns, and road junctions. During the artillery preparation the infantry worked its way forward into the jump-off position by infiltration, and from that point made a mass advance. When the first objective, which was still within range of the supporting artillery, was reached, a long halt was called since the Russians were not in a position to displace their artillery and heavy weapons forward in a manner that would allow a continuous forward thrust. The infantry immediately dug in and felt its way forward only by combat reconnaissance. During the halts, the infantry had to rely almost exclusively on local support from accompanying tanks and mortars. The Russian heavy mortar battalions (probably 120mm) were an ideal direct-support artillery for infantry. However, they also were too slow for continuous support of the infantry in an attack. The infantry-support tanks acted very cautiously and fought more in the manner of self-propelled assault guns, or like armored artillery pieces of the infantry.

Even at the beginning of the Eastern Campaign the Russian infantry was very clever at utilizing terrain features. If the Russians could not continue their current main attacks with the desired success by day, they proceeded to launch local attacks at night. In that case, they either launched sudden mass attacks, or infiltrated at many points through the German lines which for the most part were lightly manned. Thus, in a night attack on the 97th Light Infantry Division in the winter of 1941, they broke through east of Artemovsk in the Donets Basin with an entire cavalry division. However, the next day this division was cut down to the last man. Also in the battle of encirclement at Uman in 1941, and at Beli—southeast of Toropets—in November 1942, thousands of Russian soldiers without equipment or heavy weapons penetrated the German lines during hours of darkness by piecemeal infiltration. Well-prepared night attacks were rare.

Low-flying aircraft, supporting the main efforts, picked as their principal targets the defending infantry, batteries, reserves, supplies, and villages in the divisional combat sectors. The attack planes did not venture far into the rear area.

In order to develop the war of position into mobile warfare later in the Eastern Campaign, the Red Army command concentrated its forces, which were numerically far superior to those of the Germans, into more and more powerful masses at the points of main effort and, after heavy artillery concentrations, broke through or sent the German front reeling. The Russian command attempted to conceal strategic preparations for large-scale attacks from German reconnaissance, and therefore carried them out only at night. Preparations could thus be detected only by night aerial reconnaissance. Night truck transport operations on a grand scale (2,000 to 3,000 trucks in each direction in the course of one night), which usually took place shortly before a large-scale attack, were the first reliable indication of an imminent Russian offensive.

IV. The Use of Armor

The Russian armored force played only a subordinate role at the beginning of the war. In the advance of 1941, most German troops encountered only small units which supported the infantry in the same manner as the German self-propelled assault guns. The Russian tanks operated in a very clumsy manner and were quickly eliminated by German antitank weapons. The Russians carried out counterattacks with large tank forces, either alone or in combined operations with other arms, only at individual, important sectors.

On 23 June 1941 the German Fourth Panzer Group, after a thrust from East Prussia, had reached the Dubysa and had formed several bridgeheads. The defeated enemy infantry units scattered into the extensive forests and high grain fields, where they constituted a threat to the German supply lines. As early as 25 June the Russians launched a surprise counterattack on the southern bridgehead in the direction of Raseiniai with their hastily brought-up XIV Tank Corps. They overpowered the 6th Motorcycle Battalion which was committed in the bridgehead, took the bridge, and pushed on in the direction of the city. The German 114th Armored Infantry Regiment, reinforced by two artillery battalions and 100 tanks, was immediately put into action and stopped the main body of enemy forces. Then there suddenly appeared for the first time a battalion of heavy enemy tanks of previously unknown type. The tanks overran the armored infantry regiment and broke through into the artillery position. The projectiles of all defense weapons (except the 88mm Flak) bounced off the thick enemy armor. The 100 tanks were unable to check the twenty enemy dreadnaughts, and suffered losses. Several Czech-built tanks (T36's) which had bogged down in the grain fields because of mechanical trouble were flattened by the enemy monsters. The same fate befell a 150mm medium howitzer battery which kept on firing until the last minute. Despite the fact that it scored numerous direct hits from as close a range as 200 yards, its heavy shells were unable to put even a single tank out of action. The situation became critical. Only the 88mm Flak finally knocked out a few of the Russian KV1's and forced the others to withdraw into the woods.

One of the KV1's even managed to reach the only supply route of the German task force located in the northern bridgehead, and blocked it for several days. The first unsuspecting trucks to arrive with supplies were immediately shot afire by the tank. There were practically no means of eliminating the monster. It was impossible to bypass it because of the swampy surrounding terrain. Neither supplies nor ammunition could be brought up. The severely wounded could not be removed to the hospital for the necessary operations, so they died. The attempt to put the tank out of action with the 50mm antitank gun battery, which had just been introduced at that time, at a range of 500 yards ended with heavy losses to crews and equipment of the battery. The tank remained undamaged in spite of the fact that, as was later determined, it got fourteen direct hits. These merely produced blue spots on its armor. When a camouflaged 88 was brought up, the tank calmly permitted it to be put into position at a distance of 700 yards, and then smashed it and its crew before it was even ready to fire. The attempt of engineers to blow it up at night likewise proved abortive. To be sure, the engineers managed to get to the tank after midnight, and laid the prescribed demolition charge under the caterpillar tracks. The charge went off according to plan, but was insufficient for the oversized tracks. Pieces were broken off the tracks, but the tank remained mobile and continued to molest the rear of the front and to block all supplies. At first it received supplies at night from scattered Russian groups and civilians, but the Germans later prevented this procedure by blocking off the surrounding area. However, even this isolation did not induce it to give up its favorable position. It finally became the victim of a German ruse. Fifty tanks were ordered to feign an attack from three sides and to fire on it so as to draw all of its attention in those directions. Under the protection of this feint it was possible to set up and camouflage another 88mm Flak to the rear of the tank, so that this time it actually was able to fire. Of the twelve direct hits scored by this medium gun, three pierced the tank and destroyed it.

The Russian had not taken advantage of the critical situation of the German division which had resulted from the employment of the heavy sixty-five-ton tanks. His infantry, which had broken through, did not become active again, but passively watched the proceedings. Therefore, it was possible to withdraw strong forces from the northern bridgehead and send them against the rear of the attacking tank corps. The latter immediately abandoned its success and retired to the east bank of the river. There, despite the fact that strong neighboring armored forces had already enveloped it and were attacking from the rear, it again held out far too long. The result was that the Russian tank corps lost the bulk of its tanks in the swamps. The infantry scattered and made its way through the woods along swamp paths.

On 26 June 1941 the Russians, by a tank corps thrust, wanted to relieve their forces which were encircled near Rawa Ruska, north of Lwow. This tank corps consisted only of tank chassis mounting machine guns and guns up to 150mm; it had no motorized infantry support. Near Magierow it encountered organized defense of the German 97th Light Infantry Division in a day and night attack, and was repulsed. Sixty-three Russian armored vehicles were knocked out.

In the thrust on Vyazma (early in October 1941) the German 6th Panzer Division, committed in the main effort, reached the upper Dnepr and captured the two bridges there by a *coup de main* (Map 6). That maneuver cut off Russian forces which were still west of the river and assured a continued thrust to the east.

On the following day the Russians attempted to parry this

severe blow by a flank attack. One hundred tanks drove from the south against the road hub of Kholm. They were, for the most part, medium tanks, against which the Germans could send only forty light tanks and one armored infantry company. However, these weak forces were sufficient to contain the dangerous thrust until antiaircraft and antitank guns could be organized into an adequate antitank defense between Kholm and the southern Dnepr bridge. Split up by tanks in forest fighting, the Russians never succeeded in making a powerful, unified tank thrust. Their leading elements were eliminated as they encountered the antitank front. As a result, the Reds became even more timid and scattered in breadth and depth in such a way that all subsequent tank thrusts, carried out in detail by small groups, could be met by the German antitank front and smashed. Kholm and the Dnepr bridge, as well as their connecting road—which the Russians had already taken under intermittent tank fire—remained in German hands. After eighty Russian tanks had been put out of action, a break was made through the strongly fortified position on the east bank of the Dnepr, which was occupied by Red reserves, and the thrust from the southern bridgehead continued without concern for the Russians. The flank attack in detail by 100 Russian tanks near Kholm succeeded in delaying, but not in stopping, the advance of the German 6th Panzer Division.

While the German division with all its combat elements rolled along a road deep into Russian territory, hastily assembled Russian tank units and infantry, supported by several batteries, attempted to attack the twenty-five-mile flank of the march column and stop its advance. Some of the Soviet batteries remained in their former positions and merely turned their guns around, while others rushed up at full speed and assumed fire positions in the open. Infantry and tanks advanced in a widespread chain against the German column, and the artillery immediately opened fire with every battery as soon as it had shifted its front.

The attack turned out badly for the Russians. In an instant the German division was firing all its weapons. The division resembled a mighty battleship, smashing all targets within reach with the heavy caliber of its broadsides. Artillery and mortar shells from 300 throats of fire hailed down on the enemy batteries and tanks. Soon the Soviet tanks were in flames, the batteries transformed into smoking heaps of rubble, and the lines of skirmishers swept away by a swath of fire from hundreds of machine guns. In twenty minutes the work of destruction was completed. The advance continued and on the same day reached Vyazma, its objective. This completed the encirclement of 400,000 Russians.

The Russian clearly recognized and twice tried to prevent the division's intent to break out of the bridgehead and push eastward from Kholm. He failed each time, although he had adequate forces and means at his disposal. In both cases the Russian command was at fault. In the first instance it was unable to execute a coordinated blow with a force of 100 tanks; in the second, it did not succeed in readying and coordinating all the available forces and antitank defenses in time.

The command of large tank units was usually difficult for the Russians even in later years. They had only a few competent armored commanders. In the tank force, too, successes were achieved only by the reckless use of masses. However, those tactics failed whenever even relatively adequate defense means were available to the Germans.

In the winter of 1942–43 the Russians employed four tank corps for a breakthrough near Kemenka on the Donets. By a thrust on Voroshilovgrad, the Russians would have been able to strike a crushing strategic blow at the deep left flank of Army Group von Manstein on the south bank of the Donets. Instead, they were attracted by Kamenka and Millerovo and therefore made an assault only against the wings of a provisional army which were strongly defended at that point, and in spite of their superiority achieved only a tactical success. At that time the attack of the Russian main force came as a surprise. In minor thrusts launched during the preceding days the Russians had probed the front of the provisional army, which consisted only of separate strong points (a frontage of 120 miles, and held by one infantry division, one reinforced mountain infantry regiment, one SS regiment reinforced by armor, one panzer battalion, and several Flak batteries). The Russians proved that they were still unable at that time to employ large tank units strategically.

During the course of the well-commanded Russian counter-offensive of Byelgorod, massed Russian tanks reached the area around Bogodukhov, northwest of Kharkov, and Graivoron on the first day (5 August 1943), and then flowed like lava into the broad plain east of the Vorskla, where they were halted by German counteroperations from the Poltava–Akhtirka area (Map 8).

Kharkov constituted a deep German salient to the east, which prevented the enemy from making use of this important traffic and supply center. All previous Russian attempts to take it had failed. Neither tank assaults nor infantry mass attacks had succeeded in bringing about the fall of this large city. Boastful reports made by the Russian radio, and erroneous ones by German pilots, announcing the entry of Russian troops into Kharkov at a time when the German front stood unwavering, did not alter the facts. When the Russian command perceived its mistake, Marshal Stalin ordered the immediate capture of Kharkov.

The rehabilitated Russian Fifth Tank Army was assigned this mission. The German XI Infantry Corps, however, whose five divisions firmly sealed off the city in a long arc, recognized the new danger in time. It was clear that the Russian Fifth Tank Army would not make a frontal assault on the projecting Kharkov bastion, but would attempt to break through the narrowest part of the arc west of the city, the so-called bottleneck, in order to encircle Kharkov. Antitank defenses were installed at once. All available antitank guns were set up on the northern edge of the bottleneck, which rose like a bastion, and numerous 88mm Flak guns were set up in depth on the high ground. The antitank defense would not have been sufficient to repulse the expected mass attack of Russian tanks, but at the last moment the requested 2d SS Panzer Division ("Das Reich") arrived with strong armored forces and was immediately dispatched to the sector most endangered.

The ninety-six Panthers, thirty-five Tigers, and twenty-five self-propelled assault guns had hardly taken their assigned positions when the first large-scale attack of the Russian Fifth Tank Army got under way. The first hard German blow, however, hit the assembled mass of Russian tanks which had been recognized while they were still assembling in the villages and the flood plains of a brook valley. Escorted by German fighters, which cleared the sky of Russian aircraft within a few minutes, wings of heavily laden Stukas came on in wedge formation and unloaded their cargoes of destruction in well-aimed dives on the assembled tanks. Dark fountains of earth erupted skyward and were followed by heavy thunderclaps and shocks which resembled an earthquake. These were the heaviest, two-ton bombs, designed for use against Russian battleships, which were all the Luftwaffe had to counter the Russian attack. Wing after wing approached with majestic calm, and carried out its work of destruction without interference. Soon all the villages occupied by Soviet tanks were in flames. A sea of dust and smoke clouds illuminated by the setting sun hung over the brook valley. Dark mushrooms of smoke from burning tanks, victims of the heavy air attacks, stood out in sharp contrast. The gruesome picture bore witness to an undertaking that left death and destruction in its wake. It had hit the Russian so hard that he could no longer launch the projected attack on that day, in spite of Stalin's order. A severe blow had been inflicted on the Russians, and the time needed for organizing German measures had been gained.

The next day the Russians avoided mass grouping of tanks, crossed the brook valley at several places, and disappeared into the broad cornfields which were located ahead of the front, but which ended at the east–west main highway several hundred yards in front of the main line of resistance. During the night motorized infantry had already infiltrated through the defense lines in several places and made a surprise penetration near Lyubotin into the artillery position. After stubborn fighting with the gun crews, twelve howitzers without breechlocks—which the crews took with them—fell into Russian hands. The points of the infiltrated motorized infantry already were shooting it out with the German local security in the wood adjoining the corps command post.

During the morning Red tanks had worked their way forward in the hollows up to the southern edges of the cornfields. Then they made a mass dash across the road in full sight. The leading waves of Russian T34's were caught in the fierce defensive fire of the Panthers, and were on fire before they could reach the main line of resistance. But wave after wave followed, until they flowed across in the protecting hollows and pushed forward into the battle position. Here they were trapped in the net of antitank and antiaircraft guns, Hornets (88mm tank destroyers), and Wasps (self-propelled 105mm light field howitzers), were split up, and large numbers of them put out of action. The last waves were still attempting to force a breakthrough in concentrated masses when they were attacked by Tigers and self-propelled assault guns, until then mobile reserves behind the front, and were repulsed with heavy losses. The first thrust of the Russians was repelled. The price they paid for this mass tank assault amounted to 184 knocked-out T34's.

In the meantime, German infantry reserves supported by self-propelled assault guns from the 3d Panzer Division had captured the lost battery positions together with all pieces and, west of Lyubotin behind the main line of resistance, had bottled up the battalion of infiltrated enemy motorized infantry. Stubbornly defending themselves, the Russians awaited the help that their radio had promised.

The Russian changed his tactics and the next day attacked farther east in a single deep wedge, using several hundred tanks simultaneously. But even while they moved across open terrain along the railroad, numerous tanks were set on fire at a range of 2,000 yards by the long-range weapons of the Tigers and Hornets. The large-scale Red attack was not launched until late in the forenoon. As the tanks emerged from the cornfields this time, they were assailed by the concentrated defense of all Tigers, Hornets, Panthers, self-propelled assault guns, and antiaircraft and antitank guns, and the attack collapsed in a short time with the loss of 154 tanks. The weak rifle units

which followed were mowed down by the concentrated fire of
German infantry and artillery as they emerged from the cornfields. The encircled Red motorized battalion had waited in
vain for aid, but continued to fight on with incredible tenacity.
In the late afternoon its radio announced the defeat of the unit
and then fell silent forever. After forty-eight hours of heroic defense, the Red battalion was killed to the last man, including
radio operators.

The losses thus far incurred by the Russians were enormous.
However, they still possessed more than a hundred tanks, and
experience had taught the Germans that further attacks were to
be expected, even though they were predestined to failure in
view of the now vastly superior defense. The few tankers taken
prisoner were aware that death, or, if they were lucky, capture,
awaited every one of their comrades.

Contrary to all expectations, an eerie calm prevailed throughout the following day. Several Red tanks crawled about in the
cornfields and towed the damaged tanks away in order to reinforce their greatly depleted ranks. Summer heat shimmered
over the bloody fields of the past days of battle. A last glow of
sunset brought the peaceful day to a close. Might the enemy
have given up his plan, or even refused to obey the supreme order to repeat the attack?

He came back, and on the same day. Before midnight, considerable noise from tanks in the cornfields betrayed his approach. The enemy intended to achieve during the night what
he had failed to gain by daylight attacks.

Before he had reached the foot of the elevated terrain, numerous flashes from firing tanks had ripped the pitch-black
darkness of the night and illuminated a mass attack of the entire Russian Tank Army on a broad front. Tanks knocked out at
close range already were burning like torches and lighting up
portions of the battlefield. More tanks joined them. The German antitank guns could no longer fire properly, since they
could hardly distinguish between friend and foe; German tanks
had entered the fray, ramming Russian tanks in a counterthrust
or piercing them with shells at gun-barrel range in order to
block the breakthrough. A steady increase in the flash and

thunder of tank, antitank, and antiaircraft guns could be perceived after midnight. The main force of the German tanks had launched a counterattack. Many tanks and several farm buildings went up in flames. The plateau on which this great night tank duel was fought was illuminated by their pale light. This made it possible to recognize the contours of Red tanks at a distance of more than 100 yards, and to shell them. The thunderous roll turned into a din like the crescendo of kettledrums as the two main tank forces clashed. Gun flashes from all around ripped the darkness of night throughout an extensive area. For miles, armor-piercing projectiles whizzed into the night in all directions. Gradually the pandemonium of the tank battle shifted to the north. However, flashes also appeared farther and farther behind the German front, and fiery torches stood out against the night sky. Not until two or three hours later was calm restored in the depth of the German front. The conflict also gradually subsided in the battle position.

After daybreak the Germans could feel the battle was won although there were still Red tanks and motorized infantry in and behind the German position, and here and there a small gap still remained to be closed. The mopping up of the battle position, however, lasted all morning. By noon the position was in German hands and again ready for defense. Only a small patch of woodland, close behind the main line of resistance, was still occupied by Red motorized infantry supported by a few tanks and antitank guns. All attempts to retake this patch of woods had failed with heavy German losses. Even heavy, concerted fires of strong artillery units could not force the Russians to yield.

The tenacious resistance was ended only by an attack of flamethrowing tanks, which burned the entire strip of woods to the ground. The foremost of the Red tanks which had made the deep forward thrust was captured at the western outskirts of Kharkov by a divisional headquarters, and the crew members were taken prisoner. All the rest were put out of action by Flak teams.

The Red plan to take Kharkov by a large-scale night attack of the entire tank army had failed. The losses were more than eighty burned-out tanks, many hundreds of dead, thousands of wounded, and a considerable amount of equipment in this night of battle. The Russian Fifth Tank Army in the effort to recapture Kharkov lost 420 tanks in three days of fighting, and suffered such heavy losses of men and equipment that it ceased to be a combat factor for the foreseeable future. Kharkov remained in German hands until the high command ordered the troops stationed there to retire.

Blunders on the part of the leaders were only partially responsible for the fact that every one of the Red rank attacks failed, although the troops fought with extraordinary bravery. It was striking that the enemy had only weak infantry and artillery forces, and that his air forces did not participate effectively enough in operations. For these reasons the tank forces could not be adequately supported and their successes could not be exploited. The Fifth Tank Army seems to have been forced to premature action for reasons of prestige by orders of the Russian Supreme Command.

In the winter of 1943–44 the German XXX Infantry Corps' 16th Panzer Grenadier Division experienced a breakthrough of strong Russian tank forces with a long-range objective in the Dnepr bend south of Dnepropetrovsk. Here the Russians, with tank divisions followed by motorized forces, made a deep thrust against the left flank of the German Sixth Army forces which were withdrawing in front of Nikopol. At that time, the German front enclosed Nikopol in a semicircle east of the city. As this strong tank thrust gained in depth, it decreased in power because it split up. It did not achieve its strategic objective. In spite of the fact the Russian forces were many times superior in number, the German Sixth Army succeeded in containing the thrust in the depth of its sector and in forming new fronts. Even after a double envelopment by far superior tank forces (nine tank corps), the Russians, after encircling the German Sixth Army in Bessarabia, did not succeed in blocking the road over the Transylvanian Alps against the remnants of the Sixth and Eighth Armies. In the tank battle of Debrecen (summer 1944), too, Russian tanks and motorized units split up in such a manner, without being reconcentrated, that weak German panzer divisions succeeded not only in preventing a breakthrough but also in throwing the Russians back again toward Debrecen. The leadership of these large, strategic armored forces was inadequate. In this instance only the enemy's enormous numerical superiority, and his mobility, brought him local successes.

Even in the last months of the war the Russians committed blunders in the command of their armored forces. They continued either to advance timidly when there was scarcely any resistance left, or else they carried out deep, isolated tank thrusts which the infantry was unable to follow and which, consequently, could not lead to permanent success. Russian armored forces always incurred severe losses wherever they encountered German armor still organized in units of any appreciable strength. Thus, as late as April 1945, the battle-weary German 6th Panzer Division succeeded, in what was probably the last tank battle, in repulsing vastly superior Russian tank forces in the plains of the lower March River, and in knocking out eighty tanks.

If the Russian tank forces with their vastly superior numbers had had proper leadership, the Russians would have been able to bring about the end of the war at a much earlier stage.

CHAPTER 10

Defense

I. General

There are two conspicuous characteristics of the Russian soldier, both of which are inherent in the Russian people, both of which were in evidence during the course of the two world wars: stubbornness and tenacity in the defense, inflexibility and little adaptability in the attack.

During World War I the power of resistance of the Russian

soldier was gradually paralyzed because of a lack of heavy weapons, the great inferiority of Russian artillery, the almost complete lack of aircraft, and because the morale of the Russian Army was undermined more and more as time went on. As early as 1915 Russian units left their trenches at the onset of German attacks, came toward the attackers, and surrendered. Such incidents, however, were not characteristic of the Russian soldier, but rather an indication of conditions prevailing at that time. Elite units, such as Guards, and ably commanded troops defended themselves with extreme doggedness even in World War I.

During the first phase of World War II there were also numerous examples of Russian soldiers showing but little power of resistance, throwing away rifles, and surrendering or deserting by the thousands. This, however, occurred only in great battles of encirclement where the Russian soldier became demoralized by Stuka attacks and heavy, concentrated artillery fire and realized the impossibility of continuing the battle successfully. In general, in this war, firm leadership, good equipment, emphasis on patriotism, and the fear—stimulated by propaganda—of falling into enemy hands, resulted in a tenacity of defense which made German attacks without tanks, despite artillery and air support, extremely costly or even futile. This power of the Russian soldier to resist increased during the course of the war in a direct ratio to the decrease of the German power to attack. The numerical superiority of the Russians became more and more crushing, their equipment continued to improve as compared with German equipment, and continuous military successes lifted their spirit and confidence.

When on the defensive the Russian disappeared into the earth with amazing speed. Within the shortest imaginable time he constructed a system of field fortifications with numerous earthworks of all kinds. Laying mines of various types and stringing barbed wire also took very little time. The troops were deployed in depth; the Red commanders frequently changed the strength of forces occupying a position (even to the extent of varying the strength of the day and night shifts), and immediately prepared a careful plan of fire for all weapons.

Except during great battles, defensive fire was maintained chiefly by the infantry heavy weapons, particularly by mortars which the Russians employed with considerable flexibility and in great numbers. In attacks against Russian positions, it was usually quite a while before effective defense fire of the Russian artillery began. But even after a long interval the Russian artillery was unable to direct its fire precisely and flexibly. The emphasis of the defense was on the infantry weapons, including antitank and self-propelled assault guns, and on extensive mine laying.

From the German point of view, the defensive power of the Russian troops is none too good if the attacker builds up a strong superiority in air and ground weapons and provides for sufficient depth of the attacking force. Above all, the attacker must start determinedly and must know how to exploit each success quickly and flexibly in order to achieve freedom of movement as rapidly as possible. The Germans believe that a resourceful commander who knows how to take advantage of the initiative will certainly be successful, because the Russian command does not possess the necessary speed of action in unexpected situations.

In World War II the Russian was a master of the defense. He attained excellent results not only in construction of positions, but also in camouflage and in the construction of dummy installations. By unscrupulous use especially of the civilian population (including women and children), he created well-developed zones in depth. In open terrain he dug wide and deep antitank ditches, often many miles long. Mine fields, wire obstacles, entanglements, and other obstacles were immediately set up everywhere. If, because of the nature of terrain, he expected tank attacks, the enemy developed points of main effort. He was very adept at using villages as strong points. Wherever he could, he set up flanking weapons. He conducted his infantry defense in a mobile manner, but within his defense trenches. He made considerable use of roving guns. He accomplished surprise fires mostly with heavy mortars and numerous multibarreled rocket projectors. He made little use of methodical artillery harassing fire. Upon the loss of parts of a position, reserves for a counterthrust were always quickly at hand. Counterthrusts and counterattacks were in most instances supported by tanks. The Russian did not often conduct counterattacks that were based on a preconceived plan since, from the standpoint of leadership, they were too difficult for him. From 1943 on, he strengthened his defense by mass employment of antiaircraft guns and flame throwers in so-called antitank gun fronts, which were superbly camouflaged and dangerous for tank attacks. Daytime observation was made difficult, because he showed almost no movement. In general, one might say that the Russian undertook his defense in open terrain, as well as wooded areas, according to principles rigidly drilled into the soldiers, and that he showed little imagination in developing new methods of battle. He relied, in attack as well as in defense, on reckless employment of manpower.

Another peculiarity to be mentioned is the fact that the Russian proved himself to be very well disciplined in opening fire. He waited calmly until the Germans had approached to a favorable range, and then he opened surprise fire. German combat reconnaissance always had to be on the lookout to avoid unnecessary losses. The Russian sniper battalions particularly excelled in fire discipline.

In 1941 the Russians also supported defense action in the Parpach position in the Crimea very adroitly and effectively from the sea by artillery flanking fire.

II. Use of Mines

The Russian made extensive use of mines. As a rule, a protective mine belt was to be found about eight to ten yards in front of the most forward trench. Terrain particularly favorable for an enemy approach likewise was heavily mined. The Russian preferred to employ wooden box mines which could not be detected by the standard mine detectors. In the depth of the battle position, mines were laid in unexpected places. In favorable terrain, antitank mines were numerous.

Difficulties in transporting Teller mines because of the lack of transport space were solved in a very primitive manner. When marching up to the front as relief, every man had to carry two antitank mines. At the front, these mines were laid by the engineers according to a diagrammed mine plan.

In 1944–45 the Russians, while on the move, also scattered mines around points of main effort in order to block tank attacks. In the southern Ukraine, following a successful tank thrust, the Russians immediately protected the terrain they had gained with a belt of antitank mines blocking all roads and approaches. On one day alone, 20,000 such mines were laid. German counterattacks ground to a halt and collapsed in mine fields of that type.

The Russian cleared mines in front of German obstacles during the night, and used them for his own purposes. Later on, the Germans laid mine fields only behind their own front, at points at which a tank breakthrough or an enemy offensive was to be expected.

When the Russian intended to give up a previously defended zone, he used many tricks. For example, he attached demolition charges with push-pull igniters to abandoned field kitchens, weapons, corpses, and tombstones; he connected explosive charges to doors, windows, or stoves in the winter; he installed pressure mines under stairs and floors, and booby-trapped abandoned trucks and other equipment.

When the Germans took Kiev and Vyborg in 1941, and Sevastopol in 1942, the Russian used remote (radio) control mines to blow up entire blocks of houses as soon as anyone entered. This type of remote control ignition seemed to be the most effective solution to the problem. The apparatus consisted of three parts, each of which was not much larger than a full briefcase. It was easy to move, could easily be built into a hidden spot, and was at first hard to find. Built-in safety devices prevented an accidental or untimely detonation. The ignition apparatus included a clock, which ran only on a certain signal for a certain length of time, and permitted detonation only during certain minutes. There was, furthermore, a code which, when given at a certain speed, was the sole means for setting off the mines. The ticking of the clocks, however, could be heard with sensitive sound detectors and often led to discovery.

During the autumn offensive in 1941 against Moscow, the

Russian employed so-called mine dogs for destroying German tanks. In the manner of pack animals, medium-sized dogs carried demolition charges which were connected to a spindle fastened to the dog's back. The dogs were trained to hide under approaching tanks. In so doing, the animal inadvertently brought the upright spindle which was about six inches long into contact with the belly of the tank and set off the charge.

News of this insidious improvisation caused some alarm in the German panzer units and made them fire at all approaching dogs on sight. So far, there is no evidence of any case where a German tank was destroyed by a mine dog. On the other hand, it was reported that several mine dogs fleeing from the fire of German tanks sought protection underneath Russian tanks which promptly blew up. One thing is certain: The specter of the mine dogs ceased just as abruptly as it had begun.

III. Conduct of Battle

The Russian defended every inch of his soil with incredible tenacity. At the beginning of the war he was conversant only with long defense lines, which he strengthened by employing an amazing number of personnel for digging trenches. Artillery confined its activities to minor fire concentrations. However, it proved to be more mobile than the infantry and employed many roving guns which sometimes became very annoying to the Germans, since they fired only a short time from one position and then reappeared elsewhere. The Russian required a long period of time to bring effective fire to bear against an attack already in progress.

In 1943 new methods of tank and antitank warfare were introduced, though the methods of the infantry remained the same. Heavy machine guns and dug-in tanks frequently were encountered deep in the battle position. The latter were particularly dangerous because they were well armored and difficult to hit. In sectors in which the terrain was passable for tanks, antitank gun fronts would be set up in nearly all instances. They were developed to extraordinary strength and foiled many a German armored attack. They were also used against infantry, in which case they fired high-explosive shells.

In most cases, tank counterattacks without infantry support were certain to fall victim to German antitank defense. Infantry counterattacks were infrequent and generally too late. For the rest, no important changes took place in Russian defense methods up to the end of the war. The multibarreled rocket projectors, which the Russians employed more and more, certainly were very effective psychologically but their physical effect was much less impressive. The most dangerous weapons continued to be the medium and heavy mortars, particularly after the heavy mortars were concentrated in battalions in 1944.

Areas of great importance were surrounded with heavy fortifications. For instance, the German armored units before Leningrad encountered fortification systems up to six miles in depth, including innumerable earth and concrete bunkers with built-in guns and other heavy weapons. There were even concrete pillboxes with disappearing armored cupolas for artillery and machine guns. They were constructed in the rear area from standard concrete forms, assembled at the front, and equipped with the armored cupolas. The cupolas were raised and lowered by wooden levers, which had to be operated manually by the pillbox crew. A speedy elimination of these concrete pillboxes with the means available in mobile warfare was difficult.

The forward edge of such a defense system was generally situated behind an antitank ditch several miles long and up to twenty feet wide and twelve feet deep. Embedded in the rear wall of this ditch were dugouts housing the riflemen with their defense weapons. A second and third antitank ditch frequently would be located in the depth of the system, and connected by a cross ditch so as to prevent enemy tanks that had penetrated the position from rolling it up. A machine-gun or antitank bunker in every bend of the antitank ditch afforded flank protection. It was not unusual to encounter dammed-up watercourses close to the fortified position. They were up to a hundred yards wide and several yards deep, and presented an obstacle difficult to overcome. The Russians eliminated all favorable approaches to their front (forests, underbrush, tall grain fields, etc.) by laying extensive mine fields.

Outposts were located ahead of the fortified position wherever possible. Such outposts always had engineers attached whose mission it was to block routes of approach with mines or other obstacles.

The area of Krasnogvardeysk, south of Leningrad (Map 7), had been developed according to the above-mentioned principles into an outlying fortress. During early September 1941, it presented great difficulties to the advance of several German corps. Krasnogvardeysk blocked all highways and railroads leading to Leningrad from the south, thus constituting a main bulwark of Russian resistance. The Russians defended it persistently. Repeated attacks by several infantry divisions were repulsed. Only in the course of a general attack on the Leningrad Line, and after bitter pillbox fighting in the area immediately surrounding Krasnogvardeysk, was that town finally taken from the rear by a carefully prepared surprise breakthrough to the west of it. This typical example of the Russian method of defending a methodically fortified zone, and its capture by an adroitly led attack, will be discussed in detail in the following paragraphs.

The defense system of Krasnogvardeysk had been prepared long in advance and consisted of an outer belt of concrete and earth bunkers, with numerous intermediate installations which were interconnected by trench systems that could easily be defended. There were tankproof watercourses or swamps almost everywhere in front of the outer defense belt. Where this natural protection was lacking, wide antitank ditches had been dug.

At a distance of 1,000 to 3,000 yards behind the outer defense belt there was an inner one consisting of a heavily fortified position encircling the periphery of the town. Just north of the town ran the continuous Leningrad Line, with which the defense system of Krasnogvardeysk was integrated. It constituted, simultaneously, the rear protection of the town and the covering position in case the town should have to be evacuated. Beyond the open, elevated terrain immediately west of Krasnogvardeysk lay an extensive forest zone. Within that zone, a few hundred yards from its eastern edge, ran the western front of the outer defense belt. At that point it consisted of wood and earth bunkers, trenches, and strong points—all approaches to which were barricaded by extensive mine fields, abatis, and multiple rows of barbed wire. Located from two to three miles farther west were mobile security detachments. Attached to these were engineer units used to lay scattered mines.

The cornerstone of this position was the heavily fortified and mined village of Salyzy, located at the southern end of the forest zone. It covered a road leading to Krasnogvardeysk from the west, and another one which branched off the former to the north within Salyzy. The latter road served as supply route for all the troops situated west of it in the forest position. It crossed the dammed-up Ishora River via a bridge located in front of the Leningrad Line, traversing the line in a northwesterly direction. At that point the line consisted of four trench systems, one behind the other, with numerous machine-gun, antitank-gun, and artillery bunkers.

The German 6th Panzer Division, advancing on Krasnogvardeysk from the west via Salyzy, had the mission of breaking through the Leningrad Line in the above-described area, and attacking Krasnogvardeysk from the rear. Following a plan of attack based on precise aerial photos, the division decided to push with concentrated force through the outer defense belt at Salyzy, to follow through with a northward thrust and break through the Leningrad Line, and then to roll up the latter to the east. The main body of the division attacked on the road and along the edge of the forest running parallel to it, took the antitank ditch after a brief engagement, and, during the noon hour, also captured the village of Salyzy after having stormed a large number of bunkers. A bunker at the edge of the forest continued to offer resistance until late afternoon.

Immediately after breaking into the village, the armored elements of the division, supported by an artillery battalion, advanced through the rear of the enemy-occupied forest position against the Leningrad Line. Under cover of tank fire, the engineers took the undamaged bridge in a *coup de main* and removed prepared demolition charges. About four miles north of Salyzy, panzer grenadiers (armored infantry) following them penetrated the antitank ditch, which began at the bridge and ran at a right angle to the front, and formed a bridgehead. During the evening the main body of the division cleared the surrounding forests of Red forces and, with a front turned 90°, assembled in the woods for a northward thrust to join the forces at the bridgehead, which meanwhile had been cut off by the enemy. On the evening of the same day a German panzer grenadier battalion succeeded in breaking through the inner defense ring located east of Salyzy behind a river arm, in the area of the neighboring SS Police Division, which had been stalled along its entire front. The bridgehead thus established by the battalion opened a gateway to Krasnogvardeysk for the SS Police Division.

On the second day of attack the bulk of the 6th Panzer Division advanced along the road to the armored units in the northern bridgehead. Some of its elements mopped up enemy forces on the plateau west of Krasnogvardeysk, while others rolled up the Russian forest position which was pinning down a unit that had been detached as a flank guard on the previous day. During the forenoon the entire attack area south of the Leningrad Line was cleared of the enemy. Along the northern wing of the position on the forest edge alone, 40,000 Russian mines were picked up and disarmed. Then, battalion after battalion was pushed through the bridgehead into the two-mile-long antitank ditch which ran up to a forest area. These battalions were pushed so far to the north that the four parallel defense systems of the Leningrad Line could be rolled up simultaneously from the flank by one battalion each. A desperate enemy attempt to repel the advance of the battalions and tanks by a cavalry attack was easily foiled. The antitank ditch, four yards wide and deep, had made it possible to change the attack front of the entire division again by 90° at one stroke. Under cover of flank and rear protection, bunker after bunker and strong point after strong point was now blasted by Stukas, medium artillery, antitank and antiaircraft guns, and captured; step by step the trenches and nests of resistance were cleaned out. All the German artillery was still in the old front south of the Leningrad Line, and its fire thus formed a complete flanking curtain in front of the attacking battalions.

The railroad running through the attack area was reached on the second day of battle, and the Krasnogvardeysk–Leningrad highway on the third day. There, the German forces took a group of artillery pillboxes equipped with disappearing armored cupolas. At that point the division stood directly in the rear of the town. The enemy, forced to retreat hurriedly, had only one side road available for a withdrawal, and that road lay under the effective artillery fire of the panzer division. With serious losses, the Russian divisions poured back over this road and the adjoining terrain. The attempt of the motorized medium artillery, the first of the Red forces to disengage, to escape on the wide asphalt road via Pushkin, failed. The road was already blocked by German armor. All the Russian artillery, as well as all other motor vehicles, was set afire by German armor when it attempted to break through at this point. During the following night the Russians, although badly mauled, managed to evacuate the town and escape. They then reestablished themselves with strong rear guards on high terrain between Krasnogvardeysk and Pushkin.

The next day, pursuing German infantry divisions bogged down before the heavily fortified positions. Here the enemy had employed the most modern system of field fortifications ever encountered on the Eastern Front. All of the fortification installations were underground. The defense was carried out in subterranean passages which were established along terrain steps and were equipped with well-camouflaged embrasures. The heavy weapons likewise were in subterranean emplacements which were invisible from the outside. There were also subterranean rooms quartering ten to twenty men each, ammunition dumps, and medical and supply installations. All installations were interconnected by underground communication passages. The entrances were situated several hundred yards farther to the rear, well camouflaged by shrubbery and groups of trees, and protected by open squad trenches and several standard bunkers which could only be recognized from nearby. Neither the best ground nor air reconnaissance could spot this fortification system even at close range. Not even after its guns had opened fire could it be located, as a result of which it proved very difficult to neutralize. All frontal assaults of the infantry were unsuccessful.

Not until two days later was it possible to clarify the situation and to capture the position. By that time the 6th Panzer Division, committed as an encircling force maneuvering via Posyolok Taytsy, was pivoting into the rear of the Russian fortifications. An odd coincidence played into the hands of the division. The previous evening strong reconnaissance patrols had advanced into the high terrain. Suddenly encountering the rearmost outlying bunker of the position, the patrols took it by storm without orders. Among the captured garrison was a Russian military engineer, the builder of this fortification system. With him, the plans of all the installations fell into German hands, and it was easy to plan the attack for the next day.

However, the attack of the lead-off panzer grenadier regiment had hardly begun when a new difficulty arose. The Russian had recognized the danger to his frontally impregnable position, and launched an attack from Pushkin against the rear of the 6th Panzer Division. A long column of tanks, the end of which could not even be surmised in the dust, rolled against the German rear guard unit. The first of the Russian tanks had already passed a narrow strip between swamps and turned against the defended elevations. However, except for one 88mm Flak battery and the antitank guns of the rear guard panzer grenadier battalion, the German division had at that moment only one panzer battalion with light Czech tanks available for its defense. The heavy Flak guns were already thundering. Flames from tanks that had sustained hits rose straight toward the sky. The vanguard of Red tanks consisting of fifty-four KV1's spread out, but kept moving ahead. Suddenly it was attacked and destroyed from very close range by a hail of fire from the tank destroyer battalion which had just arrived with twenty-seven heavy antitank guns. Fourteen columns of black smoke announced to the main body of the enemy the destruction of his vanguard. Thereupon the main body suddenly stopped and no longer dared to pass the swamp narrow. Rear elements fanned out and disappeared into the adjoining terrain. Heavy tank fighting indicated that the German panzer regiment, which had been summoned by radio, had gone into action. Soon the din increased. The panzer regiments of the neighboring 1st and 8th Panzer Divisions which had also been summoned attacked the flank and rear of the Red forces. The Russian realized his precarious situation and felt himself no longer equal to the task. His losses and his retrograde movements bore evidence to that fact. Even the heavy tanks, only fourteen of which had been reached and destroyed by the heavy Flak guns, turned and retreated. The enemy had avoided a showdown. The threat to the rear of the panzer division had thus been eliminated.

In the meantime, however, the German panzer grenadier attack, supported by a panzer battalion, continued according to plan. In heavy fighting, the bunkers and squad trenches which protected the enemy's rear were taken one by one, and the entrances to the subterranean defense system reached. During the fighting for the first entrance, the crew resisted from an inner compartment with fire and hand grenades. In this action three Russian medical corps women in uniform, who defended the entrance with hand grenades, were killed. When their bodies were removed, several hand grenades were found on them.

Mopping up the subterranean passages was time-consuming and difficult. It had to be carried out by specially trained shock troops with hand grenades and machine pistols. German attempts to clear out the strong bunker crews led to bitter underground hand-to-hand fighting with heavy losses on both sides. The enemy defended himself to the utmost. The attack stalled. Only after engineer demolition teams had succeeded in determining the location of the subterranean bunkers by noting the sparser growth of grass above them, could these bunkers be blown up by heavy demolition charges from above, and taken. But the closer the shock troops came to the front position of the enemy's defense system, the more serious became the losses. The engineer demolition teams and all the other units were advancing above the Russian defense system, into the heavy artillery fire supporting the frontally attacking German infantry divisions of the neighboring army. Only when roundabout telephone communications had been established, and the devastating fire ordered to cease, was it possible to take the entire subterranean defense system. A junction was then effected with the infantry on the other side. Subsequently, German forces also occupied Pushkin.

With that, the most tenacious Russian defensive battles of 1941, between Krasnogvardeysk and Leningrad, came to an end. Only the flexible leadership of battle-tested armored forces, attacking with elan, made it possible to overcome the defense zones which had been set up in an all-out effort of the latest Russian defense technique. Within a week the German 6th Panzer Division had had to break through and roll up twelve positions, repel several counterattacks, and take more than 300 heavily fortified bunkers.

Equally instructive was the Russian conduct of battle in the defense against the German pincers attack (Operation ZITADELLE) on Kursk in July 1943. The exhaustion on both sides after the preceding long winter battles led, at this sector of the front, to a pause of three months which both opponents used to replenish their forces and to prepare for Operation ZITADELLE. The Russians expected the attack precisely at the location and in the manner in which it was undertaken, and prepared their defense accordingly.

Behind the most endangered sectors, opposite Byelgorod and Orel, they constructed defense systems of hitherto unknown depth, and strengthened them with all kinds of obstacles. To be prepared against surprise armored thrusts, all points susceptible to penetration were safeguarded up to a depth of thirty miles by fully manned antitank gun fronts, antitank ditches, mine fields, and tanks in emplacements, in such numbers and strength that to overcome them could have called for great sacrifices and much time. Behind the pressure points north of Byelgorod and south of Kursk, sufficient local forces stood ready everywhere. Noteworthy were the numerous alternate firing positions, and the fact that the bulk of the numerous Russian artillery pieces were kept as far to the rear as their maximum range allowed, so as to escape counterbattery fire from German heavy howitzer batteries and to be able, in case of reverses, to support the infantry as long as possible. The Russian batteries preferred firing positions in forests, or in orchards adjacent to inhabited localities. For mobile operations, the Russians very adroitly employed multibarreled rocket projectors. Strong strategic reserves were assembled farther east, in the region of the Oskol River, in such a manner that after the attacking German divisions had exhausted themselves in the above-mentioned defense system, the reserves could launch a counterattack, or, at worst, contain an enemy breakthrough. In the bulge extending far to the west, however, the enemy had stationed only weak and inferior forces, which were not backed by any deep defense system. During the long waiting period each side learned about the other's situation and intentions down to the last details. The Russians, for instance, broadcast to the German lines by loud-speaker the secret day and hour of attack well in advance, and in the same manner announced two postponements of the offensive. Nevertheless, the German attack was carried out at the precise point at which the Russians expected it. As anticipated, it did not develop into a dynamic offensive, but became a slow wrestling match with an enemy firmly clinging to a maze of trenches and bunkers—an enemy who, unshaken by preparatory fire, offered dogged resistance. Many positions could only be taken after prolonged hand grenade duels. The Russians employed stronger tank forces only against what they guessed to be the weakest point in the German attack wedge—the flank of XI Infantry Corps which attacked on the right wing. Every one of these counterattacks was repulsed.

On the very first day of the attack, 5 July 1943, several German divisions each sustained losses up to 1,000 dead and wounded. The German armor, too, suffered substantial losses each day from the strong antitank defenses and mine fields. This, as well as the divergent directions of thrust of the various corps, visibly diminished the momentum of the German attack. When, after about two weeks of bloody fighting, there was no longer any hope of reaching the desired objectives, and when German forces even began to meet reverses in the Orel area, the attack was called off, and previous territorial gains were relinquished. By excellent organization of defenses and adroit conduct of battle, the Russians had brought about the collapse of the German offensive. Shortly thereafter they launched a counteroffensive with fresh reserves and effected a major breakthrough.

Conditions were entirely different for the Russians in their defense against the German relief thrust on Stalingrad in December 1942 (Map 9). Here, there existed only temporary field positions, and the defense had to be conducted in a mobile manner. At first the Russians pushed a cavalry corps, strengthened by armor and camel troops, forward along the Don to the Kurmoyarskiy Aksay River for reconnaissance and for screening the movements of their infantry and tank forces assembling in the rear.

The German 6th Panzer Division was 10 to 20 percent overstrength and had to conduct the main thrust. When its leading elements arrived, the vanguard of the Red cavalry corps was just moving into Kotelnikovo (about 26 November 1942). It was driven back, and the assembly of German forces continued. The attempt to take Kotelnikovo in an assault by the entire cavalry corps on 5 and 6 December 1942, ended in a smashing defeat of the corps at Pokhlebin. Meanwhile, the enemy cautiously advanced two rather weak infantry divisions along both sides of the railroad onto the elevations north of the city, and pushed back several outposts. After the bitter experience of Pokhlebin, however, he did not dare attack Kotelnikovo again. He assembled his main force, the Third Tank Army and additional infantry forces, between the Aksay River and the Mishkova River sector. His entire defense forces were drawn up in three echelons, one behind the other, twenty miles in width and forty-five miles in depth. The impression was gained by the Germans that the enemy would move up under the protection of his advance infantry and cavalry divisions, and then, with his entire tank army, attack the 6th Panzer Division which was marching up alone, in order to destroy it in the wide forefield of Stalingrad before it reached the city. The move, however, did not materialize. On that occasion the Russians either missed a chance, or else did not as yet feel strong enough to attack the division, which was equipped with 200 tanks and self-propelled assault guns as well as a large number of antitank weapons. Neither did he act to save his reinforced cavalry corps from destruction on 5 and 6 December, and also looked on idly on 12 December while the beginning of the relief thrust of the German 6th Panzer Division rolled over his advance infantry divisions and scattered them. The northernmost of the two divisions here lost its entire artillery. The weak remnants of the Russian cavalry corps were also caught on the fringes of the mighty assault and so badly mauled that they played no further part in the course of the offensive. Thus the 6th Panzer Division without protection on its northern flank was able to cross the Aksay River as early as the third day. Its southern wing was protected by the 23d Panzer Division (in regimental strength with fifteen to twenty tanks), which followed in echelons.

The crossing of the Aksay River met only weak resistance from advance elements of a Russian mechanized corps, which was soon overcome. In an immediate follow-up thrust by all German armored units, Verkhniy–Kumskiy, the key point of the assembly area of the Russian Third Tank Army, was taken. Not till then were the enemy tanks stirred to action, but now they displayed very spirited activity. Speed was imperative. Therefore, the Russian commander was compelled to radio all his orders and reports in the clear. Because the Russians were forced to put their cards on the table, the German forces, although numerically far inferior, were able during the ensuing several days of bitter tank fighting to attack Russian elements in lightning moves and beat them decisively before they could receive help. In the melee that followed, the Russians occasionally succeeded in concentrating greatly superior forces which threatened to become dangerous to the division. The German armored forces then immediately withdrew, only to attack the Reds from the rear again the moment an opportunity presented itself.

Both sides made large-scale shifts under cover of darkness. By lightning-like feints and changes of direction, it was repeatedly possible for the Germans to attack strong Red tank concentrations simultaneously from all sides in the larger hollows of the hilly terrain, and to destroy them to the last tank. In this manner a number of so-called tank cemeteries originated, where from fifty to eighty knocked-out tanks, mostly T34's, stood in clusters within a small area. German bomber wings repeatedly bombed them by mistake. Neither German nor Russian aircraft could take any part in the seesaw tank battles, since the opposing tanks were frequently so intermingled that they could not be differentiated. Although air activity on both sides was very lively, it was forced to limit itself to attacking motor pools and supply lines. The air arm was of no decisive importance.

While the tank battle north of the Aksay River was still in progress, Russian tank and motorized brigades crossed the river in a southerly direction and attempted to cut off the bridge crossing, which was strongly held on both sides of the river. This had to be avoided under all circumstances, but without depleting the German armored forces then engaged in crucial battles. Soon the bridgehead was surrounded. Although more than a dozen Russian tanks were knocked out, just as many surviving tanks overran the entrenched German infantry and penetrated to a rather large village located in the center of the bridgehead and defended by the German 57th Armored Engineer Battalion. Not a single engineer or rifleman deserted his post. Each man became a tank buster. Just as fast as Russian tanks entered the village, they burst into flames. Not one escaped. Three times the Russian repeated this assault, and three times he was repulsed. Then a reinforced infantry regiment attacked him from the rear, scattered the entire force, and knocked out fourteen tanks. That opened the route of advance again and assured the free flow of supplies across the bridge.

When strong Russian motorized infantry with numerous antitank weapons entered the battle at Verkhniy–Kumskiy, the German armored infantry forces were tied down supporting their neighbor and other forces engaged at the Aksay River, leaving the German armored units so severely restricted in their freedom of movement that they had to be withdrawn to the Aksay River. The Russian, however, had suffered such heavy tank losses that he did not dare risk the rest of his tanks in a pursuit. He contented himself with defending a long ridge south of Verkhniy–Kumskiy. The premature attempt, ordered by a higher command, to roll up this ridge position from the flank with the combined armored elements of the 6th and 23rd Panzer Divisions failed. Its failure was caused by lack of sufficient infantry to silence the numerous antitank guns and rifles which were entrenched in deep antitank pits and well camouflaged by high steppe grass. Although it was perfectly possible to roll from one end of the ridge to the other, the Russian motorized riflemen popped up again afterwards like jack-in-the-boxes and, with their numerous antitank rifles, knocked out many an armored vehicle. The combined German armored force suffered considerable losses and had to be recalled in the evening without having accomplished its mission.

Not until two days later did a planned attack of the entire 6th Panzer Division succeed in taking the position and cleaning it out. In the subsequent night attack the German armored infantry recaptured the stubbornly defended village of Verkhniy-Kumskiy, destroyed a number of emplaced tanks, numerous antitank guns, and over 100 antitank rifles. At dawn of the following day the elevated position north of the village was taken in cooperation with the newly arrived 17th Panzer Division which had only the combat strength of a reinforced battalion. The 11th Panzer Regiment, which up to this time had been held in reserve, was employed in the pursuit and inflicted heavy losses upon the Russian who was retreating through a single defile.

In the midst of the pursuit, however, the entire 6th Panzer Division had to turn to the east to support the neighboring 23d Panzer Division on the right since it was being pushed back beyond the Aksay River by a newly arrived Russian file corps. The further pursuit toward the north had to be left to the weak 17th Panzer Division, which lacked sufficient driving force to destroy the beaten Russian forces.

The turning of the 6th Panzer Division against the rear of the new enemy had decisively changed the situation in the 23d Panzer Division. The Russian corps immediately broke off its attack and hastily retreated eastward in order to escape the deadly blow that would have been dealt it very soon, had it remained. The Red tanks and antitank gun fronts thrown against the German 6th Panzer Division had been scattered before, and

German armor was about to cut off the Russian escape route. At this critical moment, too, the Russian corps commander radioed his urgent orders in the clear.

But the objective of the German panzer division was Stalingrad, not the pursuit of a corps in a different direction. As soon as the 23d Panzer Division, relieved of enemy pressure, could again advance, pursuit of the corps was halted. The 6th Panzer Division then turned north and, after hard fighting, reached the Mishkova River sector at Bolshaya Vasilyevka. At that point the Stalingrad garrison was supposed to make contact with the division. Two bridgeheads were quickly formed, the village taken, and the entire division concentrated in a small area for mobile defense. It had already covered two-thirds of the distance, and stood thirty miles from Stalingrad; the flash of signal rockets from the city could be observed at night. It remains a puzzle why the German Sixth Army (Field Marshal Paulus) did not break out at that time (20 December).

In forced marches the Russian brought up additional strong forces from the Stalingrad front and the Volga in order to support the beaten Third Tank Army and throw back the German forces. Since he no longer had sufficient tank forces available for this purpose, he hoped to overwhelm and destroy them with the newly formed infantry main-attack army. The Red riflemen surged forward in multitudes never before encountered. Attack wave followed attack wave without regard for losses. Each was annihilated by a terrific hail of fire without gaining so much as a foot of ground. Therefore, the Russians went around the two flanks of the German division in order to encircle it. In the course of this maneuver they came between the German artillery position and the panzer regiment. Firing from all barrels, 150 tanks and self-propelled assault guns attacked the Russian masses from the rear when they tried to escape the fire from the artillery. In their desperate situation many Russians threw down their weapons and surrendered. Succeeding elements flowed back; Red forces which had penetrated into the village were driven out again by a counterthrust of the German infantry, and Russian tanks which had broken through were knocked out. The Russian mass assault had collapsed.

On 22 December the German 6th Panzer Division had regained its freedom of movement. By a further forward thrust of eighteen miles on 24 December, the division was to help the encircled Sixth Army in breaking out of Stalingrad. That operation, however, never materialized, because the division suddenly had to be withdrawn on 23 December and transferred to the area north of the lower Don (Morosovskaya) to bolster the collapsed Chir front. This move definitely sealed the doom of the German forces at Stalingrad. The remaining two weak panzer divisions, the 17th and 23d, were not even sufficient to make a stand against the Russian forces, let alone repulse them. But also the enemy was so weakened by his losses, which included more than 400 tanks, that he was unable to make a quick thrust against Rostov, an action which would have cut off the entire Caucasus front.

Here is another example that confirms very emphatically the characteristic fighting method of the Russians: not great achievements by small units with clever leadership, but by sacrifices of masses. Only when the Russians attacked with a tenfold to twentyfold superiority could they achieve temporary successes. In the assault, however, the individual performance of the German soldier triumphed over the masses.

The Russian high command had assigned more than sufficient forces to prevent the relief (five corps and one main-attack army against one German panzer corps). The Russian corps were organized very effectively, but were poorly led. If properly led, these superior forces would have sufficed to defeat the weak German relief force before it could launch its attack. At the very least, the combined Russian corps should have attacked and beaten this German corps which was making an unsupported forward thrust, when it crossed the Aksay River. But the commitment in detail of the Russian forces enabled the German units to attack the individual Russian corps by surprise and defeat them one after another. During the last days, the Russians hastily formed a new main-attack army and threw it against the German 6th Panzer Division in the Mishkova River sector in order to halt its further advance. This army also sustained heavy losses, and would have been unable to prevent a further advance of the German armor. It had no effective tank support because the pivotal element in the whole struggle, the Russian Third Tank Army, had already been beaten. The Third Tank Army was the most dangerous opponent on the route to Stalingrad. It had more than twice the number of tanks the Germans had, and far superior antitank weapons. Its motorized troops were well trained and fought with exemplary valor. But neither numerical superiority nor valor could make up for the mistakes of the intermediate and lower commands. Only the repercussions of the great successes which the Soviet Supreme Command was able to achieve on the Chir and Don fronts caused the German relief thrust to fail.

An indirect but very significant role was also played by the Allied invasion of North Africa. The German armored forces stationed in France (the 6th, 7th, and 10th Panzer Divisions and the 1st, 2d, and 3d SS Panzer Divisions) were among the crack troops of the German Army. They had been brought up to full effectiveness, but were not transferred as a whole to the East for fear of an Allied landing in southern France. Finally, after several days' hesitation, only the 6th Panzer Division was transferred to the sector south of Stalingrad. The 7th Panzer Division followed at a later date, but arrived too late for the relief thrust. Its timely arrival would have been sufficient to carry the thrust through to its objective.

CHAPTER 11

Retreat and Delaying Engagements

Observations of Russian fighting methods in retreat could be made particularly during the first years of the war. When the Russians had been defeated on a broad front, they reestablished their lines only after they had retreated a considerable distance. They marched very quickly, even when retreating in extremely large numbers. Precisely at such times it was important to pursue them energetically, and to give them no opportunity for renewed resistance. The German conduct of delaying action, with leapfrog commitment of forces in successive positions, was apparently not known to them; at least, this method of fighting, requiring great mobility and competent leadership, was not used by the Russians. The Russians always sought only simple and complete solutions. When they decided to withdraw, they did so in one jump, and then immediately began an active defense again. When German armored forces which had broken through chased them off the roads, the Russians disappeared into the terrain with remarkable skill. In retreating, retiring from sight, and rapidly reassembling, the Russians were past masters. Even large forces quickly covered long distances over terrain without roads or paths. In 1941 certain Russian rifle regiments which had been thrown back by German armor crossing the border at Tauroggen, again opposed the same panzer division south of Leningrad, after a march of 500 miles.

Even if time was of the essence, the Russians succeeded in carrying off large numbers of cattle, as well as a substantial amount of equipment and supplies. They shot thousands of undesirable persons in the Baltic countries before the retreat, and took other tens of thousands with them. In retreating they did not hesitate to burn to the ground the cities and towns of their own native land, if it seemed that any advantage was to be gained (scorched-earth policy). Thus, in the retreat of 1941, they almost completely destroyed the cities of Vitebsk, Smolensk, and many others, leaving nothing of value to fall into the hands of the Germans and delaying their advance. All that remained for the Germans of the Russian collective farms, state farms, machine tractor stations, and manufacturing plants of all kinds, were ashes and ruins. For that reason it even became difficult in some sectors to quarter larger headquarters organizations to assure their ability to function.

Russian tactics of stopping or slowing down the German

offensive by uncoordinated counterattacks have already been treated in the preceding chapter.

CHAPTER 12

Combat under Unusual Conditions

The Russians systematically exploited all difficulties which their country presented to the enemy. In villages, woods, and marshes, and in fog, rain, snow, and storm, the Russians combined the tricks of nature with their own innate cunning in order to do the greatest possible harm to the enemy.

I. Fighting in Towns and Villages

The Russians were very adept at preparing inhabited places for defense. In a short time, a village would be converted into a little fortress. Wooden houses had well-camouflaged gun ports almost flush with the floor, their interiors were reinforced with sandbags or earth, observation slots were put into roofs, and bunkers built into floors and connected with adjacent houses or outside defenses by narrow trenches. Although almost all inhabited places were crammed with troops, they seemed deserted to German reconnaissance, since even water and food details were allowed to leave their shelters only after dark. The Russians blocked approach routes with well-camouflaged antitank guns or dug-in tanks. Wrecks of knocked-out tanks were specially favored for use as observation posts and as emplacements for heavy infantry weapons, and bunkers for living quarters were dug under them. It was Russian practice to allow the enemy to draw near, and then to fire at him unexpectedly. In order to prevent heavy losses of personnel and tanks, the Germans had to cover the outskirts of inhabited places with artillery, tanks, or heavy weapons during the approach of their troops. Fires resulted frequently, and in many instances consumed the whole village. When the front line neared a village, the inhabitants carried their possessions into outlying woods or bunkers for safekeeping. They did not take part in the fighting of the regular troops, but served as auxiliaries, building earthworks and passing on information. The Russian practice of raiding inhabited localities during mobile warfare, or converting them into strong points for defensive purposes, was responsible for the destruction of numerous populated places during combat.

Since the defenses on the outskirts of a locality were quickly eliminated by the above-mentioned German countermeasures, the Russians later led their main line of resistance right through the center of their villages, and left only a few security detachments on the outskirts facing the enemy. Permanent structures destroyed by artillery fire or aerial bombs were utilized as defense points. The ruins hid weapons and served to strengthen the underlying bunkers. Even the heaviest shelling would not drive the Russians from such positions; they had to be dislodged with hand grenades or flame throwers. The Russians upon retreating frequently burned or blasted buildings suitable for housing command posts or other important military installations. Quite often, however, they left castles, former country seats, and other spacious dwellings intact, after they had mined the walls in a completely conspicuous manner with delayed-action bombs, which were often set to explode several weeks later. These were meant to blow up entire German headquarters at one time. The possible presence of time-bombs in cities, railroad stations, bridges, and other important structures always had to be taken into account.

When the Russians were on the offensive, they tried to encircle fortified towns in order to bring about their fall through concentric advances. Only during major offensives would the advance forces bypass inhabited places in order to gain ground rapidly, leaving the job of mopping up to the reserves following behind. If the Russians were encircled, they defended themselves very stubbornly, capitulating only in rare cases. The large-scale battles of encirclement of 1941, when hundreds of thousands surrendered in hopeless situations after previous attempts to break out, were exceptions.

Fighting for the possession of villages played a still greater role in the winter. The villages blocked the few roads which had been cleared of snow, and offered warm quarters. Cleared roads and warm quarters are the two basic prerequisites for winter warfare. Therefore, inhabited localities retained their outstanding tactical importance even though they could easily be bypassed by ski troops even in deep snow. Experience had shown that ski and sleigh forces might seriously harass the enemy, but they would never be able to bring about major decisions.

The tactics of winter warfare therefore centered around contests for the possession of roads and inhabited places. In Russia, villages and roads were infinitely more important than they were on the rest of the Continent. In other German theaters of war any one particular road never became a crucial factor, since the well-developed road net always offered a choice of alternate routes. In the East, the possession of a single road often was a life or death matter for an entire army. To be sure, inhabited places were also tactically important in France and along the Mediterranean, and offered welcome shelter. Properly clothed, however, the troops were able to remain in the open for a long time without freezing, or even endangering their health—an impossibility in the East. The extreme tactical importance of inhabited places during the six months of winter explains the fact that the Russians frequently would much rather destroy them than surrender them to the enemy.

II. Forest Fighting

The Russians favored forests for their approach marches and as assembly areas for an attack. They came and disappeared invisibly and noiselessly through the woods. Narrow strips of woodland leading to the outskirts of villages were used as concealed approaches by reconnaissance patrols. The woods also indicated the logical course to be followed for the forward assembly prior to an attack as well as for infiltrating into German positions. Outskirts of woods were a preferred jump-off position for the Soviet mass attacks. Wave upon wave would surge out of the forests. Undaunted by the losses that the German defensive fire inflicted on their ranks, the Russians continued the attack. Even small clearings were used for artillery firing positions. If necessary, the Russians would create such clearings by rapidly felling trees. Quickly and cleverly they constructed positions for heavy weapons and observation posts in trees, and so were able to lend effective support to their advancing infantry. Bringing up even medium artillery and tanks through almost impenetrable forests presented no problem to the Russians.

In June 1944, Russian tanks reached a trackless forest east of Lwow through a narrow gap in the front. The whole tank corps soon followed, although it was attacked from both flanks and heavily bombarded by artillery and rocket projectors. The Russians used their heavy KV1 and KV2 tanks as battering rams to crush the medium growth of timber. The attached engineers overcame some of the attendant difficulties by laying corduroy roads across the swamps, and the infantry and artillery were soon able to follow the tanks. Shortly before the Russian operation, the commanders of the German panzer divisions had come to the conclusion that this forest was impenetrable even for Russian tanks. The Russian advance over this hastily improvised road, constructed with the aid of the most primitive facilities, was, for a time, accompanied by the strains of band music!

In an attack across open terrain with only occasional patches of forest, the Russians endeavored to reach those patches in the shortest possible time. The Germans found that forests had the same magnetic attraction for the Russians as inhabited places. Whenever the Russians planned a river crossing, one could safely assume that it would take place where woods or inhabited localities reached down to the banks of the river.

When the Russians in the course of their great counteroffensive successfully effected a break-through sixty miles deep, west of Byelgorod on 5 August 1943, they seriously threatened the flanks and rear of XI Infantry Corps on the upper course of the Donets River. The Russians recognized the critical situation of the German corps and sought, by a thrust across the river, to cut its only route of retreat. In spite of heavy losses, the Russians managed to gain a foothold in a forest on the west bank of the Donets. On that occasion, a ruse paid the Russians handsome dividends. When the German local reserves launched a counterthrust, they suddenly faced a Russian battalion dressed in German uniforms, and immediately ceased firing. By the time the German troops became aware of their mistake, it was too late. The Russians took advantage of the resultant disorder, fell upon the deceived attackers, and took a large number of them prisoner. The Russians then entrenched themselves in a larger patch of woodland in order to continue their thrust from there. A counterattack, begun the next day and supported by the massed artillery of the German corps and a rocket projector regiment, succeeded in compressing the Russians into a small area, but not in driving them back across the river, although the concentrated drum fire killed three-quarters of their forces.

The innate aptitudes of the Russian soldier asserted themselves to an even greater degree in defensive actions fought in forests. The Russian command was very adept at choosing and fortifying forest positions in such a way that they became impregnable. On the edge of woods toward the enemy, the Russians left only outposts for guarding and screening the main line of resistance, which was withdrawn deep into the forest itself. That security line also formed the springboard and the support for reconnaissance, scouting, and other operations. The main line of resistance frequently ran parallel to the opposite edge of the woods and a few hundred yards inside the woods. Very extensive woods often concealed groups of bunkers in the central part. These bunkers, constituting an intermediate position, were to delay the advance of the enemy, deceive him as to the location of the main position, and serve as support for the outposts. The Russians also protected the exposed flanks of a forest position by groups of bunkers. Important approach routes were blocked by individual machine-gun or antitank-gun bunkers, echeloned in depth. The immediate vicinity of the bunkers was protected by mined entanglements of branches and abatis, as well as by snipers in trees. Furthermore, the Russians used to mine all bypasses and clearings in numerous places. These measures greatly delayed German progress through a forest, because the bunkers could be taken only after costly fighting, and because engineers had to be called upon for time-consuming mineclearing operations. Important forward strong points in forests had facilities for all-around defense. A forester's house or a hamlet would often form the central point of the fortified position. A defense trench surrounded by obstacles and mine fields completely encircled the position. The few sally ports were guarded by sentries and movable barriers. A ring of bunkers, connected with each other and with the fortress, enclosed the central point. The intermediate position was blocked by barbed wire, entanglements of branches, and mines. The previously described individual bunkers were placed along the approach routes.

An extensive system of bunker groups formed the battle position and made possible an unbroken defense of the front. In the battle position all the previously described defense expedients were found in even greater numbers. Entanglements of branches interwoven with barbed wire, and mined abatis to a depth of several hundred yards were no rarity. These obstacles prevented sudden thrusts along the roads. Wherever there might have been a possibility of bypassing these obstructions, one could be sure that mines or tank traps had been installed. In such cases the German troops would often end up in a swamp or an ambush. All bunkers and defense installations were so well camouflaged that they could never be discovered by aerial reconnaissance, and by ground reconnaissance only at very close range. Because of the system of advanced strong points and security positions, it was in many cases impossible for German scouting parties even to get close to the main defensive position. While reconnaissance in force by at least a reinforced battalion might succeed in breaking through the outer protective screen, it frequently would bog down at the supporting position of the Russian outposts. However, if the Russian gave way without offering much resistance, the utmost caution was indicated since a further advance was sure to end in a prepared ambush. In such cases, entire German companies repeatedly were wiped out, the prisoners being massacred.

After the capture of Sukhinichi in February 1942, the German 208th Infantry Division continued its northward thrust. The continuous threat from Red forces in a woodland, as well as raids on the supply road of the division, made it imperative that the woods be cleared of the enemy. According to reports from scouting parties, a small village occupied by a substantial number of Russians was located in the center of the woods. Since it was to be presumed that the raids were launched from that point, the division ordered the capture of the village. Half a battalion was assigned to the task. The force was partially equipped with snowshoes and reinforced by infantry heavy weapons which were taken along on sleds. The Germans advanced along the road leading from Sukhinichi to the village and, having arrived at a clearing in the woods—in the center of which lay the village—without being molested, surrounded the village. The attack met bitter resistance and failed. After having sustained heavy losses, the half-battalion retreated along its approach route. Meanwhile, Russian troops had taken up positions along the road and fell upon the retreating Germans. Only remnants of the half-battalion reached their point of origin.

Strongly garrisoned Russian forest positions were difficult to attack and always cost many casualties. They were invulnerable to attacks by the Luftwaffe, German artillery, or armor. At best, tanks and self-propelled assault guns could be employed individually or in small groups, in which case they were very useful. Very rarely could strong positions be taken if they lay deep in an extensive forest or near its far edge. Frequently whole German divisions were pinned down before such positions until they could be relieved from their plight by an envelopment by other forces. For that reason, forward thrusts by strong forces were not led through woods but around them, wherever such a maneuver was possible.

In the latter half of August 1941, the German 6th Panzer Division was to begin a thrust toward Leningrad from the Porechye bridgehead on the Luga River (Map 4). The bridgehead was completely surrounded by woods and the sector to be attacked lay in a medium-growth, partly marshy woods with thick underbrush. The sector was occupied by the 2d and 3d Russian Proletarian Divisions. The most advanced Russian position was located about 300 to 400 yards ahead of the German front. The Russian trenches were narrow and deep, and had no parapets. The excavated earth had been scattered in the surrounding rank marsh grass, and the trenches were so well camouflaged with branches that neither reconnaissance patrols nor aerial photography had been able to spot them during the preceding four weeks of fighting. The wire entanglements were no higher than the dense growth of grass hiding them. Single roads from the southwestern and northeastern ends of the bridgehead cut through the woods to a village beyond. The two roads were blocked by heavily wired abatis and mine fields. On the far edge of the woods a second position was located atop a sand dune, a third ran through the village, and a fourth lay behind the village. The second position was particularly well constructed. It consisted of a deep antitank ditch, in the front wall of which the Russian riflemen had entrenched themselves, and bunkers for heavy weapons had been installed.

The German attack was to be launched along the two abovementioned roads. A reinforced armored infantry regiment, supported by strong artillery elements and a rocket projector (Werfer) battalion, advanced along each of these roads. Individual tanks were to support the engineers in the removal of the road blocks. In spite of very heavy fire concentrations on the projected points of penetration, the Russians could not be budged from the narrow, invisible zigzag trenches. To be sure, the German tanks were able to reach the barriers, but the dismounted engineers were unable to remove the blocks in the defensive fire, which continued unabated. The infantry following up sought fruitlessly to find other weak spots in order to effect a breakthrough. Repulsed everywhere by the murderous defensive fire of an invisible enemy, it finally stopped, knee-deep in swampland, before the wire entanglements in front of the still unknown Russian position. Not until the following night did one German company succeed in crawling forward, man by man, through the deep-cut bed of a brook which was overgrown with grass and bushes, and in infiltrating through the entanglement. That particular point had not been attacked thereto-fore. Strong German reserves were immediately brought up. They widened the point of penetration, and cleared the trenches and strong points of the westerly sector after hours of hand-grenade fighting. The Soviets continued to maintain their position in the eastern sector. German forces could be directed against the rear of the enemy only after a thrust into the depth of the western sector had reached and rolled up the second position. After bitter hand-to-hand fighting the German forces were finally able to scatter the Russians also at that point, and to clear the road. Only then, after a two-day battle which exacted a heavy toll of losses from both sides, could this invisible defensive system in the woods be surmounted.

III. Fighting Beside Rivers, Swamps, and Lakes

During the course of the war, the ability of the Russians to cross even the largest rivers was always a source of amazement to the Germans. When the German armies reached the Dnepr in the summer of 1941, the problems of surmounting the obstacle presented serious difficulties to the German command, since they had no previous conception of the size and the nature of the river. How quickly and easily this problem could be solved was demonstrated a few days later by the Russians. During the course of one night a cavalry corps crossed the river—using field expedients for ferrying men and equipment to the opposite bank, and swimming thousands of horses across—and penetrated deep into the lines of the surprised Germans.

Two years later the German armies retiring westward headed for this same sector of the Dnepr and had great difficulties in reaching and crossing it ahead of the Russians. By calling on all the forces and means at their disposal, the Germans had managed to occupy seven existing bridges in a sector 300 miles long, but were able to establish only one float bridge and one improvised ferry because of the scarcity of ferrying equipment that prevailed by that time. On the other hand even before the German troops arrived, the Russians, following in close pursuit, succeeded in dropping several thousand paratroops over a 200-mile-long part of the sector, in establishing small bridgeheads at several places, and soon thereafter in building fifty-seven bridges, nine foot bridges, and other facilities for crossing the river. Thus, the Germans had a crossing over the Dnepr every forty miles, the Russians one every four miles. At one ferrying point twenty-five miles downstream from Kremenchug, the Russians established a small bridgehead and proceeded to ferry tanks across the river on rafts, by day and night. Their operations continued well when they were shelled by German artillery, and some of the tank-laden rafts went to the bottom of the river.

The Russians also made extensive use of raft bridges built by their engineers. The German engineers first learned about these from the Russians and had to experiment in order to determine their load capacity. Raft bridges could be used only for crossing waters having a slow current. The raft bridge is built of tree trunks placed side by side and fastened to each other. Depending upon requirements, a second and even a third layer of logs is added, each layer being laid at right angles to the layer below. Planking, laid across the uppermost layer, serves as a roadway. The load capacity of the raft bridge can be adapted to meet existing requirements by varying the number of layers of logs. The Russians built bridges of this type ranging from a five-ton bridge at Rogachev in 1941 to a railroad bridge of over 100-ton load capacity near Kiev in 1943. Just four days after taking Kiev, the Russians had established rail communications into the city over this heavy raft bridge across the Dnepr.

Swamps and lakes also presented no real obstacles to the Russians as was demonstrated during the battles on the Volkhov and the engagements on the Luga and Desna, as well as in many other swamp sectors. When, in February 1944, a yawning gap opened on the Pripyat River at the boundary between Army Group North Ukraine and Army Group Center, the Russians crossed this extensive marshy region during the muddy period with fourteen divisions, and pushed toward Kowel. Several of these divisions turned south through Rowne to attack

Lwow. Stopped near Dubno on the Ikwa River by the German Fourth Panzer Army, they vainly tried to take the few strongly manned crossings over the extensive swamps on both sides of the river. Nevertheless, one morning a Russian battalion appeared in the rear of Dubno. It was surrounded by German armor and captured. Interrogation of the prisoners revealed that during the night the Soviet riflemen had crawled on their bellies across the slightly frozen marsh, which was up to 600 yards wide and could not be crossed on foot, and arrived exhausted and covered with muck.

In September 1943, the German XI Infantry Corps stood on the Dnepr astride Kremenchug, and had to protect its right wing against the enemy who had broken through in the adjacent sector. A shallow lake, two-and-a-half miles long and from 300 to 500 yards wide, facilitated the flank protection. The western bank was guarded by weak German forces. One night these forces were suddenly attacked and driven back by from 600 to 800 Russians. Under cover of darkness the Russians had waded across a shallow spot of the marshy lake without a stitch of clothing, and—equipped only with small arms and ammunition—had surprised the German security. Only quickly brought up mobile reserves were able to encircle the Russians and take them prisoner.

IV. Fighting in Darkness and Inclement Weather

The Russians used darkness and fog primarily for troop movements, preparations for attack, construction of field fortifications, and supply operations. Reconnaissance in force, and raids likewise, were usually carried out under cover of darkness or hazy weather. In these instances, the Russians proceeded with patience, cunning, and perseverance. Not infrequent were Russian night attacks in strength of up to a regiment.

In the Arctic, the Russians employed commando teams specially trained in Byelomorsk for night raids into the German rear area. Appropriate to the nature of their mission, these troops were equipped only with absolutely essential items. Minutely detailed orders took care of every phase of the undertaking, and were carried out methodically and to the letter. Here, too, the Russian proved himself a fearless fighter. As in other regions, attacks on strong points in the Arctic were broken off only when the Russian casualties amounted to many times the strength of the strong point complements.

A typical example of a planned night attack was that of a Siberian division against the German 112th Infantry Division southeast of Uzlovaya toward the end of November 1941 (Map 5). After it had finished unloading, the Siberian division advanced on the 112th Infantry Division early in the night. Having gained a substantial amount of territory to the north beyond Bogoroditsk in minor engagements during the previous day, the 112th Division had bivouacked for the night. About twenty tanks led the Siberian attack. The mere appearance by night of tanks in front of the lines of the 112th Division produced a severe shock. No means of defense were on hand at that time. Any defenses would have had only a local effect at night. When the attacking Siberians appeared behind the tanks, complete panic ensued. The elements of the 112th Division hit by the attack fell back several miles, close up to the northern outskirts of Bogoroditsk. Special steps had to be taken to restore control of the situation. The territorial gains of the Siberian division remained limited to a few miles; a large-scale exploitation of their success did not follow. The Russians probably had reached their objective and had not planned any further advance.

Night attacks on a major scale, however, remained the exception to the rule. The Russians undertook such attacks only when they had orders from a higher command, or when they failed to take an important objective in a day attack in spite of a mass commitment of men and equipment. Night attacks were generally acts of desperation, where everything was staked on one card.

During the polar winter only small-scale warfare was possible which, however, the Russians as well as the Germans waged zealously. Security and reconnaissance activity had to be greatly increased. Surprise attacks were always to be expected because it remained dark throughout the day. The generally known principles of defense against night operations held true under those conditions. Almost the only new feature was the fact that fighting was not limited to mere local actions, for raiding parties consisting of smaller units did not hesitate to thrust far into the depths of the enemy front (the Russians to the Turku– and Helsinki–Petsamo highway (Eismeerstrasse), the Germans to the Murmansk railroad). Both sides frequently employed specially trained troops in these operations. The Russians used troops trained in Byelomorsk; the Germans used special Finnish units.

Attempts to break out of pockets, such as took place in 1941 at Maloryta, Vyazma, Bryansk, and other encirclements, were another type of night surprise attack. Here, the Russians made no long preparations, but hurled themselves into the open without any definite plan. In tightly packed hordes they struck at whatever points they believed there was a chance to break through. At Maloryta the Russians, after a successful breakout of part of their forces, spent thirty-six hours encircling and storming a village still held by the Germans. This village was to the rear of the Russians, and by their pointless operation they lost the advantage of their nighttime breakout. Possession of the village would have been completely unimportant for the success of the breakout. Their orders, however, probably read that way.

Russian large-scale offensives always started by daylight. Usually the early morning hours were chosen. H Hour remained the same even if dense fog obscured everything all day long as, for instance, at the beginning of the second battle of East Prussia on 14 January 1945.

It was, however, highly advantageous for the German to attack heavily fortified Russian strong points, and antitank gun and tank fronts by night. Attempts to take them by day would have cost large numbers of lives. Night attacks were almost always successful when carried out by troops specially trained for this type of combat, and usually cost only a few casualties.

In the spring of 1943 during the war of position north of Tomarovka, an assault detachment in company strength of the German 16th Infantry Division succeeded in infiltrating the

Russian front by night, raiding a strongly garrisoned village from the rear and driving the enemy out. During the previous day, two battalions had been unable to take the village despite strong artillery support.

In January 1943 a company of the 6th Panzer Division supported by six self-propelled assault guns was similarly able to take an important fortified village north of Tatsinskaya by a night assault from the rear. Previously, a panzer grenadier regiment and a sixty-tank panzer battalion of the neighboring division had vainly endeavored all day to take this village.

Verkhniy-Kumskiy, the bitterly contested key point of Russian defense against the German relief thrust on Stalingrad, also was taken in a night attack by a panzer grenadier battalion with but minor losses.

Even the Russians began no far-reaching operations in really bad weather, but such weather suited them very well for local operations. During fog and blizzards the Russians always developed lively reconnaissance activity and raided advanced security posts. Not infrequently the Russians would attack in battalion or regimental strength during driving thundershowers to effect reconnaissance in force, to improve their position, or to gain a favorable jump-off position for a major offensive. In winter they exploited the cold eastern storms of the steppes for such assaults, especially in the southern sector. On those occasions the Russians often succeeded in entering the German trenches without firing a shot, and in taking many prisoners. Indeed, the Russians knew very well that the easterly gales drove such clouds of powdered snow ahead of them that the German soldiers were unable to observe and take aim against the wind. They were, therefore, practically defenseless. Only by a ruse were the German divisions fighting there able to regain mastery of the situation. Those front sectors particularly threatened during the easterly gales were simply evacuated and the forces quartered in the villages situated along the sides of the gaps. When the Russians rushed forward into, or over the empty trenches, the German forces wheeled against the rear of the Russians and attacked them from the east; the Russians were then just as defenseless as the Germans had previously been and were often captured *en masse*. As a result, the Russians later ceased attacking during easterly gales.

CHAPTER 13

Camouflage, Deception, and Propaganda

Camouflage, deception, and propaganda were expedients much used by the Russians. These, too, reflected in every aspect the oriental character of the people. The Russians carried out measures conforming to their natural talents, such as camouflage and deception, with great skill and effectiveness. Their front propaganda, however, was crude and naïve for the most part. Because it did not correspond to the psychology and mentality of the German soldier in any way, it was ineffective. Although pursued zealously, and with a great variety of media, it attained no appreciable success for precisely those reasons.

I. Camouflage

The Russians were excellent at camouflage. With their primitive instinct they understood perfectly how to blend into their surroundings and were trained to vanish into the ground upon the slightest provocation. As illustrated in the preceding pages, they skillfully used darkness, vegetation, and poor weather conditions for concealing their intentions. Their movements at night and their advances through wooded terrain were carried out with exemplary quietness. Now and then they would communicate with each other by means of cleverly imitated animal cries.

Noteworthy, too, was their camouflage of river crossings by the construction of underwater bridges. For this purpose they used a submersible underwater bridging gear, which could be submerged or raised by flooding or pumping out the compartments. The deck of the bridge was usually about one foot below water level, and was thus shielded from aerial observation.

Artificial camouflage was another device used by the Russians. Even at the beginning of the war the Germans came across Russian troops wearing camouflage suits dyed green. Lying prone on the grass, these soldiers could be spotted only at a very short distance, and frequently were passed by without having been noticed at all. Reconnaissance patrols frequently wore "leaf" suits of green cloth patches, which provided excellent camouflage in the woods. Russians wearing face masks were no rarity.

The Russians enforced strict camouflage discipline. Any man who left his shelter during the day was punished severely, if it was forbidden for reasons of camouflage. In this way the Russians were able to conceal the presence of large units even in winter, as the following example illustrates.

In January 1944 the Russian First Tank Army attempted to take the important railroad hub of Zhmerinka in a surprise attack. The attack was repulsed, and the army encircled to the southeast of Vinnitsa. It broke out of the encirclement during the very first night, and disappeared. The bulk of this Russian army escaped completely unnoticed through the gaps left by the insufficient German forces engaged in the encirclement. In spite of deep snow and clear weather, it could not even be determined in which direction the Red forces had escaped. From the situation, it was to be assumed that they had hidden in the immediate vicinity in a group of numerous, rather large villages with extensive, adjoining orchards. Since German armored units had previously driven through those villages, the tank tracks gave no reliable evidence that the Russians were hiding there. For two days and nights the Luftwaffe scouted for the whereabouts of the First Tank Army, and in this connection took excellent aerial photographs of the entire area in which the villages were located. But neither aerial observation nor the study of aerial photographs provided any clue. Not until the third day, when a strong German tank force pushed into the group of villages, was the hiding place of the entire army established in that very area. All tanks and other vehicles had been excellently camouflaged in barns, under sheds, straw piles, haystacks, piles of branches, etc.; and all movements during the day had been forbidden, so that nothing gave away their presence.

II. Deception

Prior to offensives the Russian made extensive use of deception. In order to mislead the enemy as to the time and place of impending large-scale offensives, the Russians feigned concentrations in other sectors by preparing a great number of fire positions for artillery, mortars, and rocket projectors. They strengthened this impression by moving smaller bodies of troops into those sectors by day and night, as well as by setting up dummy artillery pieces, tanks, and aircraft, and making appropriate tracks leading up to them. The Russians were also known to place an entire tank army behind an unimportant sector, so as to create the false impression of an impending attack from that point. By running their motors at night they sought to create the impression that tank and motorized columns were on the move. Artillery trial fire and the use of roving guns likewise were among the most commonly used Russian deceptive practices.

For purposes of deception on a more limited scale, the Russians frequently used German uniforms for whole units as well as for individuals. That method of deception was almost always successful.

In the summer of 1943 a German-speaking Russian in the uniform of a German officer succeeded in driving a German truck right up to headquarters of the Rowne military government detachment (Ortskommandantur), and in obtaining an audience with the commandant, a general. He gagged the commandant, wrapped him up in a big rug, carried him out to the truck which he had left idling outside, and delivered him to the partisans. Only by the words, "Thanks, comrade"—words that an officer in the German Army simply would not use in addressing a private—did he arouse the suspicion of the kidnapped officer's orderly, who had innocently helped him load the heavy carpet into the truck. Although an immediate report was made by the orderly, it did not lead to the apprehension of the kidnapper.

In Lwow, in the spring of 1944, apparently the same Russian, dressed as a German officer, succeeded by similar trickery in killing the deputy governor of Galicia as well as a lieutenant colonel, and a later sentinel who wanted to inspect his truck. Each time he succeeded in escaping.

Similar surprise raids and deceptions of combat troops through the misuse of German uniforms occurred at all sectors of the front in ever increasing numbers.

III. Propaganda

The propaganda of the Russians exploited military and political problems and used all the technical means by which modern propaganda is disseminated—radio, press, leaflets, photographs, planes flying by night towing illuminated streamers or equipped with loud speakers and photographs, loudspeakers set up on the ground, leaflet shells, rumors spread by agents, Russian PWs, and Germans pretending to have escaped from Russian captivity. Since there were also Finnish troops on the Arctic Front, to whom different things were of importance, Russian propaganda at that front sometimes met with difficulties, and was not properly coordinated. One also had to differentiate between propaganda aimed at higher military commanders, the troops, and the German people. The various groups to be propagandized were dealt with and approached from entirely different angles. From a literary and artistic standpoint, much of the Russian propaganda was of high caliber.

The Russian intelligence service covered events in the German Army with amazing speed and accuracy. Photographs, for example, taken by one of the German propaganda companies for various reasons, appeared almost simultaneously in the pertinent Russian army newspapers. The propaganda at the front, however, was crude and clumsy. For that reason, it made but little impression. Political and military satire were used a great deal.

The Germans obtained information on Russian propaganda addressed to their own troops from captured Russian army newspapers. It, too, employed words and pictures. Nationalism and ideological fanaticism were exploited with equal intensity. The Russians seemed to criticize quite frankly some of the events at the front. Conditions among German troops in opposing positions were treated satirically for the most part. In the propaganda directed at their own front lines, the Russians pounded into their soldiers' heads the story that the Germans shot every PW on the spot. This propaganda-induced fear of being taken prisoner was to make the Russian soldiers stand their ground to the very end. The story was believed, and that particular line of propaganda accomplished its purpose. There were relatively few Russian deserters. On the other hand, older Russian soldiers who had worked in Germany as prisoners during World War I were immune to such atrocity stories and deserted very frequently.

A large part of the Russian propaganda effort was devoted to studying and counteracting German propaganda activities. Reading and passing on German propaganda leaflets was forbidden under penalty of death.

By erecting signs, by loudspeaker messages, or by dropping propaganda leaflets from aircraft, the Russians made extensive use of frontline propaganda urging the Germans to surrender or desert. Often the commander was addressed personally, sometimes by captured German officers of all ranks, who allegedly belonged to the "Free Germany" organization. Many propaganda leaflets were dropped that represented pictorially the Russian superiority in men, weapons, and matériel, as well as in armament potential. Also alleged German atrocities and acts of destruction were shown. It was, however, not quite clear just what propaganda purpose the exhibition of nude women standing on the breastworks of Russian trenches was supposed to accomplish. They supposedly were German girls who had fallen into Russian hands.

The German command had little reason to be concerned over Soviet propaganda. Neither the spoken nor the printed Russian propaganda inspired any credulity, for it contained too many obvious lies. Besides, the German soldier had seen the dubious blessings of Bolshevism at close range, and had discussed this dictatorial system with its opponents among the Russian people. There were a great many anti-Communists among the Russian intellectuals. Those people voluntarily joined in the German retreat in 1943, because they wanted to have nothing more to do with the Russian system.

Even before the Eastern Campaign, strong anti-German propaganda was disseminated. In the schools of many Russian cities and villages German language texts were found which contained the most coarse invectives aimed at Germany. That was the manner in which communism spiritually prepared for war against Germany. In a fairly large village south of Leningrad, half-grown, German-speaking boys naïvely admitted that they had been selected as *Komsomoltsy* (the Soviet counterpart of the German Hitler Youth) for Magdeburg.

Occasionally the Russians also doubled back German PWs with false reports. The Germans frequently picked up particularly well-trained Russian deserters who were supposed to supply them with false information. This type of propaganda was somewhat less than a success. With the exception of individual non-German soldiers in German uniform, instances of desertion from the German rank remained limited to the acts of a few desperadoes.

During the first years of the war the Russians apparently had sought to impress the German troops and lower their morale by committing numerous atrocities against them. The great number of such crimes, committed on all sectors of the front especially in 1941–42, but also during later German counter-offensives, tends to support that presumption.

On 25 June 1941, two batteries of the German 267th Infantry Division near Melniki (Army Group Center) were overrun in the course of a Russian night breakthrough and bayonetted to the last man. Individual dead bore up to seventeen bayonet wounds, among them even holes through the eyes.

On 26 August 1941, while combing a woods for enemy forces, a battalion of the German 465th Infantry Regiment was attacked from all sides by Russian tree snipers, and lost seventy-five dead and twenty-five missing. In a follow-up thrust, all of the missing men were found shot through the neck.

In January 1942, an SS division attacked the area north of Szyczewka (Army Group Center). On that occasion, a battalion fighting in a dense forest area suffered a reverse and lost twenty-six men. German troops who later penetrated to that point found all the missing SS men massacred. In April 1942, an elderly Russian civilian, a carpenter, appeared at a German division headquarters southwest of Rzhev, and reported that he had encountered a group of about forty German PWs with a Russian escort in his village a few miles behind the Russian front. The prisoners, he continued, had soon afterward been halted at the northern outskirts of the village, where they had dug deep pits. According to eyewitness reports, the prisoners had subsequently been shot, and buried in those pits. A few days later, the village was captured in a German thrust. The incident was investigated, and found to be true.

During the battle of Zhizdra, in early March 1943, a battalion of the German 590th Grenadier Regiment was assigned the mission of mopping up a sector overgrown with brush. The attack failed. When, on 19 March 1943, the sector again passed into German hands after a counterattack by the corps, forty corpses of soldiers from the battalion were found with their eyes gouged out, or their ears, noses, and genitals cut off. Corpses found in another sector of the battlefield bore signs of similar mutilations.

On 5 July 1943, during the German pincers attack on Kursk (Operation ZITADELLE), a battalion on the southern flank of the 320th Infantry Division lunged forward without being supported by other units. It ran headlong into the counterattack of an enemy division, and was repulsed. About 150 men were taken prisoner. Shortly thereafter the Germans monitored a telephone conversation between Russian lower and higher headquarters (probably regiment and division), which went about as follows:

Regimental commander: "I have 150 Fritzes (derogatory term for German soldiers) here. What shall I do with them?"

Division commander: "Keep a few for interrogation, and have the others liquidated."

In the evening of the same day, the presumed regimental commander reported the order executed, stating that the majority of the Fritzes had been killed immediately, and the remainder after they had been interrogated.

The Russians sought to intimidate their own civilian population by similar atrocities. In March 1943, after the recapture of Zolochev, a small city twenty miles north of Kharkov, the inhabitants told the German military police that the Russians, before their retreat, had herded and whipped a rather large number of local boys between the ages of fourteen and seventeen years naked through the streets in intense cold. Afterward, they were said to have disappeared into the firehouse, where the NKVD had its headquarters, never to be seen again. During a subsequent search, all of the missing boys were found in a deep cellar of the firehouse, shot through the neck and covered with horse manure. The bodies were identified and claimed by relatives. All had severely frostbitten limbs. The reason for this particular atrocity was assumed to have been the alleged aid rendered the German occupation forces.

One medium of propaganda employed frequently by the Russians during the last years of the war were German PWs who would be doubled back to the German lines, usually to sectors held by their own regiments, with the mission of inducing their comrades to desert by telling them how well they would be treated as Russian prisoners. That type of propaganda failed, as did similar attempts on the part of the Germans with Russian PWs who had volunteered for this assignment.

Few Russian soldiers, on the other hand, believed German propaganda. Whenever it fell on fertile soil, its effects were promptly neutralized by counterpropaganda and coercion. Except during the great encirclement operations, there were only isolated instances of wholesale desertion of Russian units. If it did occur, or if the number of individual deserters increased, the Soviet commissars immediately took drastic countermeasures.

During the protracted period of position warfare along the upper course of the Donets in the spring of 1943, a front-line unit of the German XI Infantry Corps south of Byelgorod was able to take a large number of prisoners. The prisoners were taken in midday raids, since it had been ascertained from deserters that the Russians in this terrain sector—which could be readily observed from the western bank of the river—were allowed to move only at night, and therefore slept during the day. The prisoners admitted that many of their comrades were dissatisfied and would like to desert; however, they were afraid of being fired upon by the Germans and would have difficulties crossing the deep river to the German lines. Contact with the company of malcontents was soon established, and the necessary arrangements made. Unobtrusive light signals on the chosen night informed the Russian company that the necessary ferrying equipment was ready, and that German weapons stood ready to cover their crossing. All necessary precautions had been taken in case of a Russian ruse. Just the same, the company really dribbled down to the banks of the river, and in several trips was ferried across the Donets in rubber boats; the company commander, an Uzbek first lieutenant, being the very first. Part of the company, however, ran into Russian mine fields, suffering considerable losses from exploding mines as well as from the fire of the alerted Russian artillery.

The result of this undertaking and the above-mentioned incidents was that, having become unreliable, the 15th Uzbek Division was immediately withdrawn from the front, disciplined, and committed elsewhere.

THE RED AIR FORCE

CHAPTER 14

A Luftwaffe Evaluation

Numerically, the Red Air Force was greatly underestimated by the Germans before the beginning of the Eastern Campaign. But in spite of its numerical strength, which increased considerably during the course of the war, it had no decisive influence on the outcome of the battles in the East.

Russian air force tactics were inflexible and strictly followed a fixed pattern. They were wanting in adaptability. Only in late 1944 and early 1945 could the first beginnings of strategic air warfare be observed. The Russian Long Range Force (*Fernkampffliegerkorps*), which came under the surveillance of German radio intelligence as early as 1941, was employed primarily in transport operations. Although the Red Air Force was an independent service of the Russian armed forces, it was employed almost exclusively on the battlefield, in joint operations with the army.

The Germans detected impending Russian attacks by—among other clues—the early assembly and concentration of combat aviation on airfields near the front. In this connection, the Russians proved very adept at building auxiliary airfields. Ruthlessly exploiting labor forces drawn from the civilian population, and using the most primitive equipment, they would have the airfields completed and ready for take-offs within an amazingly short time. Neither winter nor the muddy periods interfered with their work. The Russian Air Force made liberal use of dummy airfields and aircraft, as well as of numerous methods of camouflage.

In combat, the direction and commitment of aviation was assumed by command posts near the front, one of the most ably handled phases in this respect being the control of fighter aircraft from the ground. On the other hand, cooperation between fighter and ground-attack aircraft or bomber formations left much to be desired. Fighter escorts seldom accompanied them on their missions; if they did, they scattered upon first contact with the enemy.

The Russians proved to be excellent bad-weather pilots. Although not equipped for instrument flying, fighters and ground-attack aircraft hedgehopped over battlefields in the most inclement weather. They liked to take advantage of low ceilings and blizzards in order to surprise the enemy.

Russian night fighters as a rule confined themselves to attacks on those targets on which they had been briefed, and were equipped with only the most basic navigation aids. The Germans were amazed to discover that Russian night fighters almost always flew with their position lights burning.

Air force formations concentrated for major operations always revealed a rapid decline of fighting potential once they had joined action. The number of planes capable of flying combat missions decreased rapidly, and a rather long time was required to restore them to flying condition. The Russians made extended use of artificial smoke for camouflaging and protecting industrial plants, railroad junctions, and bridges against strategic air attacks.

The rapid repair of bomb damage was noteworthy, especially in the case of railroad installations. Again, labor forces for this purpose were ruthlessly commandeered from the civilian population.

Air supply operations assumed substantial proportions during the course of the war. Planes either landed the supplies, or dropped them by parachute. Agents and armed saboteurs dropped behind the German lines likewise played a special role.

At the beginning of the war, Russian ground troops were extremely vulnerable to air attack. Very soon, however, a change took place. Russian troops became tough and invulnerable to attacks by German dive-bombers and ground-attack aircraft.

Training in defense against low-level attacks was well handled. Every weapon was unhesitatingly turned against the attacking aircraft, thereby constituting a formidable defense. Whenever the weather permitted, the Russian troops avoided billets and concealed themselves masterfully in the terrain. If, in exceptional cases, they sought shelter in inhabited places, they had strict orders not to show themselves outdoors in the daytime.

In keeping with Soviet ideology, the Russians employed an increasing number of female pilots and other female air crew members as the war went on. Women not only flew transport missions, but manned combat planes as well.

In conclusion, it may be said that the Red Air Force, although conceived and built up on a large scale, was very primitively trained. Its will to fight, its aggressive spirit, and its mastery of technical aspects left much to be desired. Although constantly superior in numbers to the Luftwaffe, it was always inferior when it came to combat. Usually a small number of German fighters sufficed to clear the skies of Russian planes.

CHAPTER 15

A Ground Force
Evaluation

I. Tactical Employment

With regard to matériel and training, the Soviet Air Force in World War II was always much inferior to the Luftwaffe despite the fact that the number of its planes increased steadily and had outnumbered those of the Luftwaffe as early as 1942. Not even the introduction of new Russian types of planes was able to effect any decisive change in the disproportionate performances of the belligerents. For that reason, the Russian Air

Force often was no factor at all in ground warfare. Sometimes it played a secondary role, but never one as decisive as that of the air forces of the Western Allies.

At the beginning of the great German offensive in the East, the ground troops saw only flights of three or four reconnaissance planes, individual bomber squadrons, and only a few fighters (Soviet I-16 single-seat pursuit planes, dubbed "Rata" in the Spanish Civil War). They quickly became victims of German fighters. Seldom did one of the reconnaissance planes return from a mission. No sooner had they been sighted than a long trail of smoke told of their annihilation. Their crews followed them down in parachutes, they being among the first Russian prisoners who with bitter hate, or, in individual cases, with uncontrolled sobbing, awaited their fate: they expected to be shot, as their propaganda had led them to believe. They became all the more confused when the Germans treated them in a friendly manner. The same thing happened to the bombers which flew straight toward their targets, without fighter escorts, in single squadrons of five or six planes, or in from two to three squadrons, one right behind the other. They did not change their course even when the powerful German Flak played havoc with them. Direct hits frequently tore planes into shreds. The rest of the squadron would continue toward its objective until it was shot down by German fighters during the bombing run or the return flight. It happened repeatedly that a whole squadron would be shot down in a few minutes. At that time, an attack by Russian bombers meant nothing more to the German ground troops than an exciting spectacle, which always ended in tragedy for the Russians. Not until the Russians had realized the futility of their efforts did they attempt to ward off their fate by jettisoning their bombs and quickly turning tail upon the approach of German fighters. In that way at least some of their planes succeeded in reaching the home base, only to be finished off the next day.

The Russians were in a fair way to lose their last aircraft by this completely futile commitment in detail. True, the Russian Air Force was able to replace the lost planes, but it never did recover from the shock effect of the German fighters. The superiority of German fighters over Russian planes of any type was evident right up to the end of the war.

Soon, however, the bloody lessons began to bear first fruit. During the battles on the frontier, the Russian planes could be neutralized almost completely, but later, when the German troops were crossing the Dnepr and Dvina Rivers, concentrations of bomber units with fighter escorts did make their presence felt. Skillfully maneuvering, they hit the bridges and crossing sites in surprise attacks; coming in from the flanks or from the rear they harassed the German troops crossing the rivers and were responsible for the first German losses. However, the German crossings of the two rivers were not stopped nor even delayed. At the Luga the Russians employed their new technique by using all aircraft available in the Leningrad area in shuttle raids, in order to destroy individual, isolated bridgeheads of advanced German armored elements. The Germans suffered considerable losses, because their troops were squeezed into a narrow area, and no air support was to be had to counter the Russians because the ground organization of the Luftwaffe had not yet caught up. Nevertheless, the tactical effect was nil, for the Russian Air Force carried on its own private war, as did the artillery, the tanks, and the infantry; of the latter, each division attacked in detail. The result was that in July 1941, for example, the Russian forces, eight to ten times superior in strength to the Germans, were not able to take the Porechye bridgehead (seventy miles southwest of Leningrad) which had been cut off completely during the first days. The Russians did not succeed in destroying even one of two wooden bridges that were located within 300 yards of each other, after bombing them daily for a period of weeks, and sending 2,000 heavy shells in their direction every day, thus attesting to the meager technical skill of the artillery and the bombers.

The initial lack of any cooperation between the various Russian arms and the deficiency in technical skill, led to continuous failures in the above-mentioned sector as well as on all other fronts. The Russians, gradually recognizing these mistakes, obviously strove for improvement. They developed appreciable technical skill. Cooperation between the combined arms also improved visibly. Nevertheless, this particular aspect remained their weakness to the end of the war. The art of cooperation presupposed a measure of personal initiative, knowledge of tactics, and acute perceptory faculties that the Russian did not seem to possess because those qualities ran counter to his national character and his upbringing. He attempted to compensate for those serious weaknesses by mass commitments of forces and matériel also in the case of his air force. In the air, however, his efforts were not crowned with the same degree of success as on the ground. Eventually, the endeavor on the part of the air force led to the formation of main efforts which became more pronounced from year to year, and which made themselves felt all the more during the Russian large-scale offensives of the last war years when the fighting strength of the Luftwaffe was ebbing visibly because of fuel shortage and grievous losses in other theaters.

The Russian Air Force missed its first great chance in the winter of 1941–42 when the Germans were withdrawing before Moscow. A concentration of most of its air power on the German columns, confined to the few roads that were free from snow, would have had a devastating effect.

Even during the great Russian offensive in the winter of 1942–43 between the Don and the lower course of the Dnepr, as well as during the defense against the German relief push on Stalingrad, the concentrations of Russian aircraft were as yet not strong enough to influence the course of events to any appreciable extent. Air operations properly coordinated as to time and place with those of the ground forces were likewise an exception to the rule.

In the summer of 1943, on the other hand, the concentrations of Russian planes were much greater and their activity much more vigorous. The Russian Air Force played an important role in the battle south of Kursk (the German ZITADELLE attack, July 1943) and in the Russian counteroffensive in August 1943. But its activity soon dwindled and a month later the German armies succeeded in escaping across the few Dnepr bridges to a position behind the river barrier without any interference on the part of the Russian Air Force.

Similar mass sorties were repeated in the battles of Lwow and Vitebsk in 1944, and in the second battle of East Prussia in 1945. The main efforts, however, though clearly recognizable at the start, always dissolved within a short time, and the Russian Air Force would disappear.

II. Combat Techniques

At the start of the war, missions were flown at high altitudes. Fighters (Rata) attacking at low level were first encountered by the Germans on the northern front at the Luga River. They strafed and dropped small bombs on batteries or marching columns, without accomplishing any noteworthy results. During the breakthrough of the Leningrad Line in September 1941, there appeared for the first time small groups of Russian fighters equipped with rocket bombs. Their accuracy and effectiveness was inconsequential.

The IL-2, a very effective and unpleasant ground-attack plane, made its debut in February 1943. It could be identified by a cockpit armored with bulletproof glass about four inches thick. The pilot was protected by steel plates in the rear and bottom of the cockpit. This type of airplane was invulnerable to rifle and machine-gun fire of any caliber. Its armor also withstood 20mm Flak projectiles. It is, therefore, understandable that these ground-attack aircraft were used at danger points, and unceasingly harassed ground troops once they had caught them in a low-level attack. In that manner they were able to bring daylight movements of motorized troops to a standstill, and to inflict considerable losses on them with their twin-barreled machine-gun fire and small fragmentation bombs. Flak guns of 37mm or heavier caliber were of no use in the defense against their hedgehopping attacks because they flew too fast for allowing proper aim. Thus, it was necessary to use the 20mm armor-piercing ammunition, the use of which had previously been forbidden for any other purpose than antitank defense. Once this special-purpose ammunition was used by the

20mm Flak, the Russian IL-2's suffered such heavy losses that they rapidly disappeared from the scene.

By the winter of 1944–45, Russian antitank weapons in aircraft had become so highly developed that they represented a seriously growing menace to German tanks and self-propelled assault guns. By January 1945, for example, during the second battle of East Prussia, at least eight self-propelled assault guns were set afire on one day by Russian antitank planes.

That year, too, Russian aircraft began to hunt down German locomotives and individual motor vehicles which they suspected of carrying senior officers. The locomotive hunts led to serious losses on railroad lines located close to the front. The losses ceased only after the trains on those lines had been armed with light Flak. On the Arctic Front, the destruction of locomotives had particularly troublesome consequences. Since the Finnish supply of locomotives was very limited, the Finnish Railroad Ministry wanted to discontinue operations on the Kemijaervi line which was seriously endangered, but urgently needed for German supply operations.

Hunting individual German motor vehicles also led to losses. On Easter Sunday 1944, for example, a Germany army commander was traveling to the front north of Buczacz, Galicia, when Russian fighter squadrons attacked his car. They made repeated runs on the lone automobile, killed the commander's entourage, blew the car to bits with eighty bombs, and prevented the commander himself from continuing his journey. Only when the higher German commanders used old, nonidentified cars did the attacks cease.

Russian daytime bombing raids even in the later years of the war were carried out mostly by small groups at altitudes of 7,000 feet or higher. Raids by whole wings were an exception to the rule. Carpet bombing by large bomber formations was unknown to the Russians. On the other hand, during the last two war years, they frequently dropped clusters of small fragmentation bombs on live targets. The bombs would fall within a radius of a hundred yards in such a dense pattern that no living object within the effective beaten zone could escape the splinters. The bombs fell into even the narrowest trenches and, because of their great fragmentation, were very dangerous and greatly feared. German planes surprised on the ground often would be set afire or destroyed by the fragments of bombs dropped in such patterns. The effect of these bombs on the morale of the German troops was likewise serious.

The Soviet bombers displayed poor marksmanship. For example, in an attempt to help their sorely pressed infantry on the edge of a forest by bombing the German lines, all the bombs fell on the Russian position and wreaked such havoc that, after the second salvo had been dropped, the German infantry was able to take the position without losses. In most Russian bombing attacks the planes would fly over a troop-filled road at a right angle, so that some bombs would be fairly certain to hit the target. In flying along the course of a road it often happened that all the bombs fell so far to the sides of the road that they were completely ineffective.

Bomber attacks at night bore the stamp of nuisance raids. In nearly all instances they were flown by individual planes and directed against targets located close to the front, such as billets, highway traffic, artillery positions, and other points occupied by troops. They were annoying to be sure, but seldom caused major damage. In order to make it difficult for the night bombers to locate their targets, especially on moonlit nights, the Germans smeared all whitewashed houses with mud and conducted all movements without lights. Installation of small Flak units at persistently attacked points caused heavy losses of Russian night planes, since their silhouettes in the moonlight made them easy targets. The attacks ceased immediately.

Night attacks directed against large German installations, such as railheads, airfields, factories, cities, etc., lasted all night. They were carried out by a chain of individual aircraft following each other at short intervals. Flights to and from the target followed different routes. Whenever the Russians aimed at destroying extensive installations, they repeated their bombing raids for several consecutive nights. In the summer of 1944, for example, most of the city of Tilsit in East Prussia was destroyed in a long series of Soviet night attacks.

On dark nights, Russian aircraft used parachute flares resembling Christmas trees to mark the direction of the bomb run and the target areas for the attacking bombers. Frequently, however, inhabited places thus bracketed by a rectangle of flares could be evacuated before the arrival of the first bombers. In other cases, the wind blew the rectangles so far away before the bombers appeared that all the bombs fell into open fields and caused no damage.

The Russians used German searchlights and other guide lights as navigation aids, and for that reason never attacked them. Russian night fighters seldom appeared and were of very minor importance.

A faulty sense of orientation in the air, or an inadequate knowledge of map reading, repeatedly caused Russian pilots accidentally to land behind the German lines. In January 1943, for instance, a Russian pilot accompanied by an engineer was supposed to repair another plane which had made a forced landing. Despite perfect visibility, the repair-shop plane strayed across the clearly recognizable river which formed the front and landed in German territory. Much more distressing to the Russians was the accidental landing in the German Buczacz bridgehead of a liaison plane with courier mail and an *Armeeintendant* (administrative official of an army) aboard. That incident took place shortly before the Russian summer offensive east of Lwow in 1944. The pilot was flying from Kolomea to Tarnopol, but landed at the halfway mark because the similarity of terrain and the brown uniforms of a Hungarian unit, which he mistook for Russians, had confused him.

The Russians repeatedly used captured German planes, with the German insignia retained, for purposes of reconnaissance and for occasional special missions.

PARTISAN WARFARE

CHAPTER 16

Partisan Combat Methods

Generally speaking, Russian partisan groups on the Eastern Front were formed early in 1942. At first they were mainly isolated bands of little strength, frequently dropped from aircraft, operating in rear areas well behind the German front. During the summer of 1942, however, these bands were gradually combined into more closely knit groups, put under a unified command, and continuously reinforced. Accordingly, their operations grew in scope and impact.

Partisan group activities seldom covered areas near the front except when extensive, pathless forests favored their approach. In general, the partisan groups would maneuver in the rear areas of the German armies, in woods and swamps next to highways and railroads. They avoided open territory and regions occupied by German troops, but kept the latter under surveillance.

From the outset the German troops had difficulty defending themselves against this type of warfare. Its effectiveness had been underestimated. Apart from the fact that, considering the vast areas, the German forces were not numerous enough to combat the steadily expanding partisan groups, the frontline troops, which had been trained for orthodox warfare, all lacked experience in antipartisan warfare.

During large scale enemy breakthroughs, or German withdrawals, strong partisan groups frequently managed to coordinate their operations with those of Soviet cavalry, ski units, infiltrated infantry, or paratroops. Substantial German forces (usually several infantry and panzer divisions) had to be mustered in order to combat the joint enemy efforts. Prior to large-scale Russian offensives, strong bands would often migrate to the areas that the Red Army soon hoped to take. Such movements, therefore, gave some indication of Russian intentions. Prior to the beginning of the large-scale Red Army offensive in East Galicia in July 1944, for example, numerous bands worked their way into the Carpathian Mountains southwest of Lwow, which were among the objectives of the Soviet operations.

On the other hand, during each Russian withdrawal, as well as subsequent to battles of encirclement, innumerable soldiers cut off from their own forces, and sometimes entire combat units, made their way to the partisans and fought with them. In such instances, too, partisan activities developed into a serious threat.

During the winter, strong bands, well organized from a military standpoint and commanded by specially trained leaders, developed intense activity in the extensive woodlands of the Eastern Front.

The bands were generally organized into groupments of from 3,000 to 5,000 men each. As long as the front remained static, these groupments would remain in a fixed location; they were quartered in winterproofed camps, excellently constructed and heavily guarded. Smaller groups, varying greatly in strength, comprised at least 100 men. Attached to each groupment was a number of these smaller partisan groups. They branched out through the entire rear area and frequently were only in loose liaison with the groupment. They constantly changed their position and therefore were difficult to locate in the vast rear area, which was only sparsely occupied by German troops. They had contact men in all the larger villages of importance to them. Dispersed and cut-off Russian units gave them even tactical striking power. In 1941, for instance, in the area of Army Group Center, 10,000 men under General Kulik operated very skillfully and could not be cornered. Another example was the remnants of the 32d Kazak Division, whose destruction required the commitment of German frontline troops on 6 and 7 August 1941. In 1944, activities of partisans, reinforced by infiltrated troops, had reached such proportions west of the extremely swampy Narva River that the left wing of the northern front (III SS Panzer Corps) had to be pulled back in order to form a shorter and more easily guarded line.

Every camp of the larger partisan groups was secured on all sides—in some sections to a depth of several hundred yards—by thick underbrush, brier obstacles, or abatis and wire entanglements. All roads leading to the camp were blocked or camouflaged, or detours were built which led in another direction. Traffic to the camp was conducted on paths known only to the initiated. Sometimes these paths were protected by bodies of water, with crossings built eight to twelve inches below water level, or by large stretches of swamp which could be crossed only on swamp skis. All movements of strangers were carefully controlled by sentries stationed far from camp and disguised as peasants. Strangers were also kept under close surveillance by a network of spies active in all villages in the vicinity.

The camps were well supplied with weapons, ammunition, explosives, and rations. Only very reliable partisans were put in charge of these supplies.

The camps procured their food supplies by forced requisitions in nearby villages. Villages refusing food contributions were ruthlessly put to the torch by the partisans; the men were dragged into the woods, and the women and children dispersed. Supplies were also received by aircraft, which dropped the rations in the immediate vicinity of the camp when prearranged light or fire signals were displayed. Looting vehicles during partisan raids likewise provided ammunition and small arms for the bands.

Excellent camouflage prevented any aerial observation of the camps. The shelters were allowed to be heated only at night, so that no smoke would disclose the existence of the camp during the day. The partisans succeeded in maintaining the secrecy of the camps for a long time by having small bands appear in remote villages and by disseminating false rumors concerning partisan movements. The mere suspicion of betrayal was sufficient cause for execution of the suspect. The same fate threatened the family of the condemned. These measures explain why all partisans operations were kept secret.

Whoever joined a partisan group, voluntarily or involuntarily, could leave it only at the risk of his life.

The partisans also had signal communications at their disposal. The larger partisan units received their directives by short-wave radio, so that they had up-to-date information about current military developments in their respective sectors. Air couriers were also used. There was a carefully camouflaged landing place for liaison airplanes in the immediate vicinity of almost every major camp.

Practically without exception partisan operations were carried out at night. Daytime raids seldom took place, and then only in areas in which no German troops were stationed for miles around. Raids of that type were usually confined to individual motor vehicles.

A major partisan operation, with the demolition of a railroad bridge as its objective, would proceed as follows: A long column of women and children would move along the right of way in the direction of the bridge. Presuming them to be refugees, the German sentry would take no action. When the head of the column had reached the bridge, heavy surprise fire was directed against the bridgehead from the end of the column. Machine guns, set up on the roadbed in the direction of the bridge, pinned down the German guards. Under this fire cover, and by utilizing women and children in violation of international law, the partisans succeeded in installing prepared demolition charges and in destroying the bridge.

Partisan operations generally included mining main highways, demolition of railroad tracks, mining railroad beds and arming the mines with push and pull igniters, surprise fire attacks on trains, looting derailed railroad cars, raids on trucks and convoys, and burning ration, ammunition, and fuel depots. Less frequent were raids on command posts of higher German headquarters.

The partisans followed the practice of avoiding open combat as much as possible. This practice was indeed the guiding rule upon which their method of warfare was based. Unusual developments at the front would immediately result in extremely lively partisan activity, essentially aimed at the disruption and destruction of railroad lines. During a major German attack, for instance, the main line of a railroad that had to handle the supplies for three German armies was blasted at 2,000 points in a single night and so effectively disrupted that all traffic was stalled for several days. Such large-scale operations, carried out by small partisan teams and numerous individuals, at times seriously hampered the supply of the German troops.

CHAPTER 17

Defense against Partisan Activity

The German forces in Russia took both passive and active defense measures to protect their rear areas against the surge of partisan activities.

I. Passive Antipartisan Measures

Each army group created a special staff whose duty it was to collect all information concerning the appearance and movement of partisans by close contact with the military authorities in the rear areas and with Russian community heads, as well as by a network of agents in areas threatened by partisans. All information thus gathered would immediately be passed on to the German military authorities concerned.

Small headquarters were combined to protect them more effectively against partisan raids.

Local defense units were drawn from among the Russian population in threatened areas. Often Russian civilians urgently requested this measure because they suffered from confiscation of cattle, forceful removal of men, etc., by the partisans.

All traffic was halted on especially endangered roads at nightfall; such roads were used in daytime only at certain hours and in convoys escorted by armed guards.

Railroads, bridges, and trains were protected. Outguards within sight or earshot of each other were posted along railroad lines in threatened areas. The outguards were quartered in blockhouses protected by wire entanglements and abatis, behind which lay also the entrenchments for defense. Wherever the railroad line led through wooded terrain, all trees within fifty yards of either side of the right-of-way were felled to provide a better field of vision.

Reinforced outguards equipped with infantry heavy weapons protected all bridges. Another precaution, however, had to be taken in addition to furnishing local protection for bridges and adjacent bridgeheads, particularly whenever larger bridges were to be safeguarded. Strong guard detachments had to be posted at a great enough distance to permit them to spot approaching partisan bands, and to allow time for an orderly preparation of countermeasures. Precautions of that nature had not been taken prior to the previously mentioned partisan operation against the railroad bridge.

All trains going through danger zones had two sand-filled gondola cars coupled in front to protect their locomotives from mines. Each train was escorted by a guard detachment of about forty men.

Furlough trains were guarded by the soldier-passengers themselves. For that reason, all men going on furlough had to carry their small arms. Night traffic on particularly imperiled railroad lines was discontinued from time to time. During the day, the trains on these lines sometimes traveled within sight of each other. This procedure, however, was possible only because Russian air activity in the rear area was very limited.

II. Active Antipartisan Measures

Units such as security divisions and forces particularly organized for that purpose were normally assigned the mission of fighting the partisans. The great depth of area required a substantial number of such units, and since they were not available in desired numbers, security divisions frequently had to be assigned zones that they were hardly able to control.

In the forest terrain of Baranovichi and Minsk, for instance, the German 707th Security Division had to guard an area of 40,000 square miles (larger than all of Austria). Its duties usually consisted of protection of important points in seriously threatened wooded areas; surveillance and protection of zones and villages through which led military supply routes, and which were constantly imperiled by partisan bands; reconnaissance of partisan camps and roads leading to them; daily dispatch of as many combat patrols as possible into partisan territory to prevent the partisans from uniting into groups and establishing permanent bases; and operations against detected partisan camps.

Whenever the Germans planned a major operation against a detected partisan camp, the project had to be kept a strict secret from the troops. Experience had taught that if such plans were revealed, even larger partisan groups immediately dissolved, only to assemble again at a different location. It happened repeatedly that in carefully prepared operations partisan camps, which shortly before had been fully occupied, were found deserted. The troops, therefore, could only be informed of the actual plans after they had reached the outer line of encirclement.

The assembly of the attacking troops had to take place at least one day's march away from the partisan camps. The advance toward the outer line of encirclement had to be so timed that all troops could reach it simultaneously and occupy it immediately. As far as possible, the outer line of encirclement was anchored on natural obstacles that were easy to block and to keep under surveillance (for example, rivers). The troops were deployed in the outer line of encirclement in such a manner that they formed a continuous line of sentries, with each soldier within calling distance—and at night, within sight—of the next. Behind this line of sentries, pursuit detachments were kept ready for immediate employment against partisan bands which might break out. As soon as the encirclement had been completed, leaflets were dropped over all inhabited places within the ring, ordering all inhabitants to evacuate at once and to assemble at a designated point.

The contraction of the ring of encirclement proceeded during daytime only, in phases covering not more than two to three miles per day, and the territory was carefully combed. Individual sectors had to be occupied by at least two hours before twilight, so that the troops could establish themselves and become acquainted with the terrain ahead while it was still light.

Sectors easily distinguishable in the woods (glades, paths, railroad lines) were designated as the new line of encirclement. Close contact between individuals had to be maintained. Nighttime security at the sector boundaries was of particular importance. The procedure of detailing forces for guarding unit boundaries, as well as the command over those forces, had to be clearly regulated. The further contraction of the ring up to the final encirclement of the camp followed the same pattern as described above.

As soon as the encirclement had started, the surrounded area was kept under constant aerial observation. By dropping messages, the planes immediately notified troops and officers in command of any observed breakout attempts. Since breakouts were to be expected mainly at night, sufficient security detachments had to be posted in front of the sentry line. With the contraction of the ring of encirclement a proportionate number of reserves could be withdrawn, and their follow-up had to be properly regulated. If the partisans still remained in their camp by the time the troops had reached the final line of encirclement, a heavy air attack would usually enable the troops to score a quick success.

Experience had taught the Germans that this type of antipartisan warfare, though requiring large numbers of troops and much time, promised the greatest success. No other methods proved themselves in wooded terrain, since breakouts at night could hardly be prevented. Rigid discipline was a prerequisite for success of such an operation. The designated objective for the day could not be changed during the operation, and the slightest independent changes on the part of the troops would disrupt the line of encirclement and make the breakout of partisans possible.

Winter proved to be the most favorable season for antipartisan operations because all movements could be more readily observed in snow-covered terrain. In summer the dense foliage of the woods made such operations very difficult. As far as possible they were to be carried out during bright nights, best of all during a full moon. Liberal armament with machine pistols proved advantageous. Mortars were found to have more of a demoralizing than actual effect, since their shells burst in the trees. Artillery could hardly be used during advances in woods. As a rule it could be put into action only during the battle for the fortified camp itself. Depending upon the terrain, the Germans found it advisable to have individual guns follow directly behind the leading elements. The employment of tanks, where the terrain was suitable, produced excellent results. In such operations the troops had to have an adequate supply of signal pistols and cartridges. In the case of swampland, the troops were to be equipped with swamp skis.

The wooded terrain, which afforded poor visibility, and deceptions at night often caused shooting frays that started a panic among German units or resulted in their firing on their own troops. The Germans therefore found it advisable to prohibit the firing of all infantry light weapons except during partisan attacks. Special regulations for opening fire also were required when the final ring of encirclement had been closed and the troops were facing each other at a short distance.

CHAPTER 18

Non-Russian Partisans

In addition to the Russian partisan groups, there also existed in the East strong Ukrainian and Polish groups, as well as a few weak Czech and Jewish groups. The latter two were of no great importance. Some of the bands were for, and others against, Russia. They fought each other cruelly and ruthlessly to the point of annihilation. In 1944, for instance, at the Polish–Ukrainian linguistic frontier, Polish bands raided Ukrainian villages, and Ukrainian bands raided Polish villages, burned them, and massacred the entire populations including women and children. There were insufficient German troops to occupy the entire territory densely enough to prevent such raids. Emergency detachments usually came too late.

Behind the German front, severe fighting, even to the extent of employing heavy weapons, frequently broke out between the partisan groups of different camps. Such disturbances at times caused a local paralysis of Soviet partisan activity.

The very active bands of the Ukrainian Nationalist Movement (UPA) formed the strongest partisan group in the East except for the Russian Communist bands, which they fought bitterly. The UPA repeatedly offered its cooperation against the Soviet partisan bands to the German Army and asked for a German general to act as organizer and tactical leader, but the High Command of the German Army, very much to its disadvantage, continually refused these requests. Only tacit, local agreements were therefore made between the UPA and German military authorities. They proved advantageous to both parties. Sometimes the UPA would participate in fighting the Soviet bands even without any previous agreement (as in 1944 north of Lwow and at Stanislav). The UPA forces were deployed in groups of several thousands each in the rear of the Russian, as well as the German, armies. Although they fought the German political organizations and their police forces, they never fought the German troops, and they seriously harassed the Soviet Army. Not only did they severely impede its supply, they also attacked Russian headquarters and rendered them powerless by encirclement (for example, in 1944 at a Russian corps headquarters in Korosten, which had to be liberated by motorized troops). Furthermore, they incited revolts of the Ukrainian population in the rear area (in Kiev, for example), the quelling of which required the withdrawal of several Russian divisions from the front for an extended period of time.

Although seriously disturbing German supply operations,

and thereby also the conduct of battle, even the strongest partisan movement, that of the Soviets, had little influence on the overall operations in the East. This is illustrated in the report on the protection of supply lines near Kirovograd against partisan raids (1942–43).

The Kirovograd region was administered by German civilian authorities, with the aid of municipal and regional commissioners who had their seats in the larger towns. The former town and community boundaries were retained as much as possible. The security of the region was the responsibility of the regional military government officer (*Feldkommandant*) and the local military government officers (*Ortskommandant*) under him. It included mainly the security of railroads, the two important supply routes (express highways IV and IVc), and the Bug bridges at Pervomaisk and Voznesensk. Two local defense (*Landesschuetzen*) battalions were available for these tasks.

Except for occasional minor sabotage acts against railroads, telephone lines, etc., by the native population, the area administered by German Regional Military Government Office (*Feldkommandantur*) 509 remained absolutely undisturbed throughout 1942, and substantial progress was made in the work on express highways IV and IVc. Not until March of 1943 did a sizable partisan group invade this area.

Of the railroad lines in this region, the one with the branch line to Dnepropetrovsk and Krivoi Rog, via Aleksandriya—Pyatikhatka, was the most vital from the military as well as the war-economy standpoint. The important junction and marshalling center of Znemenka was the point most vulnerable to sabotage operations. Had that place been destroyed, the entire supply of the front, and shipments of badly needed war materials destined for Germany, would have become seriously endangered for a rather long time. The terrain was level and flat, with little vegetation. It was partially steppeland. Except for a fairly large, dense patch of forest between Znemenka and Tsibulnos, only smaller strips of woodland limited the visibility along the railroad line. Features extremely favorable for sabotage operations were the extensive fields of sunflowers, growing taller than a man, and to a lesser degree, the grain fields.

Raids on the railroad line were always carried out in insidiously cunning ways by bands which found refuge mainly in the woods north of Znemenka and which were willingly aided by elements among the population of the neighboring villages. Organized into small combat patrols (*Troikas*), and carefully protecting their lines of withdrawal, they blew up railroad tracks, damaged control towers and signal installations, and terrorized the native railroad personnel. The *Troikas* disappeared upon the completion of their work of destruction, as a rule without having suffered any losses. Their activities were directed from a higher level, and they were regularly supplied with weapons, communications equipment, explosives, maps, medical supplies, etc., which sometimes were dropped by aircraft. The explosives consisted of demolition charges, mines, artillery shells, or improvised infernal machines.

The weapons of the *Troikas* were generally machine pistols, daggers, and rifles. The members wore civilian clothes, but some were dressed in uniforms of the German Army, Luftwaffe, or political organizations.

In March 1943, a partisan group, at first numbering from 200 to 300 men, with a few women as medical and signal personnel, invaded the region of Feldkommandantur 509 at Chigirin (thirty-five miles west of Kremenchug). It was very ably led and highly mobile in its conduct of battle. The group used sleighs in the winter and requisitioned horses during the muddy period. For three weeks they roamed through this region; raided agricultural centers, sawmills, and other plants; killed the managers of the agricultural centers as well as the German harvest control officers; liberated prisoners of war; and disrupted rail traffic at Sosnovka. The partisans sought shelter in villages adjacent to woodlands. Horses and vehicles were sheltered in steep ravines to protect them against artillery fire. The expertly arranged security and reconnaissance measures precluded the possibility of surprise raids by German troops. Orders and instructions were received by short-wave equipment which was kept in a suitcase. Because of their well-functioning intelligence machinery, searches of woodlands and villages for the smaller sabotage teams of partisans were almost never successful. The Ukrainian community authorities' lists of inhabitants were seldom in order, making identification of the inhabitants of a village very difficult. It was, therefore, found practicable to chalk the names of the residents of each house on the front door.

In combatting the partisans, railroad stations, control towers, wooded zones, and bridges were focal points of security. Shifting German reserves by motor vehicles was planned for a quick reinforcement of the defenses. All places that had to be defended were converted into strong points. Arrangements had to be made in buildings to permit firing from various floors, and machine-gun emplacements with flanking and alternate firing positions had to be installed. Plank walls had to be erected for protection against fragmentation, and windows had to be provided with gun shields and embrasures. Fire steps, ammunition lockers, communication corridors, and observation posts had to be established. Telephone lines were laid so as to be protected as much as possible against gun fire, and supplemented by optic and acoustic alarm signals. In the vicinity of each German strong point, the terrain was cleared of obstructing vegetation for a distance of about 1,000 yards in each direction along the railroad line; this cleared area extended some 300 to 400 yards from the tracks.

The goal of all these precautions and preparations was to assure the smooth functioning of rail traffic. In addition to military security, the railroad lines were frequently inspected by employees walking along the tracks, and patrolled by handcars, or locomotives pushing freight cars ahead of them. The speedy formation of "alert" units for fire fighting, and the procedure of transporting them by motor or rail had to be planned and practiced in drills. The use of armored trains, or the addition to trains of cars carrying troops, proved to be effective methods of antipartisan defense.

The Germans soon realized that their military forces were not sufficient for the manifold tasks of railroad security. To ease their burden, local inhabitants were assigned to the troops as so-called voice-alarm sentries. Upon spotting partisans, these sentries were to shout the information to their neighboring guard posts, stationed at a distance of 500 yards, but were not to fight. For that reason the native sentries were unarmed. Their reliability varied, since they feared the cruel reprisals of the partisans against themselves and their families. Organized indigenous forces, some of which were employed for railroad defense, likewise functioned only when they were heavily intermixed with German units. The German regional defense units were not properly armed. Their equipment, too, was completely inadequate. For reconnaissance, the *Fieseler-Storch* (liaison aircraft) proved equal to all demands. The evacuation of villages directly adjacent to railroad lines, and the establishment of so-called death zones, within which any civilian would be shot on sight, were found to be appropriate measures.

Conclusions

The success of any armed force flows from a sum total of measures not only in the military field, but also in politics, national indoctrination, economics, and other spheres, which in their entirety decide the outcome of a war. They all must therefore be analyzed and weighed against each other if one would find the ultimate causes of victory or defeat. Only the product of intensive studies would form a positive basis for the evaluation of an armed force in a past war, and thereby offer clues as to its potential in a possible future conflict.

In the preceding pages, only the military measures—in themselves important—could be taken under scrutiny. But this study, presenting German experiences as well as German views, throws light on many significant aspects that permit readily applicable conclusions to be drawn.

Not the success alone, but also the circumstances under which it was achieved form the standards by which an armed force is to be evaluated. The Red Army was successful in the last war, a good argument for the proposition that in a future war, fought under equal or similar circumstances, it would again emerge victorious. The high command was good and in its hands the troops, purely as a human mass, were a useful instrument. The prime motive force behind both was communism; the final goal, World Revolution.

Manpower and matériel were abundant, and may be presumed to be abundant in the future. The Soviet gained a wealth of war experience on the basis of which to train their leaders and masses in up-to-date methods. They also have the means to maintain quantity and quality of their equipment at a high level. Accordingly, one might think the final conclusion from this study and from the description of climatic conditions in the U.S.S.R. has to be, "Hands off Russia; the Russian combination of mass and space cannot be overpowered!"

That, however, is not the case. It should not be forgotten that much that might be said about Russia and the Russian had to be condensed here as well as in other studies. The terrain difficulties and the characteristics of the Russian soldier had to be described one after the other in such a way that both could easily be overestimated. Despite Russia and the Russian, despite cold and mud, despite inadequate equipment and a virtually ridiculous numerical inferiority, the German soldier actually had a victory over the Soviets within his grasp.

The prerequisite for a successful war against the U.S.S.R. is a systematic preparation for the undertaking. One cannot provoke such a conflict and expect to carry it through in a spirit of adventure. The equipment of the soldiers and the total amount of matériel must meet the requirements of Russian terrain at all seasons. This is a question of industrial potential which, by applying the experiences gathered in the last war, is not difficult to solve.

Training, tactical as well as physical, must comply with the above-mentioned peculiarities of combat against Russia and on Russian soil. Training aimed at imparting toughness, independence, and willingness to assume responsibility, and the molding of self-reliant individual fighters, as well as leaders who are willing to take chances, are the most essential points in this respect. Strict discipline is an additional fundamental condition for everyone who fights in Russia. Even the best athletic background is insufficient to meet the severity of this test. And, last but not least, the soldier must have an inner conviction—the indomitable will to prevent the Russian Moloch from devouring the world.

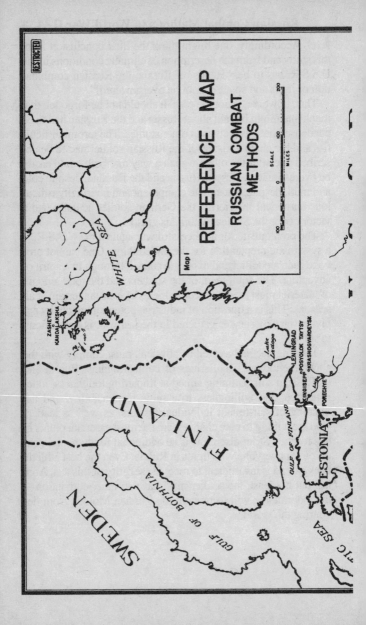

RESTRICTED

REFERENCE MAP

RUSSIAN COMBAT METHODS

Map I

SCALE

100   0   100   200

MILES

WHITE SEA

ZASHEYEK
KANDALAKSHA

FINLAND

SWEDEN

GULF OF BOTHNIA

Lake Ladoga

GULF OF FINLAND

LENINGRAD

KINGISEPP·POSTOLOK·TAYTSY

SKRASHOGVARDEYSK

POREGHYE

ESTONIA

BALTIC SEA

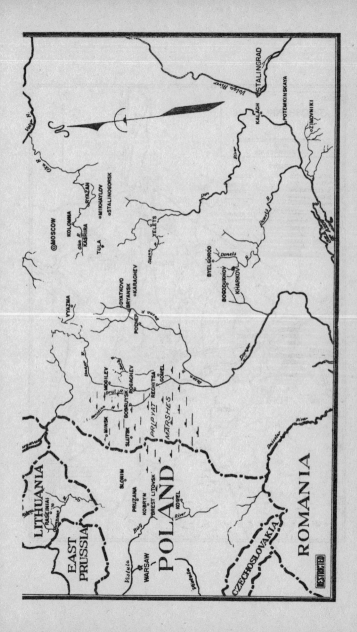

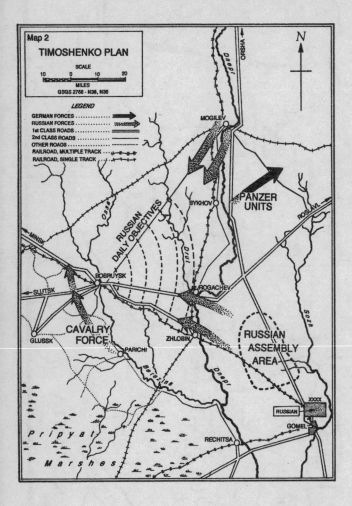

Map 2

TIMOSHENKO PLAN

SCALE
10   0   10   20
MILES
GSGS 2768 - N36, N36

LEGEND

GERMAN FORCES
RUSSIAN FORCES
1st CLASS ROADS
2nd CLASS ROADS
OTHER ROADS
RAILROAD, MULTIPLE TRACK
RAILROAD, SINGLE TRACK

N

VYASMA

Dnepr

MOGILEV

BYKHOV

ROSLAVL

PANZER
UNITS

RUSSIAN DAILY OBJECTIVES

Drut

Ossa

MINSK

BOBRUYSK

ROGACHEV

Sozh

SLUTSK

CAVALRY
FORCE

GLUSSK

PARICHI

ZHLOBIN

RUSSIAN
ASSEMBLY
AREA

Berezina

Dnepr

XXXX

RUSSIAN

Pripyat

GOMEL

Marshes

RECHITSA

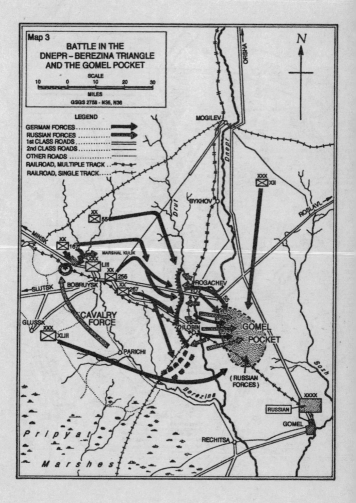

Map 3

BATTLE IN THE DNEPR – BEREZINA TRIANGLE AND THE GOMEL POCKET

SCALE

MILES

GSGS 2758 - N36, N36

LEGEND

GERMAN FORCES ....
RUSSIAN FORCES ....
1st CLASS ROADS ....
2nd CLASS ROADS ....
OTHER ROADS ....
RAILROAD, MULTIPLE TRACK ..
RAILROAD, SINGLE TRACK.....

N

ORSHA

MOGILEV

Dnepr

BYKHOV

Drut

XX 55

ROSLAVL

XXX XII

MINSK

XX 167

MARSHAL KULIK

LIII

XX 256

XX 267

ROGACHEV

BOBRUYSK

CAVALRY FORCE

ZHLOBIN

GOMEL POCKET

GLUSSK

XXX XLIII

PARICHI

(RUSSIAN FORCES)

Berezina

Sozh

XXXX

RUSSIAN

GOMEL

P r i p y a t

RECHITSA

M a r s h e s

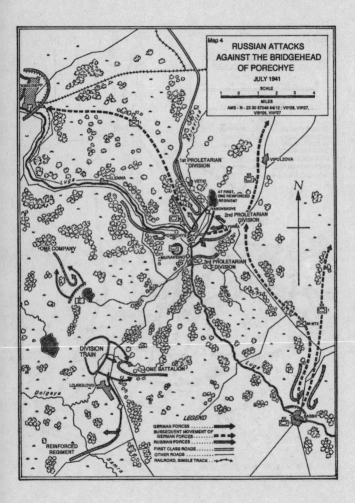

Map 4

RUSSIAN ATTACKS AGAINST THE BRIDGEHEAD OF PORECHYE

JULY 1941

SCALE
1   0   1   2   3   4
MILES

AMS - N - 23 30 57049 84/12 : VII*26, VII*27, VIII*26, VIII*27

N

KING ISEPP

Vroevka

VIPOLZOVA

1st PROLETARIAN DIVISION

Luga

YELENNA

VETKI

AT FIRST, ONE REINFORCED REGIMENT

IVANOVSKOYE

2nd PROLETARIAN DIVISION

YURKA

ONE COMPANY

PORECHYE

MURAVEINO

3rd PROLETARIAN DIVISION

36 MTZ

Luga

DIVISION TRAIN

ONE BATTALION

LOUGOLOVO

Dolgaya

RABEK

Smiria

REINFORCED REGIMENT

LEGEND

GERMAN FORCES . . . .
SUBSEQUENT MOVEMENT OF GERMAN FORCES . . . . . .
RUSSIAN FORCES . . . .
FIRST CLASS ROADS . . . .
OTHER ROADS . . . .
RAILROAD, SINGLE TRACK . . . .

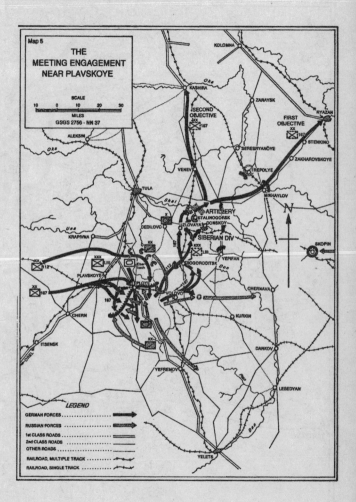

Map 5

THE
MEETING ENGAGEMENT
NEAR PLAVSKOYE

SCALE

10   0   10   20   30
MILES

GSGS 2756 - NN 37

LEGEND

GERMAN FORCES ....
RUSSIAN FORCES ....
1st CLASS ROADS ....
2nd CLASS ROADS ....
OTHER ROADS ....
RAILROAD, MULTIPLE TRACK ....
RAILROAD, SINGLE TRACK ....

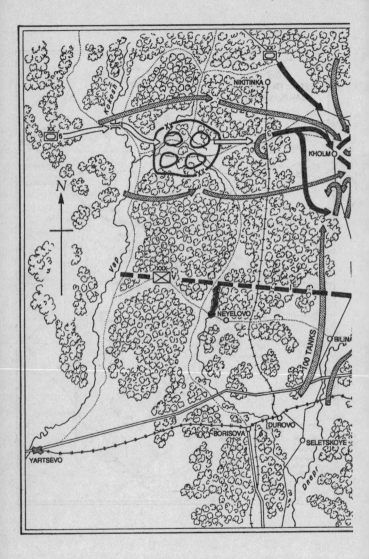

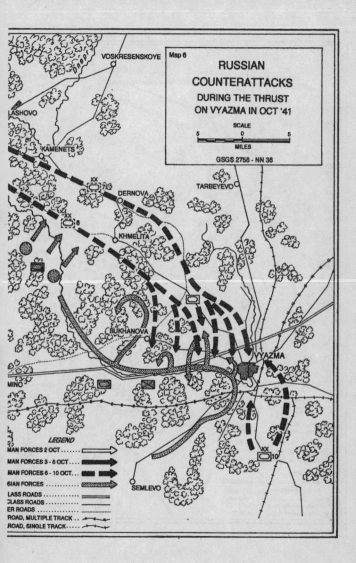

VOSKRESENSKOYE

Map 6

RUSSIAN

COUNTERATTACKS

DURING THE THRUST

ON VYAZMA IN OCT '41

SCALE

5   0   5

MILES

GSGS 2758 - NN 36

LASHOVO

KAMENETS

XX 7-3

DERNOVA

TARBEYEVO

XX 6

KHMELITA

BUKHANOVA

VYAZMA

MINO

XX 10

LEGEND

MAN FORCES 2 OCT . . . . .

MAN FORCES 3 - 5 OCT . . . .

MAN FORCES 6 - 10 OCT . . .

SIAN FORCES . . . .

LASS ROADS . . . .

CLASS ROADS . . . .

ER ROADS . . . .

ROAD, MULTIPLE TRACK . . .

ROAD, SINGLE TRACK . . . . .

SEMLEVO

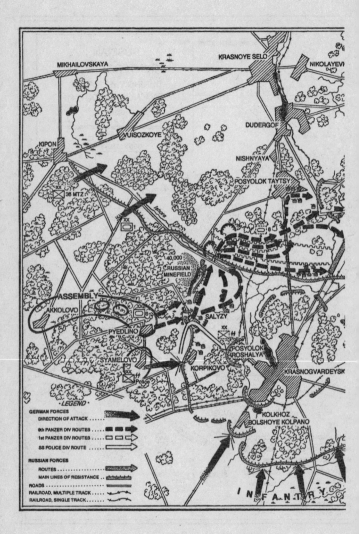

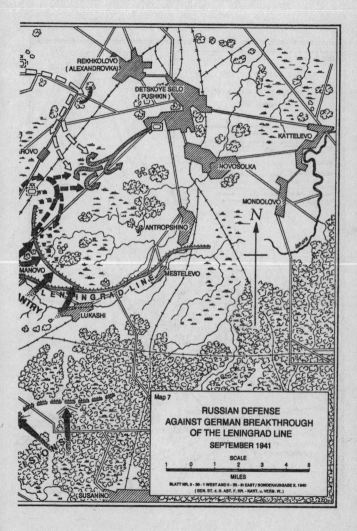

REKHKOLOVO
(ALEXANDROVKA)

DETSKOYE SELO
(PUSHKIN)

KATTELEVO

ROVO

NOVOSOLKA

MONDOLOVO

N

ANTROPSHINO

Ishora

MANOVO

MESTELEVO

L E N I N G R A D   L I N E

NTRY

LUKASHI

STONS

SUSANINO

Map 7

RUSSIAN DEFENSE
AGAINST GERMAN BREAKTHROUGH
OF THE LENINGRAD LINE

SEPTEMBER 1941

SCALE

1   0   1   2   3   4   5

MILES

BLATT NR. 0 - 36 - 1 WEST AND 0 - 35 - III EAST / SONDERAUSGABE X. 1940
(GEN. ST. d. H. ABT. F. KR. - KART. u. VERM. W.)

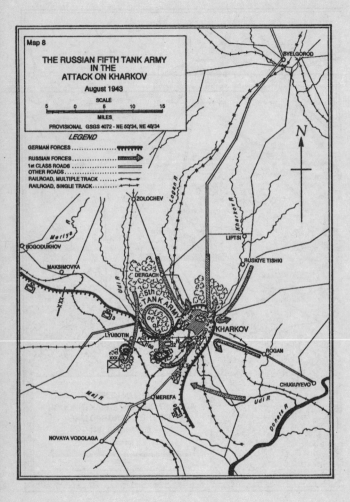

Map 8

THE RUSSIAN FIFTH TANK ARMY
IN THE
ATTACK ON KHARKOV

August 1943

SCALE

5   0   5   10   15

MILES

PROVISIONAL GSGS 4072 - NE 50/34, NE 48/34

LEGEND

GERMAN FORCES ....
RUSSIAN FORCES ....
1st CLASS ROADS ....
OTHER ROADS ....
RAILROAD, MULTIPLE TRACK ....
RAILROAD, SINGLE TRACK..............

N

BYELGOROD

ZOLOCHEV

Lopan R.

Kharkov R.

LIPTSI

Merlya R.

BOGODUKHOV

RUSKIYE TISHKI

MAKSIMOVKA

Udl R

DERGACHI

5th
TANK ARMY

KHARKOV

LYUBOTIN

ROGAN

CHUGUYEVO

Udl R

MEREFA

Donets R

NOVAYA VODOLAGA

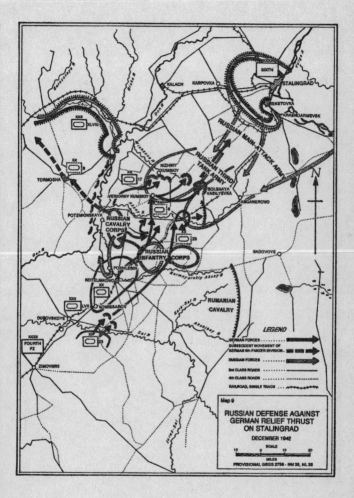

RODIONOV
KALACH
KARPOVKA
SIXTH
STALINGRAD
BEKETOVKA
KRASNOARMEVSK

XXX XLVIII

XX

TORMOSHA

IX
17
NIZHNIY
KUMSKIY

RUSSIAN THIRD
TANK ARMY

RUSSIAN MAIN ATTACK ARMY

BOLSHAYA
VASILYEVKA

ABGANEROVO

VERKHNIY KUMSKIY

POTEMKINSKAYA

RUSSIAN
CAVALRY
CORPS

23

SADOVOYE

POKLEBIN

RUSSIAN
INFANTRY CORPS

KOTELNIKOVO

XX

RUMANIAN
CAVALRY

LVII KONISSAROV

DUBOVSKOYE

XXXI

XXXI
FOURTH
PZ

23

ZIMOVNIKI

N

LEGEND

GERMAN FORCES ....▶

SUBSEQUENT MOVEMENT OF
GERMAN 6th PANZER DIVISION. ▶▶▶▶▶

RUSSIAN FORCES ....▶

3rd CLASS ROADS ....

4th CLASS ROADS ....

RAILROAD, SINGLE TRACK .....+—+—+—+

Map 9

RUSSIAN DEFENSE AGAINST
GERMAN RELIEF THRUST
ON STALINGRAD

DECEMBER 1942

SCALE

10   0   10   20

MILES

PROVISIONAL GSGS 2758 - HM 38, HL 38

PART TWO

Effects of Climate on Combat in European Russia

BY GENERALOBERST ERHARD RAUSS
Commander, Fourth and
Third Panzer Armies

Preface

Effects of Climate in Combat in European Russia was prepared
by a committee of former German generals and general staff
officers under the supervision of the Historical Division,
EUCOM. The material, based on the personal experiences of
the principal author and his associates, was written largely
from memory, with some assistance from diaries, earlier
studies, and documents. All the German officers involved
had extensive experience on the Eastern Front during the
period 1941–45. The principal author, for example, commanded in succession a panzer division, a panzer army, and
an army group.

The reader is reminded that publications in the GERMAN
REPORT SERIES were written by Germans from the German point of view. As in Department of the Army Pamphlet
No. 20-230, Russian Combat Methods in World War II, and
Department of the Army Pamphlet No. 20-290, Terrain Factors
in the Russian Campaign, the "Introduction" and "Conclusions" to this study present the views of the German author
without interpretation by American personnel. Minor changes
in form and in chapter titles have been made to obtain greater
clarity. However, passages which may reflect the authors' prejudices and defects, whatever they may be, have not been
changed, and find the same expression in the following translation as they do in the original German.

Department of the Army
February 1952

Introduction

The purpose of this study is to describe the climatic conditions encountered by the German armed forces during four years of struggle in European Russia. To this end the climate of the various regions is described together with its effects on men and equipment, combat and supply. The first three sections are concerned with European Russia south of the Arctic Circle, the last treats the European Russia north of the Arctic Circle. The study emphasizes the lessons learned and improvisations employed to surmount difficult situations.

A Western European army fighting in Russia is faced with conditions entirely different from those to which it is accustomed, conditions rooted in the peculiarities of Russia and its people. The most unusual characteristic of the country is the climate, which affects terrain and vegetation and determines living conditions in general. The climate leaves its mark upon the Russian and his land, and he who steps for the first time on Russian soil is immediately conscious of the new, the strange, the primitive.

The German soldier who crossed into Russian territory felt that he entered a different world, where he was opposed not only by the forces of the enemy but also by the forces of nature. Nature is the ally of the Russian Army, and the struggle against this alliance was a severe test for the Wehrmacht, exacting great sacrifices. To conquer the raging elements of nature was the more difficult because their fury and effect were not fully recognized by the Germans, who were neither trained nor equipped to withstand them. The German command had been under the impression that the Red Army could be destroyed west of the Dnepr, and that there would be no need for conducting operations in cold, snow, and mud.

WINTER

CHAPTER 19

General

Winter in most parts of European Russia south of the Arctic Circle sets in suddenly and lasts five to six months. The period of clear weather which follows the autumn muddy season lasts at most one month, too short a time for extensive military operations. Cold, ice, and snow may hinder operations as early as December, especially in the northern parts of the country.

Snowfall varies greatly in European Russia. It is greater in the northern and central regions than in the south. Along the lower Don and Donets, in the winter of 1942–43, the first snow fell in mid-December and did not affect mobility during the entire winter. The same winter saw more than eighteen inches of snow on the middle course of these rivers and in the Kharkov area. Snow depths of three to four feet are common in the north, where wheeled vehicles can move only on cleared roads, and huge snowdrifts build up in valleys and hollows. Here horse-mounted and dismounted troops move with difficulty except on roads, and trail breakers must be used for cross-country marches. In deep-snow country even tanks and other tracked vehicles are restricted to plowed roads.

In the Baltic and Leningrad regions the snow cover varies greatly from year to year. Leningrad and its vicinity, for example, may have as much as twenty-eight inches of snow in severe winters, while in mild winters there may be less than two inches. Water courses to the south of Leningrad often freeze over by mid-November, and temperatures there may fall as low as −40° F. Even during mild winters the mercury will drop to −20° F.

In central European Russia, the Smolensk–Vitebsk area has

noon temperatures below freezing even during average winters. The Pripyat Marshes usually freeze over in winter, and only during exceptionally mild winters, or in case of an early snow cover, will large patches of the Pripyat remain unfrozen and impassable.

The winter of the southern steppes, longer and colder than that of Central Europe, differs little from the winter of central and northern Russia south of the Arctic Circle. In the Black Sea region, where two thirds of the annual precipitation occurs between September and March, the climate is of the Mediterranean type.

The winter of 1941–42 was most severe in European Russia. In the area northwest of Moscow the mean temperature during January 1942 was −32° F., and the 26th of the month in the same area saw the lowest recorded temperature of the entire Russian campaign: −63° F. The southern part of European Russia, too, had record low temperatures during the first winter, with readings ranging from −22° to −40° F., compared with temperatures of 14° to −40° F., in the same area during the following winter. A chart of temperatures and precipitation near Rzhev for the period January through April 1942 and October 1942 through January 1943 may be found in the Conclusions.

The obliteration of landmarks in snow-covered terrain makes orientation difficult. Russian villages are hard to identify from a distance, and often a church built on high ground or a church tower is the only visible sign of an inhabited place. If neither is present, woods filled with screeching birds usually indicate that a village is nearby. The Russian peasant stores his winter supplies in advance and digs in to spend the winter completely cut off from the outside world.

Cold reduces the efficiency of men and weapons. At the beginning of December 1941, 6th Panzer Division was but nine miles from Moscow and fifteen miles from the Kremlin when a sudden drop in temperature to −30° F., coupled with a surprise attack by Siberian troops, smashed its drive on the capital. Paralyzed by cold, the German troops could not aim their rifle fire, and bolt mechanisms jammed or strikers shattered in the bitter winter weather. Machine guns became encrusted with ice, recoil liquid froze in guns, ammunition supply failed. Mortar shells detonated in deep snow with a hollow, harmless thud, and mines were no longer reliable. Only one German tank in ten had survived the autumn muddy season, and those still available could not move through the snow because of their narrow tracks. At first the Russian attack was slowed with hand grenades, but after a few days the German prepared positions in villages and farmhouses were surrounded or penetrated.

The Germans held out to the northwest of Moscow until 5 December, and on the next day the first retreat order of the war was given. In the months of the offensive, German battalions and companies had dwindled to a handful of men. The Russian mud and winter had wrought havoc upon their weapons and equipment. Leadership and bravery could not compensate for the lowered fire power of the German divisions. The numerical superiority of the Russians, aided by climatic conditions, saved Moscow and turned the tide of battle. Hitler neither expected nor planned for a winter war.

By mid-December, when the first phase of the German withdrawal ended, 6th Panzer Division was located in Shakhovskaya to refit and receive reinforcements (Map 12). On Christmas Eve the 4th Armored Infantry Regiment, which had received replacements, was alerted to counterattack Russian forces that had broken through German positions on the Lama River west of Volokolamsk, in the sector of the 106th Infantry Division.

On 26 December the regiment moved out in a snowstorm over roads already covered with deep drifts. The German troops were inadequately clothed for the Russian winter, and in every village lengthy warming halts were necessary. Two days were needed to cover the twelve miles to the line of departure.

After a meal and a night's rest, 4th Armored Infantry Regiment attacked on 28 December together with German elements already in the area. Well supported by artillery and heavy weapons, the regiment advanced throughout the day, and in the evening made contact with the 23d Infantry Division to the north, thus closing the gap. Some shelter was found in nearby villages and farmhouses. Strong security detachments were posted, and relieved every half hour because of the extreme cold.

The plan for 29 December was to regain the former German positions on the Lama by envelopment of the Russian forces that had broken through. The regiment attacked eastward while the motorcycle battalion of the 6th Panzer Division, south of the main body, advanced northward toward Vladychino. By noon the enemy breakthrough force was surrounded.

Night temperatures dropped to between −30° and −40° F., and no shelter was available to the German troops. The nearby villages were destroyed and the entrenchments of the old German positions on the Lama were buried deep in snow. To remain exposed would have meant certain death to the troops who lacked adequate winter clothing, and withdrawal to a distant village was ordered.

When the Russians observed that the encirclement had been abandoned, they concentrated for a new breakthrough which eventually forced a withdrawal of the entire German front in the area. Success had turned to failure because the Germans were not equipped to withstand extreme cold.

Periods of moderate cold alternating with thaw are particularly dangerous. At the end of March 1942, in the Lake Ladoga region, noon temperatures rose to 41° F., followed by a sharp fall of the mercury at night. Boots, socks, and trousers that had become wet during the day stiffened with the night cold and froze toes and feet.

Serious frost injuries developed when troops overheated from combat were forced to spend the night in snow pits or windswept open fields, especially when the fatigued men took even the shortest of naps. A German company that spent a day during a thaw entrenching itself lost sixty-five of its ninety-three men as a result of a sudden severe cold wave at night.

Frostbite casualties among German troops were heavy during the first year of the war. At the beginning of December

1941, Fourth Army failed in an attempt to penetrate the outer defenses of Moscow because the Russians were able to use the rail net around the city to bring up strong forces. On the morning of 4 December, after three days of heavy losses, the army fell back to its positions of 1 December to avoid further casualties.

On the same day, as the weather turned bitter cold, the Russians attacked, and by 20 December the entire army front was heavily engaged. A radio message intercepted at the time revealed that the Russian drive was an all-out effort to knock the Germans out of the war. Later information that the Russians had deployed thirty infantry divisions, thirty-three infantry brigades, six armored brigades, and three cavalry divisions on the Moscow front left no doubt as to their intent.

By 5 January, when temperatures had risen somewhat, Fourth Army counted 2,000 frostbite casualties and half as many from enemy action. At this point Hitler gave permission to pull back the army left wing in the face of a Russian envelopment, and the withdrawal was completed according to plan. There was no let-up in the battle, however, and German casualties from all causes continued to mount. A snowstorm which, since the 5th, had added to the German difficulties, stopped on the 10th, and clear cold weather with temperatures down to $-13°$ F. followed. Here and there, supplies were moved up during quiet periods, but even then at great cost in lives and equipment.

The Germans fell back steadily and in March heavy snowfalls hampered the withdrawal as the Russian offensive continued. On 18 April, the first warm, sunny day of spring, the Russian attacks ceased. Fourth Army suffered 96,535 casualties between 1 January and 31 March 1942, of which 14,236 were frostbite cases.

Frostbite was frequent among drivers and troops who were moved long distances in open trucks. So long as suitable clothing was not available, constant indoctrination in cold-weather precautions was necessary. Frequent halts were made so men could warm themselves by exercise. Front-line troops became indifferent in extreme cold; under constant enemy pressure they became mentally numbed. Medical officers and commanders of all ranks had to make certain that soldiers changed socks frequently, and that they did not wait until swollen feet made it impossible to take off boots.

Some chemical heat packets were issued, but they protected only small areas of the body for short periods. Regular use of the *sauna,* a steam bath, was helpful in preventing illnesses caused by cold and exposure, but such baths were not always available.

The Russians, too, suffered from the extreme cold when forced to remain out in the open. Their supplies did not keep up with them, and they became weak and exhausted. Consequently, they always made a great effort to capture villages for overnight shelter. For example, in the winter of 1941–42, north of Rzhev, the Russians unsuccessfully attempted to drive German forces out of a village and were forced to spend the night in the open. Cut off from supplies and stiff with cold, the Russians were so weakened by their ordeal that they were unable to hinder a withdrawal of German troops, including two batteries, from north of the village, even though the Germans passed within 100 yards of the Russian forces.

CHAPTER 20

Snow

A war of movement is difficult in deep snow. Foot marches in twenty inches of snow are slow; in depths of more than twenty inches they are exhausting. When snow was not too deep, the Germans used details, in shifts, to tramp down snow trails. Ski troops were also used as trail breakers. The Russians used T34 tanks to pack down snow; the tracks used on German tanks during the first year of the war were too narrow for this purpose.

Movements on foot or with wheeled vehicles are impossible in snow depths above forty inches. Snow crust is sometimes strong enough to bear the weight of small groups. Hard-frozen snow, however, can be used only for night movement, because the approach of troops over a snow crust can be heard at a great distance. Snow in bushland, draws, and ditches will not support much weight.

I. Infantry

A normal infantry attack cannot be made in deep snow. Advancing by bounds is out of the question, because every movement must be made in the open, exposed to enemy fire. If infantry attacks had to be made, the Germans always sought areas where the snow was less deep. If such areas could not be found, the infantry had to work its way forward under cover of darkness, digging as it went, or following a beaten path against the flank and rear of the enemy.

Without adequate snow removal equipment, infantry movement during or after a snowstorm is difficult. In December 1942, for example, the defeat of Italian forces in the Voronezh area made it imperative that this sector of the front be reinforced. A German infantry division near Siniye Lipyagi, was made available and ordered to march the fifty-five miles south to the endangered area. The march was to be made through the rear areas of several German divisions which were to assist the advancing unit by furnishing rations and quarters, and the movement was expected to take three days.

The division set out in the first flurries of what proved to be a twelve-day blizzard. The march route was over lateral roads not used for logistical support, and consequently not cleared of snow. It was just at this time that the desperate German attempt to relieve Stalingrad required all available snowplows. Instead of the expected three days the march required fifteen. A command decision to make motorized snow-clearing equipment available would have aided the movement considerably. Such equipment, always scarce in the German Army, was controlled at army or army group level.

II. Artillery

Artillery was moved on existing roads, and if no roads were available, new tracks were shoveled. In deep snow it was often impossible for the infantry to take full advantage of artillery preparation, because it could not move forward fast enough. Such an instance occurred at Gaytolovo (a few miles south of Lake Ladoga) on 21 December 1941. The German infantry attacked at 0900 after a thorough artillery preparation. It took so long for the riflemen to reach the Russian positions that enemy bunkers went into action again, and the assault was delayed. By 1500, when the infantry had penetrated at several points, a withdrawal order was given. The troops would have frozen to death if they had spent the night in the open.

The effectiveness of artillery projectiles, particularly those of small caliber, and of mortar ammunition, was seriously hampered by deep snow. Snow dampened and reduced lateral fragmentation of artillery shells, and almost completely smothered mortar fire and hand grenades. Heavy artillery weapons, such as the German 210mm mortar, remained highly effective. Because of the cushioning effect of snow, mines often failed to detonate when stepped on or even when driven over by tanks. To keep detonators effective in extremely cold weather, gun crews often carried them in their pockets.

Registration fire with aerial observation and with flash and sound was hampered because the snow swallowed projectiles and bursts. Artillery map firing was impeded by a vast difference between meteorological conditions in Russia and in Central Europe, and the resultant range dispersion. Metro corrections of German observation battalions were computed according to central European standards, resulting in less accurate fire. Checking air observation by sound and flash ranging, and checking sound ranging by flash ranging and vice versa, disclosed deviations caused by climatic factors whose ultimate causes were never fully determined. The services of qualified meteorological technicians would have been useful.

By placing fire control and radio equipment in improvised wooden containers padded with blankets it was possible to protect them against frost damage and shock. Russian peasant sleighs with built-in boxes were often used for transporting radio equipment.

III. Armored Forces

The principal shortcoming of German tanks was the narrow width of their tracks. Tanks sank deep into the snow, and because of their limited ground clearance, ultimately became stuck. Russian tanks, particularly the T34, KV1, and KV2, were able to drive through deep snow because of their good ground clearance and wide tracks, and therein lay their special effectiveness in winter warfare. After the first winter of the war, Germans started to use wide, removable tracks. These solved the problem of snow mobility, but tanks so equipped could not be moved on German railroad cars and were too wide to cross the standard German military bridge. Russian wide tank tracks were factory equipment; the broad gauge of Russian railroads with their correspondingly wide flat cars eliminated the transportation problem.

In December 1942 a German armored division, diverted from the abortive relief thrust on Stalingrad to consolidate an extremely critical situation on the Chir River front, was delayed twelve hours because the snow tracks of its tanks were too wide for a military bridge over the Don. The tracks of more than 150 tanks and assault guns had to be removed in total darkness and remounted on the far shore.

CHAPTER 21

German Tactics

Unless forced by circumstances to do so, the Germans did not launch offensives in midwinter. During local attacks communication trenches or tunnels for infantry could be dug through snow with considerable speed. While such trenches offered effective concealment if skillfully sited and camouflaged, they were practically useless for protection. Whenever artillery support was needed snow had to be cleared from firing positions and ammunition storage areas.

For individual movement through snow, skis are best. Large ski units are relatively ineffective since heavy weapons cannot be carried or supplied. The Germans did not use ski troops in units above battalion size, while the Russians used such troops up to brigade strength. Skis are a hindrance in combat; they have to be removed before going into action, and often become lost.

Ski troops are effective for reconnaissance missions. For example, in March 1942, a ski patrol of twenty volunteers from the reconnaissance battalion of 6th Panzer Division infiltrated fifteen miles into enemy territory, captured three prisoners, and gained much valuable information. Russian civilians living in the area where the reconnaissance was made, who had been well treated by Germans billeted in their villages at an earlier date, were of great assistance. Local guides led the patrol around enemy and partisan strongholds, and provided shelter in farmhouses. The mission took four days.

With the onset of the Russian winter adequate shelter is a necessity in tactical operations. His intrenching tools useless in frozen ground, the German soldier could only cower in a snow hole and wait until a dugout or similar shelter was blasted out of the frost-bound soil. Blasted shelters were usually pitch dark, and the small, open fires used for heating filled every crevice with smudge and smoke. For above-ground shelter, the Finnish-type round tent proved highly serviceable. Troops were trained to construct igloos, but this type of shelter never became popular. Native log houses in the forests of the northern and central regions of European Russia are excellent heat retainers and are highly resistant to concussion.

When German troops were attacking Tikhvin in the winter of 1941, cold set in suddenly. Lacking winter clothing and adequate shelter, the Germans suffered more casualties from cold than from enemy fire, and the attack had to be halted as the more warmly dressed and better-equipped Russians gained the initiative. The German troops were withdrawn to avoid further weather casualties.

The defender has a definite advantage in winter because, as a rule, his positions cannot be seen in snow except at very close range. He is able to keep his forces under cover and wait until the moment that fire can be used most effectively. The attacker, on the other hand, is impeded in his movements and is easily detected, even in camouflage clothing. The principal weapon of the defender is the machine gun. Its performance is not diminished by snow, in which mortars and light artillery lose most of their effectiveness.

When defensive positions were not occupied until winter, the Germans found it impossible to build shelters and emplacements in hard frozen ground. Machine guns and rifles had to be placed on a snow parapet that had been built up and packed hard. If well constructed, and water poured over it to form an ice coating, the parapet offered some protection against enemy fire.

Where organized positions are established before snowfall, parapets must be increased in height as the snow level rises, and care taken to keep trenches and approaches free of snow at all times. Trenches and dugouts provide better cover in winter than in other seasons. Snow-covered obstacles remain effective until covered by a snow crust that will bear a man's weight. Barriers against ski troops are effective only as long as they project above the snow. Obstacles must be removed when snow begins to melt, or they will obstruct visibility and fields of fire.

When swamps freeze over, the defender is suddenly faced with a situation changed to his disadvantage. German divisions that fought defensive actions when swamps were impassable barriers were at a great disadvantage against the same enemy, in the same location, when swamps froze over. The increased frontage created by the frozen swamp could be defended only by employing additional artillery and much greater quantities of all types of ammunition. Similarly, the winter freeze-up is disadvantageous to a weak defender behind a water barrier. The freeze turns rivers into routes of approach toward the defensive positions.

Since the Russians often penetrated artillery firing positions, the Germans trained artillerymen in infantry close-combat tactics. Because snow sometimes makes it impossible to evacuate guns, artillery crews were trained in demolition of field pieces.

The Russian winter covers roads, countryside, and vehicles with a crippling coat of ice and, when sand is not available, entire columns are forced to halt. Icy roads can rob an offensive of surprise or be fatal to a withdrawal. Ice conditions prevail every winter in all parts of Russia. During the German withdrawal from the Moscow area in the winter of 1941–42, ice hindered the entire operation. A few days before the order to retreat from the suburbs of Moscow, 6th Panzer Division, by building a defense around its last five tanks, held off an attack by Siberian troops who presented prime targets in their brown uniforms as they trudged forward in deep snow. This local success facilitated the disengagement of the division and provided time for the destruction of its last 88mm antiaircraft guns, necessary because no prime movers were available. Twenty-five prime movers were lost in the autumn mud of 1941, and seven had fallen victim to winter cold and snow. The withdrawal proceeded according to plan on the first day but the next day, moving over hilly terrain, vehicles skidded on icy roads, and trucks which had been abandoned during the preceding muddy season blocked the roads, adding to the difficulties.

Fearful that the pursuing Russians would overtake and destroy the rear guard if time were spent in extricating each vehicle, the Germans loaded as much matériel as possible on trucks still serviceable and put the remaining equipment to the torch. The rear guard was reinforced, and the withdrawal continued with brief delaying actions based on villages. Inhabited places were vital to the Germans, who lacked winter clothing, and attractive, too, to the Russians who preferred permanent-type shelter. The retreat became a race from village to village.

In a few days the Germans reached Klin, northwest of Moscow, which could not be used to house the division overnight, as the city was on the main route of other divisions streaming west (Map 10). However, a large quantity of explosives were found in Klin and were used to blast temporary shelters in the ground outside the city. Attempts to obtain dirt from the blasted shelters for sanding roads were useless because the explosions loosed great chunks of solidly frozen earth which could not be pulverized. The division held before Klin for one day, and then completed its withdrawal across the four-lane Smolensk–Moscow highway.

Russian air activity during the withdrawal was ineffective, because it was limited to scattered sorties of a few planes which strafed columns or dropped small fragmentation bombs. During air alerts the Germans burrowed in the snow at least 100 yards from the road. Some casualties were caused by delayed-action bombs when men failed to remain down long enough after the missiles were dropped. If the Russians had used strong bomber forces, the results would have been disastrous. In contrast to the losses from enemy air, German casualties due to cold weather and insufficient clothing were heavy.

The numerically superior enemy did not succeed in enveloping and annihilating the German rear guard, because he could not employ his heavy weapons in a frontal attack in deep snow without suffering heavy losses. Successful envelopment was difficult for the Russians because such movements were usually attempted by cavalry, ski troops, and infantry mounted on sleighs who were unable to take their heavy weapons with them. The striking power that the Russian forces were able to bring forward was not sufficient to destroy the defender.

CHAPTER 22

Russian Tactics

The Russians usually attacked along existing roads or on paths beaten down by their tanks. Frequently, the infantry followed close behind their tanks, using the trail made by the tank tracks. In other instances infantry worked its way forward in snow tunnels toward German positions, despite the heavy losses which resulted from such tactics. In mass attacks the Russians usually debouched from woods and burrowed their way through the deep snow as quickly as possible. Mowed down by machine guns, the first wave would be followed by a second attack which moved forward a short distance over the bodies of the dead before coming to a standstill. This was repeated by as many as ten waves, until the Russians bogged down from heavy losses and exhaustion or until the German defenses were penetrated.

Russian infiltration tactics were most effective in winter, because the German defense system, based on strong points, practically invited such tactics. The Germans were forced to adopt the strong point system of defense because they lacked sufficient forces to occupy continuous lines backed up by reserves. The Russians always sought to split and annihilate defending forces, and to this end cavalry, ski units, airborne troops, and, above all, partisans were used in great numbers.

I. Ski Troops

On the night of 20–21 March 1942, 600 Russian ski troops enveloped the command post of the 269th Division in a village twelve miles northeast of Lyuban. The flanking movement was made under cover of darkness over a bog which had a weak bearing surface and was therefore but lightly guarded by the Germans. As these troops assaulted the rear of the village, heavy attacks with armored support were launched against the entire division front. After a bitter fight, division service troops managed to drive off the ski troops.

Another instance of Russian use of strong ski forces occurred at the end of March 1942, after 6th Panzer Division had captured several villages southwest of Rzhev in a limited-objective attack. The area was immediately organized for defense; roads were cleared in the three-foot-deep snow, and paths cleared to the numerous bunkers taken in the action.

Under cover of darkness, a ski brigade of the Russian Thirty-ninth Guards Army, under command of a general officer, assembled in a wooded area opposite a strong point held by the 114th Panzer Grenadier Regiment plus an artillery battalion and some Flak. At daybreak, the ski brigade attacked the German position, with the main effort against the German rear. The defenders recognized the Russian intentions and withheld fire until the attackers came within 200 to 300 yards. The Germans then opened fire with 500 rifles, thirty-six machine guns, and sixteen artillery pieces. The effect was devastating. Such of the enemy as survived buried themselves in the snow in the hope of returning to the woods at night. Most of the weapons and all of the ski equipment of the force engaged in the main attack were captured. The greatest prize, however, was a map found on the dead commander which gave the disposition of the entire Thirty-ninth Guards Army.

The Russians failed in their mission because they could not achieve surprise. In cold weather sound travels a great distance, and their approach over the snow could clearly be heard. Furthermore, the attack carried across open terrain and all the roads and paths around the German positions were well guarded.

Russian ski units were more successful when used in combination with other arms. When Third Panzer Army was withdrawing west of Moscow in December 1941, a Russian force composed of ski troops, cavalry, and sleigh-mounted infantry succeeded in cutting off the 6th Panzer Division which was the rear guard of LVI Panzer Corps.

II. Unusual Russian Tactics

In October 1941 a Russian force crossed the ice-covered Gulf of Finland from Leningrad and made a surprise attack on the 212th Infantry Division. The attack, made under cover of darkness in a driving snowstorm, was thrown back to the shore after a stiff fight. The Russians had marched eastward across the ice from Leningrad to Kronshtadt and then southward to hit the German flank and rear.

Similarly, at the end of January 1945 the Russians tried to unhinge the left flank of Third Panzer Army, which was on the Deime River, by envelopment across the ice of the Kurisches Haff. Three times the enemy penetrated the army front as far as the town of Labiau, and each time was thrown back after hard fighting.

In the winter of 1941–42 the Russians supplied Leningrad day after day with food and ammunition by using an ice road over Lake Ladoga. The ice road, eighteen miles long, was nine to twelve miles from the southern shore. At night the same road was used to move regiments and even divisions from Leningrad to the Eighth and Fifty-fourth Russian Armies. The Germans fired 150mm artillery against the ice road, but could not stop the Russians. They continued moving troops and supplies despite all losses.

CHAPTER 23

Clothing, Equipment, Rations

I. Clothing

In the winter of 1941–42, the most severe in Russia in a hundred years, the Germans, if they had any winter clothing at all, carried only the regular issue overcoat, sweater, bellyband, and hood designed for winter wear in Germany. The bulk of the winter garments donated by the German people did not reach the front until the end of January 1942, after cold had done its damage. Frostbite casualties were numerous. For instance, a panzer division near Volokolamsk in January 1942 had up to 800 frostbite casualties a day.

During the inactivity of the autumn 1941 muddy period, fur pieces and felt boots were manufactured locally, purchased from civilians, or removed from dead Russian soldiers; but these sources supplied only a small number of troops. All available underwear was issued so that several sets could be worn at one time, and each man managed to obtain a piece of cloth for use as a bellyband or head protector. Some Germans acquired Russian-type fur caps, which proved dangerous, since, despite the addition of distinguishing insignia, the wearers were often mistaken for enemy and fired upon by friendly troops.

After the first winter of the war, clothing supplies improved, and although items lacked uniformity of appearance they served their purpose. Garments were worn in various combinations, such as: heavy quilted trousers, fur vest, regular jacket, and regular overcoat; quilted trousers, sweater, quilted jacket, and regular overcoat; heavy quilted trousers, sweater, regular jacket, and fur coat; or regular trousers, knee protectors, regular jacket, and fur coat. With these combinations each man wore warm underwear, gloves, scarf, and felt or felt-and-leather boots.

The Germans found the quilted suit with hood, worn over the regular uniform, plus a fur cap, felt boots with leather reinforcement or leather soles, and fur gloves best for cold weather. This was the type of winter uniform worn by the Russians. Long sheepskin coats should be worn by drivers and guards. Without winter clothing troops cannot remain out of doors in temperatures under −10° F.

White camouflage clothing should have some identifying feature. White-clad German ski formations moving at extended order through wooded areas, or advancing during snowstorms, were sometimes infiltrated by similarly dressed Russian troops.

II. Equipment

WEAPONS

Maintenance of weapons is difficult in winter. German rifles and machine guns developed malfunctions because the grease and oil used were not cold-resistant. Strikers and striker springs broke like glass; fluid in artillery recoil mechanisms solidified, crippling the piece. Light weapons had to be warmed in huts, and fires were lighted under the barrels of guns to get them back into action. Before suitable lubricants were available, troops found an emergency solution in the removal of every trace of grease and oil from their weapons. In the south of Russia, the abundantly available sunflower oil was used as a lubricant. It is acid-free and cold-resistant.

VEHICLES

The need for spare motor vehicle and tank parts increases at low temperatures. The number of broken springs, for instance, reached unusually high proportions. The Germans cannibalized broken-down and abandoned vehicles to get spare parts. The policy of furnishing as many complete tanks and motor vehicles as possible to the front was detrimental to spare parts production. It was by no means unusual that some armored regiments sent their technical personnel on unauthorized trips to factories in Germany to obtain spare parts through personal contact.

Winter temperatures in Russia render self-starters useless. The Germans resorted to prewarming engines by building fires under them. In this way a few vehicles were started for towing. During alerts motors were frequently kept running for hours.

III. Rations

During winter, particular attention must be given to proper packaging and storage of foods sensitive to cold. At extreme low temperatures the Germans found that even the relatively short haul from field kitchens to men on the line sufficed to turn food into lumps of ice. Foods sensitive to heat kept almost indefinitely in cold weather.

CHAPTER 24

Transportation and Troop Movements

I. Roads

During winter, road conditions are usually favorable except during bad weather. Roads kept free of snow are easily passable, often better than in summer. With the onset of heavy snowfalls, however, difficulties arose on all traffic routes, which were counteracted by the road services of the various German armies. The assignment of one battalion per thirty miles of road proved satisfactory for snow clearance. Civilian labor was hired for shoveling and for driving horse-drawn plows.

At certain points along roads the Germans established relay stations to provide warm quarters and food for drivers and small units that were held up by snowstorms. Other stations, manned by engineer personnel, were in telephone communication with corps and army, to which road conditions were reported by 0800 each day. Army distributed daily bulletins with maps showing road conditions.

If at all possible, each emergency station had one motorized snowplow. Two or three motorized snowplows were held in reserve by army to clear the way for important troop movements. It was the German experience that during severe snowstorms at least six power plows were necessary to keep a road open for an infantry division.

Strong winds caused snowdrifts which blocked all traffic. Shoveling during storms was futile, for the roads quickly became covered again. To avoid drifts the Germans routed winter roads through woods, where drifts rarely occur, or along the crest of high ground, where the snow is usually less deep.

SNOW FENCES

Whenever roads across open terrain must be used, snow fences should be erected before the beginning of winter. The location of snow fences is important. They must be set up on both sides of the road, fifty to seventy feet from the shoulders. After a snowstorm the fences must be placed on top of the snow wall that has formed behind them.

In most instances the prewar snow fences had disappeared, and fences four to five feet high had to be improvised out of latticework, wickerwork, or branches of coniferous trees. If materials for construction of snow fences were not available, the Germans used snow blocks.

MARKING OF ROADS

If snow roads follow a different course from those indicated on maps, they should be marked on the ground so they can be followed after a heavy snowfall or when covered by drifted snow. The Germans marked roads with tall poles topped with straw or branches. Stakes with black or red tops or colored markers were also used.

ICE-COVERED ROADS

Serious traffic jams are often caused by icy roads. It is important to have towing service ready to render assistance in icy sections. In hilly terrain the Germans set up sand dumps, and all vehicles were ordered to carry sand. Vehicles with trailers were barred from icy roads, since they often became stuck even if roads were sanded.

II. Railroads

Heavy snowfalls and drifting snow interrupt railway traffic, and the Germans used local civilian labor and snowplows to keep tracks clear. Cold reduced the efficiency of German locomotives which had been built for the milder temperatures of Central Europe. During the first winter of the war 70 percent of the German locomotives broke down. Only after a period of trial and error and protracted technical research which led to the introduction of a new type of locomotive, did the Germans overcome their difficulties. Railroad construction and maintenance requiring excavation slowed down or stopped completely in cold weather. Cold crippled operations, caused traffic congestion, and slowed supply movement.

In the winter of 1941–42, sometimes only one third, and frequently less, of the daily quota of twenty-eight trains got through to Army Group Center. The German Second Army and Second Panzer Army together required eighteen supply trains a day and received only two. In November 1941 these armies were unable to take Tula because their supply system had broken down. Even the most critical supplies did not reach the front in time.

III. Draft Horses

Most of the German horses became accustomed to the Russian winter, although they needed at least emergency shelter. In the open, horses freeze to death at temperatures under −4° F. Russian horses, with their thick shaggy winter coat can withstand temperatures as low as $-58°$ F, if they are sheltered against the wind. Some German horses, notably the heavy cold-blooded breeds, were unable to withstand the Russian winter, particularly those moved suddenly from the mild climate of France.

The Germans expected their draft horses to pull excessive loads in winter, and the animals became prematurely spent particularly when they were given insufficient care, forage, and water. Lighter breeds were better able to stand the cold, but were not strong enough to move the heavy German equipment; they became exhausted, and collapsed and died in the snow.

During the first winter of the war German horses frequently lacked winter shoeing, a factor which lessened their draft power on icy roads and caused them to fall. Sometimes ice was so bad that horses which had not been wintershod could not be led from the railroad station to the stables.

A great many horses perished for lack of forage. In quiet sectors horses were worked as little as possible when feed was short. Work teams which were given extra feed were used for routine duties.

There were no horse diseases directly traceable to or aggravated by the Russian winter. Most of the 1.5 million horses which the Germans lost in Russia were victims of battle wounds, overexertion, forage shortages, and cold.

CHAPTER 25

Health and Morale

I. Evacuation of Casualties

In some respects conditions for evacuation of casualties during winter were more favorable than during other seasons. Even after a heavy snow, road traffic was soon restored. In some sectors native sleighs were used for evacuation, and special sleighs with enclosed wooden superstructures were built and did good service. Battlefield evacuation was done with small one-man sleds which are easily pulled by one or two soldiers.

A plentiful supply of blankets is essential, and the Germans also used paper coverings to protect limbs of casualties in transit. Frost injuries rarely occurred during evacuation, and only during the first year of the war, when hospital trains were immobilized for hours by cold, did wounded freeze to death. Except for the length of time involved, evacuation generally caused little discomfort to casualties.

II. Effect of Cold on Morale

The reverses suffered at Moscow lowered the morale of both officers and men who felt that lack of preparation for winter warfare was the cause of their defeat. Although it was too late to correct the basic mistakes, officers succeeded in convincing troops that the retreat would soon end, and that defeat would not become disaster.

Many men who had become separated from their units marched westward singly or in small groups and, when apprehended, freely admitted that their destination was Germany because "the war is over." These men were turned over to the nearest combat unit for rehabilitation. More serious were the cases of deserters who concealed themselves on farms and managed to obtain civilian clothes. The number of deserters to the enemy was few.

Since gasoline was precious, thefts of fuel were common. Troops helped themselves wherever they found unguarded stocks, and even drained tanks of unattended vehicles. Spare parts were scarce and were stolen whenever it was opportune to do so.

CHAPTER 26

Air Operations

I. Aircraft

In general, German aircraft stood up well even under the worst winter conditions. However, oil became quite viscous, and placed an excessive strain on various parts, especially hydraulic equipment, and a special type of winter hydraulic fluid had to be used. Lubricating oil was heated before starting engines, and electric storage batteries were also prewarmed because cold reduced their efficiency.

Aircraft tires did not show adverse effects at temperatures down to $-30°$ F., but at lower temperatures tires started to become porous. Other rubber parts, such as self-sealing tanks and rubber packings of shock absorbers, deteriorated when exposed to prolonged, intense cold. Tarpaulins provided good weather cover for wings and tail units of aircraft parked in the open, and served as camouflage.

The Germans kept some planes in heated "alarm boxes" during periods of low temperatures to assure an immediate take-off during an alarm. Skis were installed on light liaison planes for landings away from airfields. Combat aircraft took off on wheels from packed-down runways.

II. Airfields

For winter operations, air installations must have adequate, heated working space, heating equipment, snow-removal and snow-packing equipment, and good quarters. The Germans found that aircraft maintenance in winter took several times as long as in summer unless heated working space was available.

Concrete runways and strips quickly become covered with

snow, and careful maintenance through packing and removal of excess snow is necessary. Since snow in many areas of Russia remains dry and powdery throughout the winter, excessive snowdrifts pile up whenever there is a strong wind. All obstacles must be cleared from runways, for even small bushes and gasoline drums may be the cause of drifts several feet high.

In view of possible changes in plans involving the redistribution of units and the movement of reinforcements, the Germans tried to keep even unused airfields ready for winter operation. To get fields into operation once winter had set in required a considerable expenditure of time and labor and sometimes necessitated the construction of roads if no railroad connection was available for movement of matériel.

III. Flight

The very short days of winter made night flying necessary for extended missions. German crews not qualified for night flying were therefore limited to missions of short duration.

Particular difficulties were encountered in orientation from the air because of the similarity of snow-covered ground to snow cover on frozen lakes and rivers. During winter—as well as during spring floods and mud—the Russian landscape bears little resemblance to what is shown on maps. New aerial photographic maps and sketches for each season are indispensable for navigation and for effective cooperation with ground forces.

During early winter, ceilings and visibility below the clouds are usually favorable enough to permit flights along coastal areas. Poor visibility and clouds resembling high altitude fog frequently appear within the cold continental air masses and western warm air masses over the Volkhov River and Lake Peipus. The danger of ice formation during all seasons is greater in European Russia than in Central Europe. Frequently when Germany and western Russia have good flying weather the intermediate area of eastern Poland has low overcasts, poor visibility, precipitation, and conditions which lead to formation of ice.

In the German experience the number of accidents caused

by climatic conditions in Russia was neither greater nor less than in Central Europe. Emergency missions necessitated by the ground situation, such as low-level attacks to support armor, or supply flights—especially to Stalingrad—naturally brought about increased losses attributable to weather conditions. Virtually every emergency landing in winter resulted in total loss of the aircraft.

IV. Emergency Equipment

Based on the experiences gained in the first winter of the war, normal emergency equipment was supplemented by short skis with which flight crews could cover considerable distances if forced down. Snowshoes proved unsatisfactory and consequently ski boots were issued instead of air force fur-lined boots. Equipment for emergency landings in all seasons included abundant quantities of salt and pictures of saints which were used as barter items with the local population.

V. Rations and Clothing

The campaign in Russia taught the Germans nothing basically new in the matter of rations for flight personnel. Standard preparations for long-range and high-altitude flight assured that personnel were properly fed for extreme climatic conditions.

Normal-issue cold-weather clothing was adequate for flight and maintenance personnel.

SPRING AND AUTUMN

CHAPTER 27

General

The rain and mud of spring and autumn have a decisive effect upon military operations in European Russia. Because both seasons are similar, they are dealt with in the same part of this study. Mud is the dominant climatic factor in military operations during spring and autumn. With the first thaws of spring, most of European Russia below the Arctic Circle becomes a muddy mass. The spring muddy season lasts from four to six weeks, and ends when the ground is sufficiently thawed to absorb melted snow. The autumn muddy season starts in early October and lasts about four weeks. In sandy regions or on high ground the adverse effects of mud upon military operations are less severe.

The melting snows of spring cause heavy floods in addition to mud conditions. The spring muddy season does not end everywhere at once; there are extensive wooded and swampy areas which do not dry out until summer, sometimes not even then. The autumn muddy season ends suddenly—after the first frosts mud rarely recurs again.

I. Spring

In the northern and central areas of European Russia the melting snow, often accompanied by heavy rainfall, begins between the end of March and the middle of April. During the first days of this period, recurrences of cold spells with frost or snow are likely, followed by quickly rising temperatures which rapidly melt the snow. The spring floods swell all streams. Rivers increase to as much as ten times their normal width, and floating ice threatens bridges often causing their collapse. All river traffic is suspended while rivers are at flood stage. The excess water flows off in a comparatively short time and leaves the countryside an ocean of mud. In open country one often sinks knee-deep; paved roads give way and motor vehicles become hopelessly stuck. All attempts to use force usually make matters worse, lead to useless waste of energy and terrific consumption of fuel, and end with the complete breakdown of the vehicle. Few railroads, and fewer roads remain passable during the muddy season, and often aircraft offer the only means of transportation. In swampy terrain the muddy season is particularly troublesome because all contact with surrounding areas is interrupted. Roads previously dry are saturated, and impassable even on foot.

In the south, spring begins toward the end of February in the lowlands, and in the higher regions one or two weeks later. Here the muddy period usually lasts about four weeks, and is particularly severe in the black earth belt of the Ukraine. Here, too, unsurfaced roads become bottomless, although most surfaced roads can still be used by motor traffic. In some regions of the south the muddy period does not start as suddenly; moreover in its early stages it is limited to daylight hours. Night temperatures fall below freezing, permitting only a superficial thawing; the ground underneath remains solidly frozen. This makes it possible to continue large-scale movements through the first half of the muddy period.

Along the northern coast of the Sea of Azov the muddy period, with brief interruptions, lasts throughout the winter, because in this coastal area winter temperatures fluctuate between just above and just below freezing. Although the muddy period here lasts much longer than in other areas, it presents problems no different from those in other parts of the southern Ukraine.

In the Crimea, north of the Yaila Mountains, climatic conditions at the beginning of spring are similar to those in the southern Ukraine, and are marked by warm weather and rapidly melting snow after mid-March. The coastal strip south of this mountain range has a subtropical climate because of its geographic location, being sheltered from northern winds and open to the south toward the Black Sea.

II. Autumn

In northern and central Russia the autumn season is limited to September and October, while the south benefits from an additional month of autumnal weather. During the first half of autumn the weather is dry and temperatures are moderate, and summer operations can continue through this time without interruption. During the second half of autumn temperatures drop and the rains begin, ushering in the muddy period. In the steppe regions farthest to the south the autumn muddy season is less severe, but everywhere else traffic over open terrain and on loose surface roads is tied up.

CHAPTER 28

Mud

I. General

The spring and autumn muddy seasons are the greatest obstacles to a war of movement in Russia. The attacker, who must seek to retain the initiative, is much more affected by mud than the defender. Operations are impracticable even for troops that are familiar with and equipped for the muddy periods.

The Russians are by no means immune to local climatic hardships. During World War II they made it a point not to launch or continue large-scale operations during the muddy season. They went so far as to halt their winter offensive before Moscow on the first warm, sunny day of spring (18 April 1942) despite the fact that their objective—turning the tide against the German invader—was virtually within their grasp. Whenever the situation forced them to move despite mud and mire, countless Russian tanks would wallow helplessly, and if the Russians were forced to withdraw, these tanks became a total loss. More than once an entire Russian tank corps got barely a dozen machines into combat—the rest were stuck and churned through the mud for days before catching up. But Russian tanks are designed to take the worst of punishment and usually reached their objective.

Large-scale operations are impossible during the muddy season. In the autumn of 1941, an entire German army was completely stopped by mud. The muddy season of that year began in mid-October and was more severe than any other muddy season experienced in World War I or World War II. During the first stages cart and dirt roads were impassable, and then the road from Roslavl to Orel became mud-choked. Supply trucks broke through gravel-top roads and churned up traffic lanes until even courier service had to be carried out with tracked vehicles. Finally only horse-drawn vehicles could move; all other transport and the bulk of the tanks and artillery were stopped dead. The muddy season lasted a month.

Pursuit of the enemy who had been beaten at Bryansk was impossible. Only divisions which had reached the Bryansk–Orel–Tula road could move. Units became separated and intermingled, with only scattered elements in contact with the enemy. The bulk of the force stuck fast or moved fitfully forward in short marches. Motor vehicles broke down with clutch or motor trouble. Horses became exhausted and collapsed. Roads were littered with dead draft animals. Few tanks were serviceable. Trucks and horse-drawn wagons bogged down and railroad supply was not equal to the situation.

Defense in place is effective during the muddy season. Any defensive operation involving movement is hampered by the same difficulties as offensive actions. An organized position is more easily defended during the muddy season than in dry weather—the attacker is at a disadvantage in mud and has to confine himself to local actions. The defender has time to organize his position well in advance of the muddy season. He can establish communications that enable him to shift reserves to threatened sectors. The defender of an organized position usually has rearward communications or adequate supplies at his disposal. He can counteract cold and dampness by preparing heated shelters and fortifications. His signal installations can be given regular maintenance. Defending infantry can fight from dry, well-concealed positions, while attacking infantry offers a prime target as it clumsily trudges through knee-deep mud.

A forced withdrawal from an organized position is the worst possible turn of events for a defender. All his former advantages become hindrances, and he is as handicapped by the terrain as the attacker. Further, he is pressed for time and is likely to lose his weapons, vehicles, and supplies. Defense begun without prepared positions, and a defense requiring mobile defense tactics, are normally carried on from villages or farmhouses until the situation permits establishment of a continuous line.

II. Infantry

Limited-objective attacks during a muddy period are feasible when units equipped with tracked vehicles are used in conjunction with infantry. In October 1941, for instance, such a combination of forces captured Kursk. Tracked vehicles in the lead, the Germans advanced about twelve miles eastward from Dmitryev Lgovski to the Usozha River, where the bridge had been burned and Russian labor battalions offered strong resistance on the east bank. Suddenly, Russian cavalry supported by T34 tanks made a surprise raid on the stalled German column. Only the timely arrival of German dismounted armored infantry, which succeeded in destroying a large number of T34's, prevented a serious setback. Engineers replaced the bridge and the advance continued. The Russians fought on, but the 95th Infantry Division made a wide sweep east of the road to Kursk and captured that strongly fortified city.

III. Artillery

Artillery must be light to retain mobility in mud. The German pieces were too heavy for muddy terrain, and guns became so badly bogged down that teams of horses could not budge them.

The roads, mud, and swamps of northern Russia posed entirely new problems for the German artillery. Tactical concentration, normally a routine matter, became an art in the desolate morass where new problems had to be solved each day. Reconnaissance, selection, and occupation of observation and firing positions, and the installation of wire required hours of labor and a great deal of ingenuity. Work on roads and bridges was even more time consuming. In many places extensive networks of corduroy roads had to be built, often by combat troops as there were not enough engineers to do the job. Prior training of artillerymen in road construction would have been useful, but the necessity therefor was not foreseen, much less planned for. Poorly constructed roads that constantly broke down under heavy loads of ammunition resulted. The maze of corduroy roads through swamps and thinly wooded marshy forests had but little natural cover and were easily seen by enemy air reconnaissance. To counteract this condition, roads were built far beyond gun positions and dummy roads constructed. These deceptive measures were not particularly effective since the artillery was of necessity confined to the few dry areas available.

The Russians are familiar with the swamp country and know exactly where such areas can be crossed. They often penetrated or outflanked the weak German infantry and popped up in front of artillery positions. Every gun position had to be made a strong point, and artillery troops given basic training in infantry tactics, a subject which had received little attention in artillery training up to that time.

Mud impairs the effectiveness of artillery fire, dampens splinter effect, and causes a high number of duds, making fire adjustment extremely difficult.

IV. Armored Forces

German losses of tanks and motorized equipment of all types were extraordinarily high during the autumn muddy period of

1941, the first time that the mud of Russia was encountered. For example, Second Panzer Group, operating in the Orel area at that time, lost 60 percent of its tanks in mud. A division of Fourth Panzer Group, operating in the area north of Gzhatsk during the same period, lost fifty tanks without a shot being fired, thirty-five of them within three days. These losses were most serious since no replacements were received. Germany at that time was producing only eighty-five tanks and forty assault guns monthly.

Armored operations in mud are most difficult. For instance, in February 1944 when two Germans corps were encircled at Cherkassy, an attempt by a strong armored force to crack the Russian ring from the outside bogged down within sight of the encircled corps, although the relief force did come close enough to its objective to make contact with some troops who had fought their way out on foot. In another instance, in March 1944, 6,000 German troops cut off in the city of Ternopol were lost because a tank force of thirty-five Tiger and 100 Panther tanks attempting a relief thrust were prevented by mud from reaching the beleaguered city. The task force was able to cross the Strypa River and knock out strong antitank defenses, but had covered only half of the twelve miles to Ternopol when forced by mud to give up. Thousands of hours of labor were needed to restore roads and small bridges sufficiently to retrieve the stranded armor.

In early spring major operations with limited objectives are possible if timed for the period when daytime thaws and night frost leave but a thin layer of mud on deeply frozen ground. Operations begun just before a muddy season, however, run the risk of failure because there is no way of estimating how long terrain will remain passable. For instance, in March 1943 when two panzer armies, together with two German infantry corps, started an operation to retake Kharkov, their advance carried into high country, where spring usually begins later than in the lowlands. There was still some snow on the ground when the attack was launched. Just before the Germans reached their objective—the upper course of the Donets—a sudden rise in temperature created a severe muddy condition. All vehicles except those on the only hard-surfaced road in the area, leading from Kursk to Kharkov, became helpless. The infantry was able to slog forward, but heavy weapons and artillery were delayed and finally moved up with great effort. Even the T34 tanks of the Russian rear guard became embedded and could not be retrieved by the Germans until warm weather.

Operations begun when spring mud starts to recede and roads are usable can be successful. In March 1944, one panzer division and two infantry divisions, using a main road passable for wheeled vehicles, made a twenty-five-mile thrust which liberated First Panzer Army from encirclement near Buchach.

Local, limited-objective offensives are possible during the muddy season if rail transport is available to the attacking forces. In October 1941, at the height of the autumn muddy season, the Germans determined by air reconnaissance that the Orel–Kursk railway was intact except for destroyed switches and water towers. Only partisans and weak Russian cavalry were believed to be in the area, and the Germans decided to attack from Orel to establish a supply base at Ponyri, about half way to Kursk.

Two armored trains captured from the Russians were in the Orel rail yards. One regiment of infantry, some artillery, railroad engineers, and flak were entrained and quickly moved south, completely surprising the enemy. After several minor engagements on the way, the combat team reached Ponyri and the rail lines were firmly in German hands. The operation took two days.

CHAPTER 29

Clothing, Equipment, Rations

I. Clothing

The wet and muddy weather of spring and autumn subjects clothing to excessive wear and tear. Uniforms become matted and quickly go to pieces. Accessible facilities for the rapid repair of clothing are essential, and ample supplies must be located as near as possible to the front.

Footwear rapidly deteriorates. For wearing quality and protection, the Germans found their half-length infantry boot best for muddy season wear. Rubber boots are too cold when worn alone, although they are well suited for wear over shoes. Wrap puttees are unsatisfactory because they become waterlogged and saturated with mud. Footwraps are warmer, cleaner, and more durable than socks. Adequate shoe repair facilities are necessary.

II. Equipment

SUPPLY

The inevitable paralysis of highway transportation during the muddy seasons requires long-range planning of a supply organization that remains unaffected by climatic conditions. Supply dumps and depots are best located at points which can be reached by motor transport even in the most inclement weather. It is well to remember that woods or terrain offering concealment usually become inaccessible during muddy seasons, and goods stored in such places must be removed well in advance of thaw or rains and dumped along roads. This system is disadvantageous in that it wastes manpower in moving stocks, requires dual administrative records, and calls for twice the usual number of guards.

WEAPONS

Protecting weapons against the weather is difficult during the muddy seasons. Neglect of protective maintenance, shortages of cleaning materials and protective lubricants, or failure to shield weapons from wind and weather result in such serious waste that even a well-functioning supply organization cannot replace losses. Protective coverings for small arms bolt assemblies are especially important.

III. Rations

The Germans found that a good way to prevent shortages of rations—as well as equipment—was to store a three to four weeks' reserve in depots close to the front. Withdrawals from these stores must be prohibited as long as supply continues from the rear. Similar steps must be taken to forestall shortages of forage, which are apt to be serious during autumn when railroads are busy hauling winter supplies. Expedients such as loading pressed hay and straw in crevices between other cargo are not enough to cover forage requirements.

In the autumn of 1941 German troops were without bread for days and had to live off the land and such local food supplies as the Russians had not destroyed. Requisitioning of food in unoccupied territory was possible only with strong parties, as such areas were infested with partisans and scattered Russian soldiers.

CHAPTER 30

Transportation and Troop Movements

I. Roads

The road net of European Russia is sparse and, except for a few well-built roads, is not equal to sustained use by heavy vehicles. The effect of the muddy season on roads and highways is so devastating that movement slows to a snail's pace and eventually comes to a complete standstill. Most hard-surfaced roads lack good foundations and become so waterlogged that they cave in under the smallest load. Roads need continuous maintenance, a job that requires thousands of laborers. Most of the bridges on main roads and all those on secondary roads were very weak, and the Germans had to replace them with more adequate structures. The peak of road and bridge construction and maintenance occurs during the muddy seasons.

The Germans had no conception of mud as it exists in European Russia. In the autumn of 1941, when front-line troops were already stuck fast, the German High Command still believed that mud could be conquered by main force, an idea that led to serious losses of vehicles and equipment. At the height of the muddy season tractors and wreckers normally capable of traversing difficult terrain are helpless; and attempts to plow through the muddy mass makes roads even more impassable. Tanks, heavy wreckers, and even vehicles with good ground clearance simply push an ever-growing wall of mud before them until they finally stop, half buried by their own motion. A sudden frost in the autumn of 1941 cemented a crippled, buried column into a state of complete uselessness, and it never moved again. Because it could not be reached in any other way, gasoline, towropes, and food supplies were airdropped along this line of stranded armor, but all attempts to move were futile. Often, when drivers found themselves bogged down far from any habitation, they abandoned their vehicles and set out on foot to contact friendly troops in the nearest village, or sought food and shelter from local civilians in order to remain alive until the worst of the muddy season passed.

For the muddy seasons, vehicles with high ground clearance, light weight, and low unit ground pressure are necessary. German trucks had low ground clearance, and could not get traction in deep mud. Since German supply carts had wheels too narrow for muddy terrain, they sank deep into soft ground. Even the German *Maultier* and *Ostschlepper* of the later war years bogged down in mud; their tracks were too narrow. The awkward-looking and slow Russian tractor of prewar vintage salvaged the heaviest, most deeply mired loads after German equipment failed to budge them. Russian trucks, too, were much better for muddy terrain, and the Germans promptly put captured Russian vehicles into service.

The Russians know the effect of mud upon dirt roads, and therefore restrict traffic to paved roads during the muddy seasons. Their tanks and cross-country vehicles have wide tracks, and these they allow to travel alongside dirt roads, while light traffic is permitted on roads when they are hardened by night frost.

After their first experience with mud, the Germans adopted the Russian method of preserving roads through the muddy seasons. Troops were supplied in advance with food and ammunition, and dirt roads were closed off. Single vehicles were allowed to travel parallel to roads, with the distance between vehicles regulated by a block system. Repair and maintenance of roads was assigned to engineer troops and to Organization Todt [paramilitary construction agency of the Nazi Party, auxiliary to the Wehrmacht]. Corps headquarters were responsible for roads in corps areas, although in practice army assumed responsibility for main traffic arteries. Changes were reported to the army engineer and road maps distributed daily, as during winter. One battalion could maintain thirty miles of dirt road in the muddy season. The Germans used a large number of Russian civilians, mostly women, for draining roads and making other improvements. Roads that become badly rutted during the muddy season do not dry out to a usable condition unless leveled while still soft. In dry weather graded dirt roads are as good as hard-surfaced roads, but the slightest rain makes them slippery.

The Germans sometimes had to construct corduroy roads during an attack. In the autumn of 1941, when panzer units of Army Group North were given the threefold mission of cutting off Leningrad, establishing contact with Finnish forces, and seizing the bauxite mines east of Tikhvin, the operation degenerated into a struggle against mud and swamp. Each unit had to construct its own corduroy road since the terrain was almost impassable, even for tracked vehicles. The Germans did reach Tikhvin, but did not accomplish their entire mission.

In another instance on the Leningrad front, in the autumn of 1942, when the Eleventh Army was to attack across the Neva River, the operation did not get beyond the planning stage because of the lack of usable roads through the mud and swamp of the area. Neither the time nor the materials were available to build the corduroy, concrete, or steel plank roads that would have made the terrain passable.

II. Railroads

The few railroads of European Russia are the only means of long-distance transportation during the muddy season, and overburdening their facilities is inevitable. Operating schedules are disrupted because muddy highways prevent access to railheads. Repairs to damaged sections of track consume endless time because labor and materials must be transported by rail to the damaged places. The right of way must be restored step by step, as simultaneous work on several sections of track is out of the question. Supply shipments suffer serious delay. During the German autumn offensive of 1941 the supply flow was so reduced that operations in some areas came to a complete halt.

As an expedient, supplies were sometimes shuttled over serviceable sections of track. This was difficult when intact sections of track could not be reached because of muddy roads. In such situations men and matériel were flown in by gliders to the place where rail movement could be made.

Mired roads make movement of troops and vehicles on top of dry railroad embankments a great temptation, but it must be avoided. Vehicles damage rails and switches which are hard to replace.

Russian railroad bridges are usually high enough to escape harm from spring floods. In only a few instances will the water level reach a railroad span. Even then superstructures suffer little damage, despite the fact that they are invariably of poor construction.

III. Bridges

Most rivers in Russia are not regulated, and after snow melts in the spring the rushing waters make river beds extremely muddy, especially near the banks. High water and muddy river bottoms make bridge construction difficult. For example, after the German attack across the Dnepr in 1941, a military bridge settled and broke under the weight of the first tank to cross. The trestles, which were placed on an apparently firm gravel bottom, had sunk through a layer of mud below the gravel. The small footings used were not suitable for supporting weight on a muddy river bed. The six-hour delay during which the bridge was repaired prevented a panzer corps from achieving a tactical surprise.

Flood waters carried heavy, floating ice which threatened bridges, and only high spans equipped with ice fenders withstood this danger. Well-anchored underwater bridges were widely used by the Russians. High waters can cut off bridgeheads from supplies, and for this reason both Russians and Germans repeatedly abandoned bridgeheads before spring floods.

IV. Small Boats

Flood waters form channels and sand bars in rivers, and these irregularities constantly change. Because of this the Germans abandoned the use of deep-draft motorboats and replaced them with shallow-draft assault boats for river crossings in spring. Boat crossings during high water periods are dangerous, and fording streams, other than small brooks, is hazardous.

CHAPTER 31

Health

I. Troops

During the rainy and muddy periods the humidity and cold induced mild forms of respiratory diseases which, however, rarely required hospitalization. Except for a lowering of resistance, the Germans found that the general state of troop health remained satisfactory.

Of great concern throughout the Russian campaign was the typhus plague. During autumn—and winter—the infestation of troops with lice reached serious proportions in front-line positions. Typhus was less common among combat troops than among service personnel in rear areas, because front-line troops had much less contact with the civilian population. Major outbreaks of typhus among combat troops occurred when the men occupied captured enemy positions and immediately bunked on straw they found in dugouts and other shelters. In some cases the Germans had to withdraw and quarantine whole companies.

Continuous delousing is most important in fighting typhus. During the first year of the Russian campaign the Germans did not have effective antivermin powders, and only at the end of 1942 did front-line units get mobile delousing stations. Wherever possible, *sauna* baths were installed at supply units, and a more or less effective delousing of clothing was carried out.

The benefits were but temporary; after using the *sauna*, soldiers had to be returned to the front with its vermin-infested positions, and they once again fell prey to lice.

Evacuation of wounded is so difficult during the muddy seasons that unnecessary losses of personnel can be avoided only if facilities for emergency treatment are placed well forward in the combat zone. Hours are needed to carry serious cases through a mile of knee-deep mud and marsh to aid stations. In situations where casualties could be evacuated only under cover of darkness, four litter bearers often required an entire night to bring out one man.

Motor transport of wounded to hospitals which cannot be reached via a hard-surfaced road is a torturously slow procedure; ambulances towed by prime movers must wind their way through mile after mile of vehicles bogged down in mud. A thirty-mile trip under such conditions often takes six to eight hours. So many ambulances broke down that the Germans started to evacuate wounded in supply trucks returning to rear areas, an advantageous method. Eight to ten wounded can be transported in a truck, while only four can be carried by an ambulance.

II. Horses

During spring and autumn, diseases among horses were no higher than in other seasons. Exposure of animals to dampness after sweating caused colds, and deaths from overexertion were numerous. Horses collapsed on the road and had to be given weeks of rest. Supply difficulties during the muddy season caused shortages of feed which led to the loss of many draft animals.

CHAPTER 32

Air Operations

Advance preparations must be made for draining airfields during spring thaws; otherwise, they turn to mud and remain unusable for weeks. Drainage ditches are rarely sufficient; as much snow as possible should be removed before it starts to melt. It is frequently helpful to puncture the ground frost, permitting water to drain off.

During the spring thaw the ground often heaves with such force that runways are destroyed for great lengths, seriously interfering with air operations.

SUMMER

CHAPTER 33

General

Summer comes suddenly south of the Arctic Circle, and literally overnight all traces of spring disappear. The ground hardens, roads dry out, and the mud of spring becomes a hard crust or turns to dust. Days are warm, nights are cool, and only in the southern region is the heat intense. Moors and swamps dry up, and swampy lowlands which are impassable during the muddy seasons may be used by peasant carts and, to a limited degree, by wheeled and tracked vehicles. Narrow paths emerge from swampy terrain, and islands rise out of the receding water to furnish partisans with hiding places. The paths to these island strong points are water covered in many places, and contact with the enemy is difficult. The rapid growth of vegetation, especially in the south, provides natural cover which has a definite effect upon operations.

All roads are passable in summer, and even driving in open terrain is possible, despite numerous fissures and cracks in the ground. So-called summer roads can be created at will without engineers or laborers—they form themselves by use. Speeds up to fifty miles per hour are possible on summer roads and they are often preferred to regular roads which are full of holes. Summer roads are useless after rain, but if not used while wet they dry out to a smooth surface and full-scale movement can be resumed.

Summer not only dries out roads, but reduces the level of rivers and streams as well. Rivers can be forded, and smaller streams are only minor obstacles. Swampy terrain remains a serious barrier.

Summer is the most favorable period for operations in European Russia. All arms are capable of optimum mobility. Counterattacks and raids on communications can slow an offensive, but are rarely enough to bring it to a halt. The attacker can bypass fortifications or bring up his heaviest weapons against them.

I. Sudden Changes in Ground Conditions

Sudden thunderstorms can change easily passable dirt roads and open terrain into mud traps. Near Kiev, in August of 1941, such a storm was almost fatal to a regiment of a German motorized infantry division. The division was ordered to block the last escape route of Russian forces encircled north of Cherkassy. Moving over dry roads, the division reached the area of encirclement in good time and, despite a strong attempt at breakout by the enemy, accomplished its mission. Relieved from the blocking position, the division was ordered to join Second Panzer Group for the drive on Bryansk. Hardly had the first elements moved out when a heavy rain began, and the roads became such a slippery mass that the last regiment stuck fast. At this critical moment Russian tank forces, attempting a relief thrust on Kiev, hit the rear of the mud-bound regiment; the Russian armor with its wide tracks could still move over the muddy ground, but the German motorized infantry was anchored by its own wheels. Lacking the firepower to mount a defense against the tanks, the infantry set fire to its vehicles and set out on foot to join the division which was also bogged down to the north.

In another instance, a brief rainy period at the end of July and the beginning of August 1941 prevented First Panzer Group from closing a ring around Russian forces in the southern sector of the Uman area. The Germans started their advance east of Berdichev in three columns. The first two, using tracked vehicles and horse-drawn Russian peasant carts, made slow progress; the third and strongest element, using wheeled motor vehicles, bogged down completely. Mud and the German shortage of proper equipment enabled a considerable number of enemy forces to escape encirclement.

After the return of sunshine, dirt roads dry out rapidly and can be used for normal traffic, provided undisciplined, over-eager drivers have not plowed them up while the roads are still soft. After 22d Panzer Division broke through the Parpach battle positions preparatory to seizing the Kerch Peninsula in the summer of 1942, a sudden cloudburst so mired the road that movement was impossible. A perimeter defense was thrown up, and the division sat it out until the storm was over and the summer sun had dried the road to a passable condition.

II. Dust and Sand

Right at the beginning of the Russian campaign the Germans experienced the havoc which dust can wreak with motor vehicles. Even German tanks sustained severe damage from the dust they stirred up while crossing vast sandy regions. Many tanks had no dust filters, and on those so equipped the filters soon became thoroughly clogged. Quartz dust was sucked into engines, which became so ground out that many tanks were rendered unserviceable. In other tanks the abrasive action of dust reduced engine efficiency and increased fuel consumption; thus weakened, they entered the autumn muddy season which dealt them the death blow. Sand roads greatly slowed, but did not stop trucks. The *Volkswagen* [German counterpart of the U.S. Jeep], which otherwise proved highly serviceable, stuck easily in sand because of its narrow wheels. Huge dust clouds raised by convoys frequently provoked air attacks that resulted in serious losses of vehicles and horses.

III. Water

The water supply in European Russia varies greatly from region to region. During summer it is uniformly poor. Generally, the quantity and quality of drinking water deteriorates toward the south. To the north, nearly every inhabited place has an adequate number of wells that furnish potable water. Between Leningrad and the Luga River there are many wells sunk as deep as eighty feet; the water from these sources is cold and of excellent quality. Each village in central and southern Russia has one or two wells, but during summer their water is scant and warm, and drinking water must be taken from brooks and rivers. Many wells and cisterns in southern Russia nearly dry up in summer droughts, and such water as they furnish must be boiled before drinking. The water supply in the bend of the Don River is poor. German forces that fought between the Don and the Volga in the battle of Stalingrad had practically no local water supply.

CHAPTER 34

German Tactics

I. Swamp and Sand

Even in summer, swampy and sandy terrain can have a decisive effect upon movement and combat. It is impossible to estimate the time required for a march through such areas, and careful ground and air reconnaissance must be made to compare maps with actual terrain conditions. Provision must be made for supplementary gasoline. Extra engineer troops are necessary, and portable bridging equipment is indispensable for crossing water holes and swampy areas. Wreckers must be spotted to provide help where the going is particularly rugged. The small and light column with the same organic structure as its parent unit is at a definite advantage in sand and swamp.

On 11 July 1941, 6th Panzer Division was diverted from its eastward advance toward Porkhov and Dno to assist 1st Panzer Division whose drive via the Pskov–Leningrad *Rollbahn* [road designated as a main axis for motorized transportation] toward Luga had run into stiff enemy resistance near Novoselye (Map 13). Hardly had Flying Column Raus, the leading echelon, started for the trouble spot, than the road, shown on the map as leading directly through a swampland to Novoselye, came to an end. Local residents said no such road had existed for forty years. With guides and engineers to the front, the column took up a zigzag course from village to village over the best wagon roads that could be found. At the first swampy hole, about thirty feet wide, an apparently sturdy bridge collapsed under the weight of a light tank. The advance was delayed for five hours while a new bridge was built.

Whenever possible, driving in the tracks of preceding vehicles had to be avoided, otherwise wheels sank deeper and deeper until they became completely stuck. The column had to cross twelve swampy brooks, and at each one a long delay was necessary while rotted bridges were strengthened with girders or entirely rebuilt. In trying to detour swampy spots, vehicles and tanks broke through the crusted top layer of ground and became so mired that they had to be towed out by other tanks. In many instances the towing vehicle sank in beside the one it was trying to assist. Sometimes vehicles roped together to help each other became so badly stuck that they had to be pulled out one by one by the most powerful wreckers. To get the huge wreckers to points where they were needed was an entirely separate problem. The cart roads were so narrow and clogged that there was little opportunity to turn out. Commanders had difficulty in exercising leadership because emergencies developed everywhere at the same time and bottlenecks could be reached only on foot.

To keep the column from becoming scattered, it had to be halted at regular intervals, where the terrain permitted, so that vehicles could close up. Such a halt was made ten miles south of Novoselye to let the troops assemble and recover their strength for the impending engagement. The first vehicles reached the halt point at 2000 after a day in which the only fight was made against the swamp. At 0400 next day the last truck pulled in. The rate of march had averaged about one mile an hour. Men and motors had run out of water and the troops were exhausted from the burning summer heat.

The rest of 6th Division was notified by radio of the conditions encountered and took another route. The all-day struggle with the swamp, caused by the inaccuracy of available maps and the lack of engineer equipment, prevented the column from attacking near Novoselye on 11 July.

Next morning the advance guard of the German column attacked the flank of the Russian forces, guarding the *Rollbahn*, whose presence south of a small, swampy stream had been reported the day before. After a short, sharp engagement in which both sides used tanks, the flank guard was thrown back across the river. American amphibian tanks made their first appearance on the Russian front in this action, and six of them fell victim to antitank and panzer fire at close range from a wooded area—three knocked out on land and three while crossing the small stream. Two amphibians which were still serviceable were seized by the first German troops to gain the north bank.

A bridge was constructed so that the main body of the flying column could cross the six-foot-deep, swampy stream which was not fordable. Toward 1000 the entire column was across, and after destroying more Russian light tanks, drove the enemy to a point just south of Novoselye. In the afternoon the Germans launched an all-out flank attack while another force, including a panzer battalion, hit the enemy rear. After a bitter fight the main attack caved in the enemy flank, and as the panzer thrust hit the rear, the entire Russian defense collapsed. The 1st Panzer Division took up the pursuit.

Hardly had the flying column reorganized than it was ordered to march northward to seize the bridge over the Plyussa River at Lyady and establish a bridgehead on the far bank. The order ruined all chances for a night's sleep, and early on 13 July, after three hours of rest, the march began. The advance led through many swampy places and moved forward slowly. Time and again single vehicles or whole sections of the convoy stuck in swamp or intermediate sandy areas, and motors ran hot as they were forced under the strain. Numerous halts to add water to radiators were necessary and consumed much time. At several steep places trucks had to be towed by tanks or wreckers.

South of Lyady the forward elements ran into light enemy resistance, which was quickly smashed, and the immediately following pursuit brought the bridge intact into German hands. The span was over 600 feet long, of new wooden construction, and quite sturdy. After the last remnants of enemy resistance were cleaned out of Lyady, the bridgehead was established. The objective had been reached after a march of thirty-seven miles in nine hours—a rate of slightly better than four miles an hour.

The troops had just finished a meal and completed first echelon maintenance preparatory to taking a well-earned rest when they were alerted for a new mission. The corps commander appeared and ordered the divisional column to make a quick thrust to seize and hold the two large wooden bridges over the Luga near Porechye, the so-called Gateway to Leningrad. With the order, the importance of the assignment became clear. Up to that time no German unit had been able to penetrate the Luga River line which was protected by an extensive swamp and defensive fortifications. Eighteenth Army was stalled in front of Narva to the north, and Fourth Panzer Group was held up before the city of Luga to the south.

The slogan "Open the gates to Leningrad" had a magical effect, and weariness was forgotten as unit after unit rolled toward the new objective. The road was good, and it was hoped that the sixty miles could be covered in a few hours. At the entrance to the swampy area southwest of Lake Samros hopes were dashed when the road became a swampy path of the worst type. Progress became increasingly difficult, and before dusk tanks that had tried to skirt especially bad spots and those that tried to drive through swampy ponds by main force were stuck fast. After hours of work by every officer and man to make the way passable by the use of tree trunks, boughs, planks, and the last available fascine mats, the first moor was crossed.

The column gained momentum beyond the swamp, but relief was short-lived as a burnt-out bridge loomed up to the front, its timbers still glowing. Quickly, a diversionary route was found through a neighboring village. As the leading elements approached the village, explosions were heard from all sides, followed by fires which soon engulfed the narrow road through the settlement. For the next two hours the fire made movement impossible. As the flames died the column moved slowly through the smoldering embers and falling boards. By then it was midnight and a great distance remained to be covered. Time and again radio messages were received urging speed because of the importance of the mission. With great difficulty vehicles tried to find their way in the dim light, and for a few thousand yards the column moved jerkily forward. Then real trouble started. Swamp hole after swamp hole appeared, and bridge after bridge broke under the weight of tanks and disappeared in the mud. Time and material to rebuild bridges were not available; tree trunks were gathered and thrown over the collapsed bridges until a sufficient, though precarious bearing surface was built up. This method was followed in numerous places until the hard-surfaced road near Zaruchye was reached eight hours later.

On the good road speeds up to twenty miles an hour were possible but in a short time there was another halt—the bridge across a deep swamp lake was on fire. Engineer troops rushed forward in armored vehicles and extinguished the blaze. The span was blackened, but still serviceable, and the column rolled on.

Suddenly the cry "Enemy aircraft!" was heard but the planes made no attack, and the column continued. Again the planes appeared, signalled with lights, and dropped pamphlets. "Identify yourselves or we will fire," was the Russian demand as translated by the interpreter. The march continued, nor did it halt as the pamphlets were again dropped, and the planes flew away. Their doubt was understandable. The Germans had advanced through a large, swampy area with enemy on both sides, and were deep in enemy territory. The position of the German units had given the pilots cause for suspicion, but the continuance of the column must have convinced them that the troops were Russian. This is borne out by the fact that the planes neither attacked, nor reported the presence of the column, because little less than an hour later both Luga bridges were captured without a shot being fired, the small Russian security detachments surprised and overcome, and a bridgehead was established. Shortly thereafter the last Russian in the area was rooted out of his observation post in a church tower overlooking the nearby Russian airfield. He was completely surprised and apparently had not seen the action which led to the seizure of the bridges. A German tank attack toward the airfield answered the request to "identify yourselves"—an immediate attack by planes from every airfield in the Leningrad area, including naval planes, left no doubt on that point.

In three days and nights of continual struggle against climate and terrain Flying Column Raus had advanced 160 miles, and on 14 July stood at the gateway to Leningrad, sixty-five miles from the city itself.

The movement of the flying column through the swamp area southwest of Lake Samros had so torn up the dirt roads and turned them into such a morass that the following divisions completely bogged down and required days to cover the same distance. They had to make completely new roads with tree trunks and fascine mats placed parallel to the unusable route. The first troops to get through were those of a motorcycle battalion, whose men carried their motorcycles and side cars over the swamp areas for five days and nights.

Meanwhile the flying column in the bridgehead was surrounded by three Proletarian divisions reinforced by over 100 tanks and all the air strength in the Leningrad area. Time and again the Russians attacked the bridgehead in attempts to take it at all costs. The situation was very serious. The Germans had no communication with their follow-up forces. The message which reported establishment of the bridgehead reached corps only because a signal detachment moved back about thirty-five miles to relay the news, as the German radios could not span the entire distance over the swamp. This procedure could not be repeated because the approach route had fallen to the enemy—a Russian infantry regiment reinforced by artillery hammered the German rear. The Germans could not contact their air support, whose communications center was on the move and no longer operational in its old location. [The story of the German breakout from the bridgehead area may be found in *Russian Combat Methods in World War II*, pp. 111–113 of this volume.]

II. Swampy Forests

At the close of the spring muddy season of 1942, Fourth Panzer Army attempted to destroy or rout a large enemy force which was operating between army rear and army group, and succeeded only because the Russians delayed the start of their summer campaign for almost a full month (Map 14).

Throughout the spring of that year, a force under General Belov constantly harassed the rear of Fourth Panzer Army, which was under heavy attack from the east. On 18 April, the first day of the muddy season, the main Russian attacks ceased. The Germans decided to destroy the enemy to the rear at the close of the muddy season. This decision was made even though the Germans ran the risk that Russian attacks from the east might be resumed during the large-scale mopping-up operation.

Despite this danger, army group furnished a corps with three divisions, and army made two divisions available for the undertaking. Since five divisions were not enough to completely surround Force Belov, the first phase of the operation was limited to the swampy forest of Bogoroditskoye.

The German assembly, which began in mid-May, was hampered by continuous rains which muddied roads to a great depth. No postponement to await better weather was possible, because the troops loaned by army group were scheduled for a later operation in another area.

On 24 May the Germans jumped off in a pouring rain and ran into very strong resistance, especially from the cavalry and parachute troops which were part of Force Belov. Almost worse than the enemy were the swollen rivers and muddy terrain. The large bridge at Znamenka was swept away, and the Ugra River was crossed with great difficulty. Guns sank up to the axles in mud, and as the rain continued next day even the light prime movers and horse-drawn Russian peasant carts used by the Germans bogged down. Some of the infantry slogged barefoot through the muddy water. The rain stopped on 26 May, but terrain conditions did not improve very much as the troops struggled slowly forward.

As the Russians attempted to break out of the forest toward

the west, the two German flank divisions started an envelopment which linked up at Fursovo on the afternoon of 27 May. The next few days were spent in cutting up the encircled elements of the Belov force. At this point one division reverted to army group for commitment elsewhere.

The rapidity with which the first phase was completed, plus the failure of the Russian forces facing the Fourth Panzer Army front to attack, prompted army to order the mop-up continued, with the enemy in the Yelnya area as the next objective.

The new attack was made on 3 June. On 2 June there were cloudbursts in the area of the two divisions on the right, and on the day of the attack there were numerous thundershowers. Terrain and roads were again deeply mired, and in a short time most of the tanks and all of the guns bogged down. Force Belov, which had received reinforcements by air, fought bitterly, and the German spearheads inched forward through a maze of Russian mine fields as the main bodies engaged in a series of firefights. The German armor could not gain the momentum required to carry out the army plan of quick armored thrusts which were to fan out and block the Russian forces, and the advance became a slow push instead of a quick punch.

On 5 June forces from army group thrust northward and linked up with the left division of German attack forces, cornering Russian elements in the Chashchi area and preventing their movement west. The two divisions on the right took Dorogobuszh on 6 and 7 June, and the elements of Force Belov around Chashchi were left to army group troops as the two divisions on the left continued west.

The Russians in the swampy forest and around Chashchi were no longer a factor, and the bulk of Force Belov was blocked to the west and southwest by army rear area troops. The enemy sought and found an escape route south near Yelnya, which was lightly held by two weak German security divisions. By the afternoon of 9 June 8,000 to 10,000 Russians and over 1,000 vehicles had broken through, with the apparent intention of joining with forces in the Klin forest for a drive to the east. Three divisions of the German force were now transferred to another area, and the remaining divisions plus some army rear area troops were moved quickly south to surround the Klin forest.

General Belov rallied such of his force as was in the southern part of the forest and, on the night of 16 June, broke through to the east in unknown strength. A blocking line was set up to prevent the breakout force from reaching Kirov, and German mobile units pursued and destroyed most of the Russians in the southern part of the forest. The enemy in the northern sector of the Klin forest was destroyed, and on 22 June Force Belov ceased to exist as a fighting force. Russian losses were over 4,300 dead and 9,000 captured.

The first attacks against the Fourth Panzer Army front were made on 17 June north of Kirov. The Russians had made no attempt to rescue Force Belov, and the position of Fourth Panzer Army was considerably improved.

CHAPTER 35

Russian Tactics

Entirely new to the Germans was the Russian use of forest fires as a hot weather weapon. In midsummer, when the trees were tinder-dry, the Russians attempted to delay German forces by putting forests to the torch. Not only the physical, but the psychological impact of such fires was severe. The crackling of burning trees, the acrid gray-black smoke, the increasingly unbearable heat, and the feeling of uncertainty put troops under a severe strain. Fleeing before towering sheets of flame, men would fight through mile after mile of burning forest only to be confronted by enemy bunkers and fortified positions. Ammunition dumps blew sky high and gave the impression that fierce battles were raging to the rear.

The command post of a German brigade was nearly wiped

out by a fire in a pine forest on the Luga River in July 1941.
The bivouac area was near a sand road which led through the
forest, with a cleared area thirty to sixty yards wide between
the road and the forest itself. The cleared area was overgrown
with swamp grass. All the vehicles of the brigade headquarters
and the artillery echelon were parked in the underbrush and
were well camouflaged by the high trees. The entire area was
under enemy observation, and shells continually landed within
90 to 120 yards of the camp perimeter with no hits scored on
important targets. There was no wind. In the belief that the position was secure, no thought was given to the possibility of
forest fire.

One day a strong easterly wind came up, and artillery fire
into the area ceased except toward the east, where an occasional muffled burst was heard to which no attention was paid.
Suddenly the German sentries ran out of the woods with bewildered expressions shouting "Fire! Fire!" And behind them
could be seen a high, wide wall of fire rushing and roaring
toward the command post at great speed. At the edge of the
clearing the progress of the flames slowed, but the fire crept
along through the high grass. At one point a row of trees near
the sand road burst into flames, but the threat to the wooded
area across the road did not materialize.

Brief, short orders organized the soldiers, and in a moment
everyone was battling the blaze with pick and shovel, cutting
trees, and smothering the fire with sand. Only the fact that the
command post was opposite a cleared area prevented great loss
of life and matériel.

As the danger of forest fires became apparent, bivouac areas
were more carefully selected, and precautionary measures increased. A few weeks after the fire on the Luga River, 2,000
trucks of a panzer division were dispersed in an extensive
wooded area along the only approach route to the Luga bridgehead. The forest was lightly wooded, had sandy soil with little
undergrowth, and was broken by numerous open spaces. Many
cart roads wound through the widely spaced trees to individual
parking spaces, and trucks were well dispersed in depth. Each
vehicle had room to turn in its own area, and was parked fac-

ing the road, some 200 yards distant, with drivers close by. A fire guard and signal system was set up, and a field grade officer with a small staff placed in charge of fire discipline. The evacuation plan was tested in a fire drill.

Flames broke out one day a few hundred yards north of the dispersal area and the alarm was sounded. Fanned by a light wind, the blaze advanced slowly through the woods, its progress broken here and there by the sandy open spaces. Evacuation was carried out as planned, and all vehicles were saved except a few which were trapped in the sand near the point at which the fire started.

Several square miles of forest were destroyed, and the reeking, charred hulks of the trees which still stood made the area unbearable. In any event, all natural cover was destroyed, and the site was no longer suitable for dispersal. A good fire plan saved nearly all the division's vehicles.

CHAPTER 36

Clothing, Rations, Draft Horses

I. Clothing

The clothing worn by the German soldier proved too heavy for summer. As a result, men perspired too easily, became very thirsty, and were soon caked with dirt. Only the mountain trousers and field jackets which were worn by the mountain and light infantry are practical for year round wear. For protection against dust, masks for mouth and nose and goggles should be issued. Individual equipment should include a mosquito head net. Hard-packed dirt roads cut like glass into shoe leather, and boot soles quickly go to pieces. Spare boots should be carried by every soldier.

II. Rations

Even during the first summer of the Russian campaign, the Germans were able to obtain part of their cereals and forage from local sources, although the retreating Russians burned large quantities of grain and destroyed many agricultural implements. Some grain and almost all the cattle of the collective farms were carried away in the Russian retreats.

Local procurement improved in direct ratio to the ability of the German civil government detachments to regulate cultivation and harvests. Local potato supplies were sufficient until the autumn of 1941, and thereafter they ran short. Vegetable cultivation was generally limited to small garden plots which barely covered the needs of the civilian population. Fruit was available only in the south, and then in limited quantities. Forage is plentiful in summer; sufficient pasture land is available in almost all parts of the country.

Local procurement improved after the first year of the war and the Germans were independent of grain and flour shipments from Germany. Only at the time of the great German reverses did this advantage diminish. To the very end of the war, however, the rations of the combat forces remained relatively unaffected by retrograde movements. In summer small German units used wood fires for cooking.

III. Draft Horses

During summer German horses as well as those from German-occupied western countries soon became accustomed to the Russian climate. Diseases directly traceable to the climate were extremely rare. By subjecting horses to a quarantine period before shipping them to the Russian front, communicable diseases remained practically unknown. The only exception was sporadic outbreaks of mange, which always required replacement of the entire horse strength of the unit affected.

The light and medium breeds of Western European countries proved generally satisfactory for summer duty. Heavier breeds were less hardy and needed excessive amounts of forage. It would have been better not to have used heavy breeds in Russia.

The *Panje* horses [the small native breed of Eastern Europe] proved extremely enduring, as well as easy to feed, handle, and stable. They have very hard hoofs and need not be shod for soft ground. In all seasons and in all situations this horse proved outstanding for pack and draft use. It is *the* horse for European Russia.

CHAPTER 37

Health

During summer the woods and swamplands of Russia teem with mosquitoes, including malaria carriers, which for weeks scourge man and beast. Even mosquito nets do not furnish complete protection against bites on the head and neck. Flies torment men and animals in hot weather. Many of the wooden huts in the northern and central regions are infested with vermin such as bedbugs, fleas, head lice, and body lice. The mud huts of the south are cleaner, but the dust storms of this area cause inflammation of the eyes and respiratory organs.

The health of German troops during summer remained generally good. Diarrhea was frequent during the midsummer fly plague, but seldom required hospitalization. In swamp regions there were isolated cases of malaria, and occasionally cases of cadaveric poisoning were noted. Volhynia fever appeared in 1942, some cases requiring long convalescence. Many soldiers contracted jaundice diseases which lasted two or three weeks, and sometimes required hospitalization. Gas gangrene was not infrequent. Vaccinations may be credited with preventing epidemics.

Evacuation of sick and wounded during summer was often handicapped by bad road conditions, heat, and dust. Moreover, when roads were being used for sizable troop or convoy movements, delays made evacuation trips a torture. The Germans took full advantage of air evacuation of casualties. Medical liaison aircraft often picked up casualties from right behind the front lines.

CHAPTER 38

Air Operations

Aircraft engines need special protection against summer dust. Precautions must be taken against raising dust on unpaved airfields. Dust storms in southern Russia occur immediately after the end of the spring muddy season, and visibility during takeoffs and landings is greatly reduced.

NORTH OF THE ARCTIC CIRCLE

CHAPTER 39

General

The Arctic zone of European Russia extends from the Arctic coast east of Kirkenes southward to the Bay of Kandalaksha, a distance of about 190 air miles. This area contains the southward routes of land communication from Murmansk and commands the shipping lanes to the White Sea ports. Climatic conditions in this land of midnight sun and polar night pose serious problems not only in the conduct of military operations, but also for mere survival.

North of the Arctic Circle the conduct of operations is circumscribed by time and space elements unknown in temperate regions. The midnight sun of summer, the twenty-four-hour night of winter, and the muddy transition periods of spring and autumn nullify conventional concepts of freedom of maneuver.

In the arctic a military decision communicated by an order is irrevocable. Whatever forces have been committed, whatever course of action has been initiated, an interminable time elapses between original impulse and final effect. Once started, the chain reaction must run its course. To stop, to reverse, to change direction is to run the risk of losing the initiative. First decisions must be correct. Command procedure must be adapted to the unorthodoxies of warfare in the north. Leaders at all levels, down to the squad, must make decisions far transcending the scope of their usual responsibilities.

North of the Arctic Circle the enormous land mass of European Russia, with its wide seasonal range in temperature, borders on the Barents Sea region which is moderated by the warm current of the Atlantic Drift. While the oceanic influence is strongest in the fjords on the arctic coast, the continental climate of interior Russia dominates the inland sea. A comparison of mean temperatures in northern Karelia with those in corresponding latitudes in Siberia strikingly illustrates the influence of the Atlantic Drift. In winter, for example, this warm current raises the level of mean temperatures by at least 35° F., and, though the warming influence of the sea quickly decreases toward the interior, the January mean in the inland area of the Kola Peninsula is still 18° F. higher than in corresponding latitudes of Siberia.

The mean winter temperature on the Murman coast, 13° F., is the same as the January mean at Minneapolis, Minnesota. The mean temperature during July—the hottest month—is 53° F., equal to the average May temperature on the North Sea coast of Central Europe. The comparison, however, applies only to mean values; actual day-to-day variations in temperatures are substantially greater and much more abrupt than in Central Europe. In winter a transition from thaw to severe frost may be a matter of a few hours, and the mercury may rise again just as suddenly. Winter readings on the arctic coast range from 43° to −31° F. Summer maximums on the coast vary between 75° and 85° F., with temperatures in the interior rising as high as 95° F. Night frosts are nevertheless fairly common during the subpolar summer. Only the coastal region has one whole month of temperatures above freezing—July.

Generally speaking, there are but two seasons north of the Arctic Circle: the long, cold, and dark winter; and the short summer with no night. The ideal time for large-scale ground operations is late winter, the two-month period beginning around March. At that time the days grow longer, lakes and swamps are still frozen, and ice roads can be used to move men and matériel. Early winter, right after the formation of ice, is also favorable, but an operation in early winter runs the risk of continuing into the adverse conditions of the polar night. Summer is the season least suited to ground operations. Large areas of the terrain are impassable, and the land routes of the Arctic are in the worst possible condition at this time.

Housing is virtually nonexistent in the high latitudes of European Russia. Finnish-type log huts are best for permanent quarters up to latitude 69° N., and farther north timbered dugouts are best. The Germans found collapsible wooden barracks useful throughout the north. Snow is usually too loose and powdery for igloos, and ordinary shelter tents are inadequate. The Finnish plywood tent and the Swedish cloth tent with stoves are excellent, and in emergencies snow-covered windbreaks having pine-bough roofs and heated by low reflecting fires offer good protection.

I. Infantry

Small unit actions, away from established front lines, are feasible in the desolate arctic. The limited visibility of the polar night favors operations at company, battalion, or, in exceptional cases, regimental strength. Operations are usually of limited duration, because every bit of equipment must be carried along. Only troops in excellent physical condition can be used. Fighting and marching through wasteland, forest tangle, and brush demands endurance, *esprit de corps*, and the ability to exploit every terrain feature to the utmost.

The Germans learned that only mountain and ski troops should be used in the arctic, and that such troops are most effective when organized in ski units or mobile task forces. The mobile task force should include both combat and supply elements, and a large percentage of its personnel should be equipped with skis to prevent the force from becoming roadbound. Its heavy weapons should be suitable for breakdown into one-man loads for the same reason. Ski units should be capable of at least three days of combat in any kind of terrain without resupply.

Visibility in the close terrain of the arctic is so poor that the Germans were forced to organize infantry observation battalions to direct fire of infantry howitzers and mortars. Captive balloons were also used for observation. The XXXVI Mountain Corps, on the Kandalaksha front, had a permanently attached balloon section.

FINNISH TACTICS

Finnish units in the arctic operated with what they called *Sissi* and *Motti* tactics which are planned to permit small, battle-seasoned units to fight on even terms against numerically superior forces.

Sissi combat denotes small unit actions which have the objective of hitting the enemy at one point. Each participant is briefed on the objective, and the method of execution is left up to the group.

Motti tactics are, on a small scale, analogous to the envelopment tactics of German doctrine. *Motti* uses small forces for enveloping—almost sneaking around—the enemy, and attacking and annihilating him once the ring has been closed.

Both methods take advantage of concealment, defilade, and flank protection offered by lakes and watercourses, and depend upon the self reliance, initiative, and fighting spirit of officers and men.

COMMANDO-TYPE ACTIONS

Commando-type missions in the arctic require highly trained special purpose units. Finnish troops who raided the Russian-held Murmansk railway were specially trained and equipped.

The Russians dropped parachutists, including female radio operators, behind the German lines. The presence of these Russian teams usually became known only through interception of radio messages.

II. Artillery

Artillery for the virtually roadless arctic must be light and mobile. Long-range artillery is useless in close terrain. The Germans entered the arctic campaign of World War II with divisional artillery that required ten horses for displacement and GHQ artillery that included 175mm and 280mm pieces. These were soon supplemented with light and medium mortars because the big guns had no targets at which to fire. The Germans used antitank guns to knock out enemy bunkers above ground, while the Russians used antiaircraft artillery against ground targets.

In winter, artillery can be displaced over ice. Many Russian attempts to cross ice under cover of darkness were foiled by the German method of stationing sound-ranging teams, equipped with seismological instruments, at the edge of frozen lakes to detect enemy movement.

Generally, German artillery techniques in the Arctic were no different than those used in winter in the lower latitudes of European Russia.

III. Armored Forces

Tanks and self-propelled artillery are of limited value in the arctic region of European Russia. Huge granite boulders cover the landscape, making cross-country operations impossible. Armor can be moved only on the few available roads. No German tank or self-propelled gun ever saw action north of the Arctic Circle in World War II.

The climatic conditions of the arctic can be and were mastered by the Germans who were able to learn many lessons from the Finns, but nevertheless had to go through bitter experiences of their own. The observations on polar warfare presented in this study were drawn from both sources. A number of other lessons, such as the reorganization of units for arctic warfare, special training, the flow of replacements, and Russian and Finnish combat methods are treated in Department of the Army Pamphlets No. 20-201, Military Improvisations During the Russian Campaign; No. 20-230, Russian Combat Methods in World War II; and No. 20-292, Warfare in the Far North. [For "Military Improvisations . . ." see *The Anvil of War*, ed. Tsouras (London, Greenhill, 1994). The second and third pamphlets are contained in the present volume.]

CHAPTER 40

Clothing, Equipment, Rations

I. Clothing

Winter uniforms must be designed to give protection against the extreme cold of the arctic region. The Germans found several layers of clothing better than merely thick, heavy apparel. Trousers should fit loosely enough to permit wearing of at least two pairs of drawers; trouser legs should be cut full around the calf and fit tightly about the ankle. Blouses must be large enough to be worn over extra underwear and a fur vest. Windproof, snowproof parkas are essential for ski troops. Chemical warming pads inserted under clothing add to physical comfort. Fur outer clothing is required for sentries, drivers, and others engaged in limited physical activity. Fur clothing is not suitable for ski troops because it induces perspiration; quilted uniforms are best for ski wear. A wool toque plus a felt or fur cap with ear flaps is best for winter. White camouflage coats or coveralls are essential for combat troops, and the Germans also found white face masks useful. Camouflage covers are needed for headgear.

For summer wear in the Arctic, the regular uniform plus a mosquito veil and sunglasses proved adequate.

The jagged rocks, swamps, and snow of the arctic require sturdy, waterproof boots, which should be adaptable for skiing. Only boots of top-grade, double-stitched leather give adequate protection against frostbite and trenchfoot. Russians taken prisoner complained that their U.S. army boots were not water-repellent, were inadequately stitched, and were generally unsuited to arctic wear. Ski boots must be large enough to permit extra socks and felt inner soles to be worn. The best ski boot is double-stitched with a long tongue that is securely stitched to the upper, and full leather sole under a ribbed composition sole. Soles should extend beyond the sides of the toe caps and be covered with brass inserts. Canvas leggings provide good protection in loose, deep snow.

Fur-lined boots large enough to accommodate heat packets are needed for sentries, and drivers should have felt boots. Lapp shoes, soft shoes made of reindeer hide, are needed by ski troops for tent wear.

A limited quantity of rubber boots, enough for about 15 percent of combat personnel, is required for thaw and muddy periods and for occasional summer wear.

II. Equipment

INDIVIDUAL EQUIPMENT

In the arctic the primary consideration is not how much the individual can carry, but how much he can possibly leave behind without impairing his chances for survival. The German soldier undoubtedly presented a more military appearance than the Finn or Russian, but many of the German items turned out to be mere ballast. About all the Finnish soldier carried was a rifle or submachine gun and a dagger on his belt. He carried no gas mask, no steel helmet, no bayonet.

For construction of shelter and clearance of trails combat troops need saws or hatchets that can be carried on the rucksack or pack.

The Finnish oil-filled wrist compass is best for extreme temperatures, but even this type compass is subject to serious deviations due to natural mineral deposits and the effects of the aurora borealis.

PACK EQUIPMENT

The rucksack is the best pack for the arctic. It offers less interference in passing through narrow clefts or underbush, and is more comfortable for skiing. The Germans found that forty pounds is the maximum which should be carried on lengthy missions; heavier loads impair speed and mobility.

SKI EQUIPMENT

Most ski movement in the arctic is over flat terrain, and skis should therefore be light and narrow, about two and one-half inches wide, without reinforced edges. Tips should be slightly turned, and holes provided for pull ropes. Snow should be used for camouflage, since paint dries skis and leads to damage. A simple cross-country binding is best for arctic use.

The Germans found steel ski poles with tightly woven webbing adequate, although steel deflects compasses. Ski climbers are necessary when pulling sleds or similar loads. An important item for ski troops is a small tool kit, about one per squad, for emergency repairs.

SNOWSHOES

Snowshoes are needed for personnel carrying heavy loads. The Germans found that wooden-frame snowshoes with leather webbing rendered excellent service, while snowshoes with willow webbing proved unsatisfactory.

SMALL ARMS

In the wilderness of the north, where the fire fight is usually carried on at close range, a high cyclic rate of fire in small arms is more important than accuracy. The submachine gun is ideal for arctic combat. The early type of German submachine gun frequently jammed at low temperatures and, until an improved design was brought out, German troops preferred to use the Russian model. In extreme cold air-cooled weapons are superior to water-cooled. Ammunition was usually a critical item for Germans in the arctic, and strict fire discipline was maintained. A plentiful supply of ammunition for a few weapons is better than many weapons with little ammunition. German experiences with small arms in the arctic differed little from those in Russia generally.

HAND GRENADES

The stick hand grenade was found to be unsafe in the arctic; it catches on trees and rocks, and the Germans replaced it with egg-type grenades. Deep snow renders grenade bursts harmless.

MORTARS
Ski troops effectively employed 81mm mortars. Medium mortar shells are effective, even in deep snow.

RADIO EQUIPMENT
Arctic warfare consists mostly of small unit actions, and therefore great reliance must be placed on radio communications. German equipment was too bulky and too limited in range for arctic use, and the small, powerful American-made equipment used by the Finns was much better. The component parts of signal equipment must be adaptable to pack-animal transport.

Low temperatures damage storage batteries, and the Germans cradled them between heating pads to preserve their power. Troops starting on extended missions should take freshly charged batteries.

Radio communications in the arctic are disturbed by the aurora borealis and by magnetic fields.

VEHICLES
Motor vehicles must have good ground clearance to permit passage over rocks and boulders which protrude from such roads as are found in the arctic. Roads are too narrow to allow passing, and long drives in low gear strain engines and transmissions. Starting vehicles required the same precautions as those used by the Germans in European Russia below the Arctic Circle. Fascine mats are useful in mud and snow, and adequate stocks of snow chains and sled runners are important.

German horse-drawn wagons are suited only for movement over roads, and found little use in the arctic. The two-wheeled Finnish cart drawn by one native horse is well adapted to arctic conditions. Terrain impassable for wheeled vehicles can be traversed by the *purilla*, a sledge fashioned from a forked bough or two slender tree trunks. The *purilla* can easily be pulled over rocks and mud and can carry twice the payload of a pack animal.

The Finnish peasant horse sleigh is practical for Arctic use, as are the Finnish *akja* and *loijakka*. The *akja* is a small boat-shaped sled which weighs about thirty pounds, readily glides over obstacles, and always maintains a steady balance. The *loijakka* is a larger *akja*, and is suitable for moving bulky cargo. Both are usually drawn by reindeer, though they can be pulled by ski personnel. Two men can pull 100 pounds in flat country, and three men can pull the same load in mountainous terrain.

Motorized combat sleighs armed with a heavy machine gun and carrying three to five men were extensively used by the Russians. The Germans made a few experiments with this type of equipment. The German models were successful only on frozen lakes with a thin snow cover.

III. Rations

The rigors of the arctic require foods which provide extra energy. The Germans issued extra fats and bread, while the Finns relied on extra rations of sugar. German winter food supplies consisted of frozen beef, pork, and vegetables; dehydrated potatoes and legumes; cheese and canned foods. Since the Baltic Sea was usually blocked all winter, food was stocked in advance for an entire year.

CHAPTER 41

Transportation and Troop Movements

I. Roads

There are few roads in the arctic wilderness. On the Kandalaksha front in World War II a sector extending 250 miles in a north-south direction contained only one east-west road which, by European or even Russian standards, was not a road at all.

Scouts probing into enemy territory had to mark out a route

of advance for infantry. Later, construction troops transformed the track into a wagon trail. At first, the wagon trail would be the only supply route, and thousands of hours of work were needed to widen the trail to accommodate horse-drawn vehicles and trucks. The Finns had some American road-building machinery which was most helpful.

The Germans found that a corps needed two to four battalions of engineer troops to maintain roads once they were built. Jagged rocks constantly worked to the surface, and in muddy terrain corduroy or chespaling had to be used.

During summer the numerous lakes, swamps, and rivers of the Arctic make large-scale operations entirely dependent upon man-made routes of communication. Progress is inevitably slow. Sometimes the enemy is able to control available roads so effectively that only wide envelopment, sometimes upward of ten miles laterally, can reduce his positions and open the way for the advance of friendly forces. For instance, in the summer of 1941, when the Germans were inexperienced in arctic warfare, the Russians blocked the sole route through the wilderness to Kandalaksha with a line of bunkers reinforced by artillery, while the road itself was patrolled by tanks. Any German maneuver short of wide envelopment would have meant a costly hammering at the Russian positions. Wide envelopment, however, required construction of paths for the main attack and trails for the secondary close-in envelopments. The Germans found that every one of four twelve-mile advances in the operation required four weeks of preparation for seven days of combat.

Terrain difficulties are less pronounced in winter, when frozen lakes, swamps, and rivers become good routes of communication.

SNOW AND ICE ROADS

An ice cover of three feet or more on a lake supports the heaviest loads, and the Germans made ice roads by simply clearing snow with a conventional or rotary snow plow.

Snow roads were built over swamps by removing snow and

then pouring water over the cleared surface until a frozen surface was built up. The Russians used forty-four regiments in the construction of snow roads on the Kandalaksha front in 1944. Each man was made responsible for about five square yards a day, and in this manner two sixty-five-mile stretches were completed virtually overnight.

Snow clearance was carried out and snow fences were built in the same way as in other parts of Russia.

II. Railroads

Locomotives for arctic use must be designed to burn wood, the only fuel available in high latitudes. Locomotives equipped with snow plows were used to keep railroads open, and in one instance the Germans converted a Russian tank into a motor-driven armored railway car that was equipped for double duty as a snow plow. Russian and Finnish railroads are broad gauge.

RAILROADS OVER ICE

In the winter of 1941–42 the Baltic froze over, completely cutting off German forces in Finland from sea communication with their homeland. Even the most powerful Swedish ice breakers were unable to get through. A plan for a railroad over the ice from Reval to Helsinki, similar to the Russian undertaking on Lake Ladoga, was abandoned because the ice of the Baltic was constantly in motion. The Finns attempted unsuccessfully to move motorized columns across the narrowest part of the Gulf of Bothnia in the winter of 1939–40.

III. Ski and Dismounted Movement

Ski marches are the most practical form of movement during winter. In difficult terrain with a moderately deep snow cover, the Germans found that small units should not exceed two to two and one-half miles per hour, and larger units about one and one-half miles per hour. Foot troops should move about one-half mile per hour, or about one-third mile per hour when carrying loads or evacuating casualties. Unreasonable speed on skis or on foot stimulates perspiration and induces chills and frostbite.

IV. Draft and Pack Animals

Heavy, cold-blooded horses lack the stamina required for service in the arctic. Finnish, Estonian, and the small Norwegian horses proved best for pack and draft duty. Mere windbreaks suffice for their shelter, and they readily accept thawed-out hay. Sickness among horses was rare.

The reindeer is a better work animal than the horse in the Arctic. It is efficient in deep snow, gets along with very little forage, and needs little shelter. Despite the reindeer's normal self-sufficiency, pasturage must be selected in advance of the winter season, and moss and similar forage gathered to avoid starvation in case of unusually deep snow.

Only reindeer broken to harness are suitable for military purposes. Trained reindeer are capable of pulling 150 to 250 pounds up to thirty-five miles a day, with one day's rest alternating with two days' work. As a pack animal the reindeer can carry forty to sixty pounds. In deep snow it is advisable to have skiers break trail for reindeer.

By late spring, the reindeer reverts to its wild state of roaming the forest, and does not seek contact with man until the autumn. The reindeer cannot endure a strange scent, and can be handled only by its owner. It even refused to drink except from its individual water hole.

CHAPTER 42

Health and Morale

I. Health

Lack of sunshine during the long polar night causes deficiency symptoms, and the Germans rigidly supervised daily administration of vitamins, particularly vitamin C and cod liver oil.

German troops in the Arctic suffered kidney diseases, perhaps as a result of colds, although Finnish medical authorities spoke of the presence of a communicable kidney ailment. Leptospirosis, a communicable sickness of about twelve days' duration, and having malarialike symptoms, was widespread. This disease was attributed to contact with the excrement of lemmings, molelike brown and white rodents.

The *sauna*, or steam bath, was widely used by the Germans. It toughens the body and builds up resistance to the arctic climate. Its regular use not only helps prevent colds and rheumatic ailments, but also constitutes a vital morale booster in cases of so-called Lapp-happiness, the melancholia which may be induced by the monotony of midnight sun and polar night.

German troops in the Arctic were adequately clothed, and frostbite casualties were rare. Nonbattle casualties in the arctic during the entire war amounted to only about 2 percent of total troop strength, a figure which compared favorably with that of the best health years of peacetime.

MEDICAL CARE

The Germans found that during the polar night prompt treatment and evacuation of casualties, no matter how lightly injured, was essential to speedy recovery. Early medical aid could be rendered only if skilled medical personnel were immediately available, and procedures were devised for rendering first aid on combat patrols, at strong points, and on the firing line. The difficulties were many. Casualties were often far from established positions, roads were few, and footpaths were narrow and rocky. Young, able-bodied medical officers were attached to combat troops, and only doctors able to ski were picked for such duty. Some enlisted medical personnel were given advanced training in first aid and assigned to combat troops when no medical officers were available.

EVACUATION

Finding and evacuating casualties in deep snow or close terrain is difficult, and the Germans sometimes used dogs to track down wounded or injured personnel. Evacuation was accomplished on stretcher frames slung between two horses hitched in tandem, by *purilla*, or by single-wheel mountain litter. Reindeer were also used to pull the *akja* in evacuation operations.

Emergency sleds for evacuation can be fashioned from skis, using ski adapters or ski poles. Dog teams were used for evacuation over flat or gently rolling terrain. Evacuation by litter bearers was slow, and required large numbers of personnel. Casualties located in extremely inaccessible parts of the wilderness were frequently evacuated by aircraft. In winter frozen lakes provided landing areas, and in summer lakes were used for hydroplane landings.

II. Morale

The psychological strain of the twenty-four-hour summer day and the seemingly endless polar night had an adverse effect on troop morale. The Germans found that combat personnel past their mid-twenties were more affected by arctic conditions than younger troops.

Whenever possible the Germans, to raise morale, encouraged hunting, fishing, regular use of the *sauna* bath, and provided the opportunity for soldiers to cook a meal of their own choice.

The use of distinctive insignia for arctic troops bolsters morale considerably.

CHAPTER 43

Air Operations

I. General

If proper preparations are made, air operations can be conducted the year round in the Arctic. In summer, each lake is a sheltered water landing and, in winter when frozen over, an

excellent landing field for aircraft of moderate size. With air
superiority and suitable landing areas, air transport is an important factor in supplying advanced ground units and in re-
lieving other supply facilities. Small units can be supplied by
airdrop.

It is difficult to camouflage air installations in the far north.
There are either huge wooded areas into which the profile of
an airfield cuts sharply or the terrain is bare and rocky, and
thus susceptible to enemy observation. The German remedy
in the latter instance was to hollow bunkers and hangars out
of the rocks.

Latticed wooden runways were used with success by the
Germans during the spring and autumn muddy periods. When
this was done aircraft were, of necessity, parked near the landing strips; construction of latticed taxi strips would have involved tremendous extra effort.

II. Flight

Snow covers all irregularities in the terrain during winter, ice
makes coastal boundaries indistinct, and orientation during
flight is generally difficult. Flat vapor and fog layers seen from
the air are difficult to distinguish from snow.

Warm fronts from over the Atlantic are frequent in January.
These fronts produce heavy cloud formations over land and
sea, fog that extends to high altitudes, and scattered rain or
snow. Icing and poor visibility result.

Over the Arctic Ocean ice will begin to form at 6,500 feet,
even in summer. During spring and autumn ice forms at very
low altitudes in cloud formations, and in winter this danger
increases. In winter even comparatively thin cloud layers produce snow.

In extremely cold weather, pools of very cold, dense air
form over the interior of fjords. If a strong wind blows across a
fjord at a certain angle, some of this cold air will be sucked out,
and replaced by warmer air from above. This process can cause
a violent storm in a matter of minutes, with winds of high ve-
locity accompanied by a sudden rise in temperature.

Modern air forces may revolutionize arctic warfare. In summer every lake provides a convenient water landing; in winter an extensive airfield. Anticipatory measures to use the Arctic for air operations can be taken at any time. Such preparations can counteract to some extent the difficulties presented by lack of overland routes and the inhospitality of the polar region. Even with extensive use of aircraft, the lessons presented in this study will remain valid.

Conclusions

Combat in European Russia was greatly influenced by climatic conditions. Large-scale operations and small unit actions were equally affected. The influence of climate was felt in every effort of the German military establishment, whether on land, over water, or in the air.

Climate is a dynamic force in the Russian expanse; the key to successful military operations. He who recognizes and respects this force can overcome it; he who disregards or underestimates it is threatened with failure or destruction.

In 1941 the Wehrmacht did not recognize this force and was not prepared to withstand its effects. Crisis upon crisis and unnecessary suffering were the result. Only the ability of German soldiers to bear up under misfortune prevented disaster. But the German Army never recovered from the first hard blow.

Later the German armed forces understood the effects of climate and overcame them. That victory remained beyond reach was not due to climate alone, but in great measure to the fact that the German war potential was not equal to supporting a global war. The Wehrmacht was weakened by climatic conditions, and destroyed by the overpowering might of enemy armies.

Map 10

GENERAL REFERENCE MAP
EFFECTS OF CLIMATE
ON COMBAT IN
EUROPEAN RUSSIA

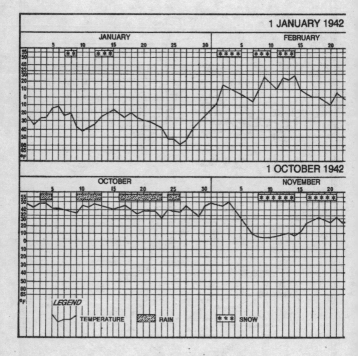

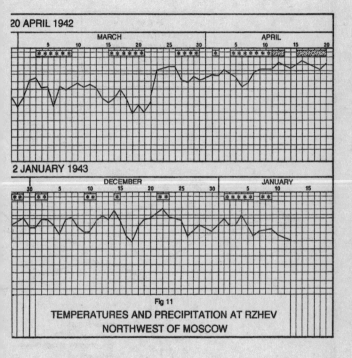

Fig 11
TEMPERATURES AND PRECIPITATION AT RZHEV
NORTHWEST OF MOSCOW

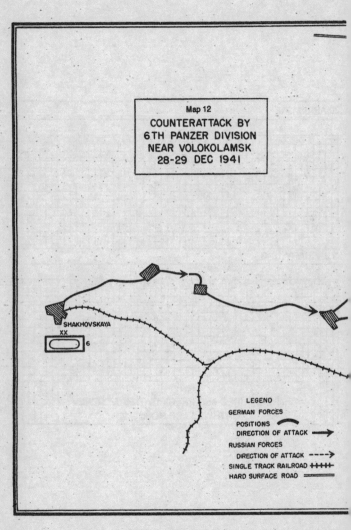

Map 12

COUNTERATTACK BY
6TH PANZER DIVISION
NEAR VOLOKOLAMSK
28-29 DEC 1941

SHAKHOVSKAYA

XX
6

LEGEND

GERMAN FORCES

POSITIONS

DIRECTION OF ATTACK ➜

RUSSIAN FORCES

DIRECTION OF ATTACK ---->

SINGLE TRACK RAILROAD ++++

HARD SURFACE ROAD ═══

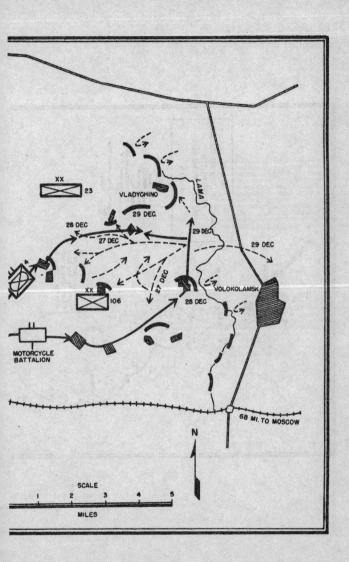

VLADYCHINO

XX
23

28 DEC

27 DEC

29 DEC

29 DEC

29 DEC

XX
106

27 DEC

28 DEC

VOLOKOLAMSK

LAMA

MOTORCYCLE
BATTALION

68 MI. TO MOSCOW

N

SCALE

1   2   3   4   5

MILES

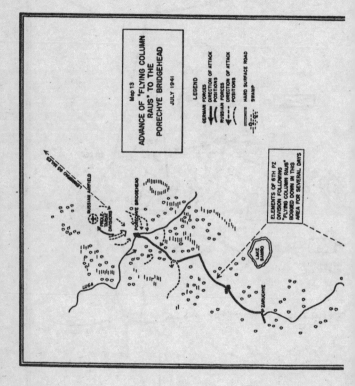

Map 13

ADVANCE OF "FLYING COLUMN
RAUS" TO THE
PORECHYE BRIDGEHEAD

JULY 1941

LEGEND

GERMAN FORCES
DIRECTION OF ATTACK
POSITIONS

RUSSIAN FORCES
DIRECTION OF ATTACK
POSITIONS

HARD SURFACE ROAD

SWAMP

LENINGRAD 60 MILES

RUSSIAN AIRFIELD

PSKOL-OSTROV
DIVISIONS

PORECHYE BRIDGEHEAD

PORECHYE

LUGA RIVER (CROSSING)

LUGA

LAKE SAMRO

ELEMENTS OF 6TH PZ
DIVISION FOLLOWING
"FLYING COLUMN RAUS"
BOGGED DOWN IN THIS
AREA FOR SEVERAL DAYS

ZARUCHYE

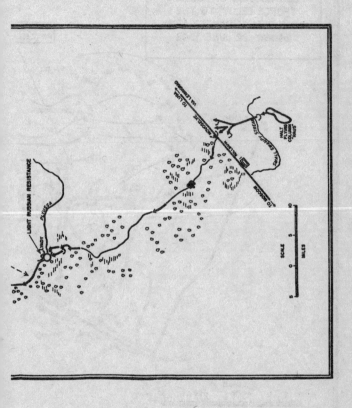

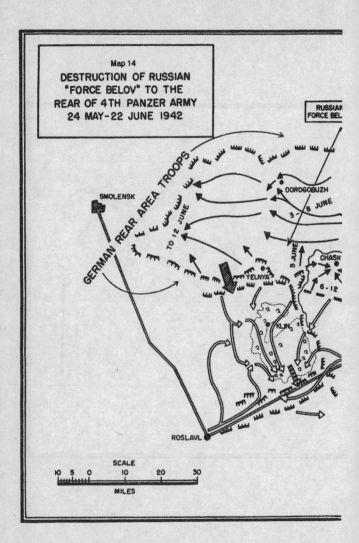

Map 14

DESTRUCTION OF RUSSIAN
"FORCE BELOV" TO THE
REAR OF 4TH PANZER ARMY
24 MAY-22 JUNE 1942

RUSSIAN
FORCE BEL

SMOLENSK

DOROGOBUZH

3 - 8 JUNE

GERMAN REAR AREA TROOPS

TO 12 JUNE

5 JUNE

CHASH

6-12

YELNYA

KLIN

ROSLAVL

SCALE

10 5 0   10   20   30

MILES

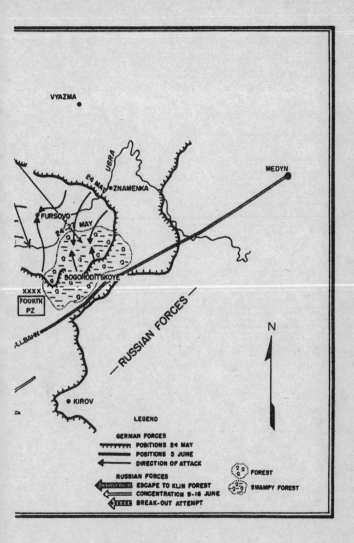

VYAZMA

MEDYN

UGRA

24 MAY   ZNAMENKA

FURSOVO

24-27 MAY

BOGORODITSKOYE

XXXX
FOURTH
PZ

...LLBAHN

— RUSSIAN FORCES —

KIROV

N

LEGEND

GERMAN FORCES

⊥⊥⊥⊥⊥⊥   POSITIONS 24 MAY
◄━━━━━   POSITIONS 5 JUNE
◄━━━━━   DIRECTION OF ATTACK

RUSSIAN FORCES

◄▭▭▭▭   ESCAPE TO KLIN FOREST
◄━━━━   CONCENTRATION 9-16 JUNE
◄□□□□   BREAK-OUT ATTEMPT

FOREST

SWAMPY FOREST

PART THREE

Warfare in the Far North

BY GENERAL DER INFANTERIE
DR. WALDEMAR ERFURTH
Wehrmacht Representative to
Finnish Headquarters

Preface

Warfare in the Far North was prepared by Dr. Waldemar Erfurth at the EUCOM Historical Division Interrogation Inclosure, Neustadt, Germany, late in 1947. Dr. Erfurth represented the German Armed Forces High Command at Finnish Headquarters from June 1941 until the Finnish surrender in September 1944. He attained the rank of lieutenant general (General der Infanterie) in the German Army, and was a United States prisoner of war when this study was written.

Like all publications in the GERMAN REPORT SERIES, this is a translation from the German and presents the views of the German author without interpretation by American personnel. Throughout this pamphlet, Finnish and Russian combat methods, organization, and equipment are compared to those of the German Army. The descriptions of Finnish climate and terrain involve comparisons with that of Germany.

In the preparation of this revised edition, the German text has been retranslated, and certain changes in typography and chapter titles have been made to improve clarity and facilitate its use. The author's views, whatever they may be, find the same expression in the following translation as they do in the original German.

Those interested in a detailed history of the war in Finland, especially its political and diplomatic aspects, are referred to Dr. Erfurth's book *Der Finnische Krief 1941–1944* (Wiesbaden, 1950). No English translation is available at this time.

Department of the Army
October 1951

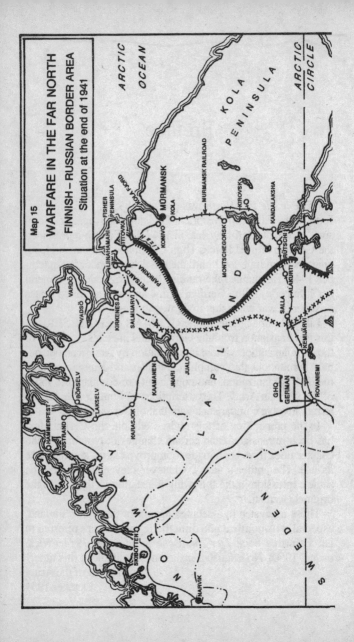

Map 15

WARFARE IN THE FAR NORTH
FINNISH–RUSSIAN BORDER AREA
Situation at the end of 1941

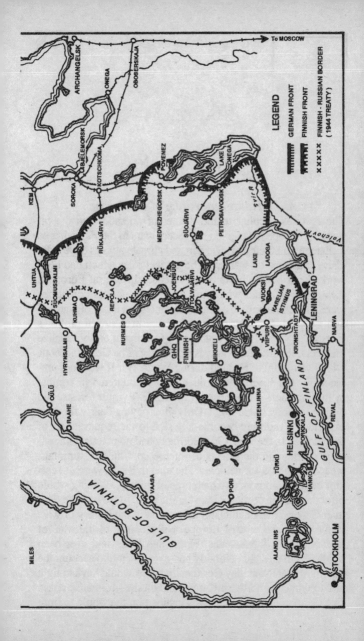

CHAPTER 44

The Climate

I. German Ignorance of the Arctic

The features peculiar to the theater of operations in the far north of Europe have given the recent wars in the Finnish area a character all their own. Terrain and climate always have a decisive influence on warfare. The tactical rules which had been worked out on the basis of experiences in central European theaters of war and which are adapted to normal conditions were applicable only to a limited extent in the cases of Karelia[1] and Lapland. In many respects warfare in the Arctic follows rules of its own. The German High Command did not realize this fact until after the war was in progress. The German troops which were sent to Finland during World War II were not prepared for the special difficulties they encountered in combat in that trackless wilderness, in the endless virgin forests, and during the long arctic night. Only after paying dearly for their experiences did they become adjusted to the requirements of that theater. In the year 1941 Germany had no practical knowledge concerning the effects of intense cold on men, animals, weapons, and motor vehicles. The men in Berlin were not certain in their minds as to which type of military clothing would offer the best protection against arctic cold. In the past the German General Staff had taken no interest in the history of wars in the north and east of Europe. No accounts of the wars of Russia against the Swedes, Finns, and Poles had ever been published in German. Nobody had ever taken into account the possibility that someday German divisions would have to fight and to winter in northern Karelia and on the Murmansk coast. The German General Staff was inclined on the whole to limit its studies to the central European region. Only a few men (for instance, Baron von der Goltz, Count von Schlieffen, Baron von Freytag-Loringhofen) had attempted to have a larger area covered in the study program of General Staff officers. However, in so doing, they had encountered the opposition of the older generation which had been brought up in the tradition of von Moltke and which considered it sufficient to study the countries immediately surrounding Germany. In the absence of any stimulation on the part of the leaders of Germany's foreign policy toward more extensive studies, the northern regions of Europe remained practically unknown to the German soldier. From the days of Count von Schlieffen to the year 1940, the German General Staff in its studies on strategic concentrations had no longer concerned itself with the problem of an offensive campaign into Russia. The fact that the German soldier, finding himself involved quite suddenly in an offensive against the Murmansk railroad, was able after a certain period of adjustment to accustom himself to the peculiarities of the theater and make the best of the difficult conditions encountered in that type of warfare is proof of the great adaptability of the German soldier and is deserving of highest recognition. The Finns and the Russians were thoroughly familiar with the organization, clothing, equipment, armament, and troop training methods best suited for the theater situated between the Gulf of Finland and the Arctic Ocean, as well as with the most suitable tactics to be employed. Both are good and tough soldiers, knowing by sure instinct what has to be done in this terrain and climate. When the German soldier first came to the Arctic, he was a tenderfoot, but by following the example of his Finnish brother-in-arms he reduced the differences between himself and his model with comparative speed.

Because of the valuable qualities of the Finnish soldier, all German commanders on the Finnish-German front tried to have Finnish units attached to them whenever independent missions were assigned to the German units. How long Mannerheim wrangled with General Dietl at the beginning of the year 1943 about the return of the four Finnish battalions which had remained under the command of the German Twentieth

Mountain Army! The endless Karelian forests had a discomforting, indeed a downright sinister, effect upon the German soldiers, many of whom had been raised in cities. They were depressed by the apparent limitlessness of the woods. On the other hand, the Finn who had grown up in the forests did not even notice the difficulties which made life hard for the German soldiers and, moreover, always knew how to act and what to do. After the heavy fighting of the summer and fall of 1941 in the Suojaervi area, near Kestenga, near Salla, and on the Liza, during which the German divisions suffered considerable losses without reaching their objective, the morale of some of the German troops had lowered noticeably. The realization that the prospects of going on furlough to Germany were becoming steadily poorer because of the crisis affecting the Finnish railroads and the freezing-over of the Baltic Sea had a depressing influence upon the German troops. Since the mail service became increasingly slower and more irregular because of winter weather conditions, a feeling of isolation was spreading among the soldiers. During that period German officers would occasionally make remarks more or less as follows: "The German soldier is anxious to leave these never-ending Karelian woods; with half the losses, the Finns will accomplish twice as much here as the Germans."

Correctly interpreting this situation, the German Army High Command turned in the fall of 1941 to Finnish General Headquarters for assistance. This was willingly and generously granted by Marshal Mannerheim. Beginning in the winter of 1941–42, courses in winter warfare of approximately twenty days' duration took place regularly in Finland. The Finns provided the instructor personnel, the school troops, and the school facilities for these courses. The students (mostly officers, but also some noncommissioned officers) were taken from the German eastern front. The instruction courses were held at several places in southern Finland: at the Kankaanpaa troop training center near Pori, at Camp Parola near Haemeenlinna, and in the Tuusola Civic Guard School near Helsinki. The German troop training center at Gross-Born was utilized on only one occasion when, owing to the freezing of the Baltic

Sea in the beginning of 1942, it was impossible to move the Germans participating in these courses to Finland by boat. In this one instance the Finnish instructors were taken to Germany by airplane.

In the beginning the purpose of these courses was training in winter warfare, since the particularly hard winter of 1941–42 had caused considerable losses and critical reverses on the German eastern front. When the Germans requested that these courses be continued also in the summer in order to make the greatest possible number of German officers acquainted with the Finnish theater of war, the curriculum was extended to include training in combat in woods. During these courses, Finnish instructors with Finnish school troops at their disposal trained German regimental and battalion commanders in the command of these units in the dense forest. Also younger officers were trained in the conduct of combat patrols and long-range reconnaissance missions. Moreover, courses in long-distance skiing were held during the cold season.

These courses took into account that the largest part of Finland and the bordering regions to the east, as well as the northern part of Russia, constitute continuous wooded regions which are for the most part completely unexplored, and that the northern winter, of a severity to which the central European is not accustomed (deep snow, all waterways solidly frozen, very low temperatures, long nights), lasts through the greater part of the year.

II. Protective Measures of the Finns

The Finn, who learns to use an axe and a saw from childhood on, was able to make use of the means available in the woods and to spend the night in the open even in the most severe cold. The clothing of the Finnish soldier (fur cap with ear and neck protector, warm underwear, woolen scarf, fur gloves, warm footgear[2]) offered good protection against the cold. The Finnish tents, which were made of plywood and could be heated, proved to be very satisfactory. They could be put up quickly and moved easily. In wintertime these tents were set up for even a rest of but a few hours. When tents could not be set up, the Finnish troops built log fires and windbreaks in the open very rapidly. Whenever a pause of several days occurred during an advance, barrack-like huts were constructed with amazing speed. These offered protection against the cold and, in case the troops stayed in the same place for some time, were improved until they were quite comfortable. Thanks to the background and appropriate training of the troops, frostbite was practically unknown among the Finnish soldiers. In December 1941, when news reached Finland about the heavy losses the German Army was suffering in Russia because of the severe winter, Marshal Mannerheim made the following remarks on the subject: "Losses among the troops because of frost weigh heavier on the commander's conscience than battle casualties. Because in this case there always remains the disturbing feeling that losses due to the cold might possibly have been avoided if greater precautions had been taken."

The Finnish Supreme Commander could not understand why the High Command of the German Armed Forces and the Army administrative agencies had not made greater efforts in proper season to increase the German Army's ability to withstand the arduous Russian winter. The impression which Mannerheim, in his capacity as a general of the Czarist Army, had gained of German soldiers on the Russian front in the First World War had given him a high respect for the careful and timely planning of the administrative agencies of the German Army. All the less could he understand the crisis which materialized in the winter of 1941–42 on the German eastern front, especially since he was not aware of the causes which had brought it about, such as, for example, the insufficient transport capacity of the railroads.

On the Finnish front, too, during the first year of joint warfare, many difficulties arose among the German troops which had an unfavorable effect upon the course of the war in the year 1941. However, the arctic climate was not the only peculiarity of the northern theater of war which made life hard for the German soldier. In comparison with the unhappy experiences of the German forces in Russia which resulted from the sudden beginning of winter, the German Army in Lapland was actually able to adjust itself to the requirements of the climate in the Far North with comparative speed and without great losses. The troops were able to cope in a surprisingly efficient manner with the inclemencies of the weather, the great variations in temperature (ranging from 95° F. in the summer to −40° F. in the winter), the heavy snowstorms, the long polar night, and the constant daylight in the summer. The ability of the German soldier to adjust to conditions on the Lapland front was enhanced by the facts that (a) the change-over from offensive to defensive in the fall of 1941 had been executed at such an early date that the construction of fortifications had progressed sufficiently by the time winter started; (b) there was an abundance of wood in the Karelian forests; and (c) supplies from Germany (winter clothing, warm quilted trousers, quilted blouses with hoods, snow shirts, a second blanket for every man, and good rations rich in vitamins) reached the troops on time despite the transportation crisis which materialized in Finland during the winter of 1941–42. There were difficulties only in the Murmansk sector, where the construction of fortified winter quarters in the rocky subsoil of the tundra was extremely difficult. Moreover, it was necessary to bring the required wood from great distances to the treeless coast of the Arctic Ocean. This instance once more proved the absolute necessity of making intensive and timely preparations for winter in the Far North. Nevertheless, it may be said that once the German troops became acclimated to Lapland their physical condition was and continued to be entirely satisfactory.

Notes

1. Karelia is a somewhat vague regional designation that applies to the area north and west of Lake Ladoga and west and south of the White Sea. The area was roughly bisected by the old (pre-1939) Russo-Finnish frontier, but most of it is now within the Karelo-Finnish Republic of the U.S.S.R.
2. In wintertime the Finnish soldier wears boots of a larger size than in summertime so that he can wear two pairs of woolen socks.

CHAPTER 45

The Terrain

I. General Characteristics

The peculiarities of the Finnish theater of war that caused the greatest combat difficulties were the absolute lack of roads and the close character of the terrain which, with its vast zone of virgin forests, is so very different from the European landscape in latitudes farther south. The Karelian woods are under no forestry management such as is commonly applied in central Europe. The primeval forest is the result of natural reseeding. Old and young stands of trees are intermingled and frequently give rise to impenetrable thickets. This boundless forest is virtually unexplored. Throughout the trackless, desolate region deepest solitude and deathly silence reign supreme. Lakes, swamps, moors, and loose rock are characteristic of the Karelian landscape. Although on the Karelian Isthmus (the corridor between the Gulf of Finland and Lake Ladoga) and in the area between Lake Ladoga and Lake Onega the woods in some places are very dense and include old stands of trees, the timber becomes lighter and weaker the farther one goes north, until at last only scattered trees and bushes extend upward from an inextricable tangle of large rocks. In the Far North, rocky ground covered with reindeer moss, lichens, and blueberry, cranberry, and juniper bushes predominates in the wilderness. In the part of Karelia between Lake Onega and the White Sea, the tree line is about five hundred feet above sea level. Birches grow on the slopes between the conifer-covered dales and the bare tops of the mountains, which are less than a thousand feet high. The conifers disappear completely north of the Arctic Circle. This is a favorable region for birch forests, so characteristic of Lapland, with their short trunks often branching out like bushes. In the Petsamo region the completely treeless tundra extends up to the coast, where it changes into bare shingle along the Arctic Ocean.

This is an heroic landscape which has remained completely untouched by modern civilization. Since the dim past little or nothing has changed there. As in those days of long ago described in the songs of the Finnish epic, the "Kalevala," the hunter and fisher, the Lapp nomad with his reindeer herds, the individual loving solitude lives in the primeval wilderness, constantly struggling with the forces of nature.

II. Effect upon Operations

Experiences gained during the Finnish-Soviet Winter War of 1939–40 had furnished certain definite indications for the conduct of operations in Karelia and Lapland. The course of this war had taught the following lessons:

1. The natural conditions along the frontier between Finland and the Soviet Union, the extremely extensive, pathless wasteland of the frontier region, the uneven terrain covered with loose rock and consequently passable only with difficulty, and the negligible development of roads are not suited to operations with large masses of troops of low mobility. Over broad stretches of country it is in many cases impossible to conduct operations involving large organizations, and in some instances it is pointless.
2. From the strategic point of view the importance of the different sectors of the frontier region varies widely. Gain or loss of areas far removed from any kind of communication is of no decisive importance to the further course of war.
3. The characteristics of terrain and climate in the Far North are such that winter is the more favorable season for offensive campaigns, while summer is more suitable for defensive operations. Early and late winter are particularly favorable for attack operations; mid-winter with its deep snow is a less appropriate time for offensive warfare.
4. The transitions from winter to summer and from summer to

winter constitute the muddy periods when use of the roads temporarily ceases or is greatly limited. The muddy period in the fall does not last as long as that in the spring. Because of the hard granitic soil of Finland and Russian Karelia, the roads usually dry out much quicker there than in southern Russia. In the Far North the principal concern is the melting of the snow which has fallen during the winter. The Finns have great experience and have developed special techniques (snowplows, road graders, etc.) to keep the main highways free from snow and open throughout the winter for the use of mail trucks and buses. The effect of brief periods of rain, which in Russia proper turn the roads into a hopeless condition, is negligible in Finland and the border area. During the muddy season, especially in the spring, there is no chance for effective air support because it is impossible for units of any considerable size to take off from the completely flooded airfields. Provisions were made to maintain flying operations on a limited scale through installation of latticed wooden runways. In these cases it was necessary to park the airplanes either on the runways or in their immediate vicinity. Such a procedure cannot be applied for organizations of any considerable size unless one accepts the necessity of expending enormous amounts of material and labor in the construction of latticed wooden runways and taxiing strips to the hardstands. Since both opponents were faced by identical conditions, air force activity, with only a few exceptions, was almost completely suspended on both sides during the muddy season.

The period between the Winter War of 1939–40[1] and the outbreak of the Finnish War against Russia in June 1941 was too short and the German Armed Forces High Command was too involved in other problems at that time to make possible the application of Finnish experiences to the advantage of the German troops. It was soon realized though that the horse-drawn and the motorized organizations of the German Army and the Waffen-SS which had been sent to Finland were too cumbersome. The Finnish Army, highly mobile both in summer and in winter because of its economical but very appropriate organization, would have been a good model for a suitable reorganization of the German troops operating in Finland. Fortunately, Dietl's mountain corps, which had been brought from northern Norway and assigned the missions first of occupying the Petsamo area and later of attacking in the direction of Murmansk, was equipped with pack animals like all German mountain troops. Even though the Karelian area certainly cannot be considered as mountainous terrain, this type of organization proved very satisfactory since the pack animals were able to proceed off the roads and were not susceptible to the cold. As a consequence, during the later course of the war the German organizations selected for duty in Finland consisted preferably of mountain troops. Nevertheless, it should be pointed out that even the trains of the mountain troops were much too bulky and cumbersome for the conditions prevailing in Finland.

During the Winter War the Finns gained experience in defensive operations conducted during the season of the year least suited for such operations. In World War II[2] Finnish and German troops took the offensive at the beginning of July 1941 along the long front between the Gulf of Finland and the Arctic Ocean. Not only during this war of movement but also throughout the entire duration of the immediately ensuing war of position, all operations in the Finnish theater in World War II took place in the same regions as did the Winter War. This facilitated the collection of certain experiences gained during both wars. The Winter War experiences of the Finnish Army were fully confirmed during World War II.

III. Individual Sectors

In both wars the attackers as well as the defenders concentrated their main forces on the Karelian Isthmus and in the area northeast of Lake Ladoga. There never were any doubts or differences of opinion at Finnish General Headquarters about the strategic importance of the Karelian Isthmus and its suitability for the operations of strong forces. The road net in that region is well developed and in good repair so that operations by strong forces can be carried out on the Karelian Isthmus in both summer and winter.

The terrain estimate of the area northeast of Lake Ladoga was not quite so clear to the Finns. During the Winter War comparatively weak Finnish forces by bold counterattacks stopped the advance of the Red Army immediately northeast of Lake Ladoga and in the wooded and lake area of Tolvajaervi. The German Army High Command wanted the main body of the Finnish forces to advance in this region in the summer of 1941. The Finns, however, felt that the number and condition of the roads in Russia Karelia northeast of Lake Ladoga would be inadequate for the advance and the supply of troops in any considerable numbers. This view proved to be erroneous in the course of the Finnish summer offensive in the direction of the Svir and Petrosavodsk. Very soon there was a lack of divisions rather than roads. Additional forces had to be brought by rail from the Karelian Isthmus, where they could be spared, to the region northeast of Lake Ladoga. Thanks to this most timely reinforcement, the objective of the Finnish offensive towards the Svir was reached in a swift operation. Farther north on the Finnish eastern border, Finnish and German troops pressed forward on the same roads over which the Red Army had invaded Finland during the Winter War. The following are the roads which run from the Murmansk railroad in the direction of the Finnish border and which were used by the Finns and the Germans:

1. The Kotshkoma–Rukajaervi road, the continuation of which via Repola toward Nurmes or Kuhmo had been inadequate for the Finns for moving troops and supplies in the year 1941. This inadequacy made it necessary to build a parallel military road for rather long distances.
2. The Kem–Uhtua–Suomussalmi road.
3. The Louhi–Kestenga–Kuusamo road (this road had been spared by the Russians in the Winter War).
4. The Kandalaksha–Alakurti–Salla–Kemijaervi road.
5. The "Russian" road along the Arctic coast, which had been built after the Moscow Treaty of 1940 from Konivo on the

Kola Fjord via Titovka up to the Finnish border and which from the summer of 1941 had been improved in the zone of the German troops. (The Russian Winter War invasion in the Petsamo region did not come from Murmansk but from the Fisher Peninsula.)

Out of this arose the well-known World War II designations of sectors:[3]

1. Rukajaervi (Kotshkoma),
2. Uhtua (Kem),
3. Kestenga (Louhi),
4. Salla (Kandalaksha), and
5. Petsamo (Murmansk).

The regions between these sectors, entirely remote from any traffic, remained completely untouched by the war. No attempt was made by either side to penetrate deeper into the vast, track-less wastes of the border marshes. After the war of movement had given way to position warfare, Russian partisan detach-ments and Finnish *Sissi*[4] patrols attempted at times to encircle the flank of one sector or another in order to interrupt the flow of supplies or to rouse the sparse population of the border zone. But these undertakings only bore the stamp of minor warfare and were of no consequence to the main task.

IV. Significance of the Murmansk Railroad

The Murmansk railroad played a very special role in World War II. It was the most important strategic objective for the Finns and Germans; only by seizing it could the Soviet Union be cut off from supplies coming from the U.S.A. and Great Britain over the shortest route by way of the Arctic Ocean.

The fight for the Murmansk railroad disclosed the undeni-able superiority of the Red Army over the Germans and Finns in the realm of transportation. The fact that all offensive plans of the Finns and the Germans came to naught in the region be-tween Lake Onega and the Arctic Ocean can be traced in the last analysis to the existence of the railroad and its undisturbed operation by the Russians. The importance of this fact warrants our taking a look at the transportation situation in the Russo-Finnish border region.

The railroad from Petrosavodsk to Murmansk was built during World War I and was a continuation of the Leningrad–Petrosavodsk line constructed back in 1899. As the means of communication with the only ice-free Russian harbor on the Murmansk coast, it was not only of great importance in marine commerce but also in a war against Finland it assured the Red Army of a great strategic superiority over its Finnish neighbor. Primarily, it enabled the Russian Army to assemble and shift troops rapidly along the eastern frontiers of Finland. The automobile road from Rovaniemi to Petsamo (the so-called Arctic Highway), built by the Finns and completed in 1929, had promoted tourist traffic to Finnish Lapland, but for military transportation it could not compare at all with the capacity of the Murmansk railroad. The northernmost Finnish railroad running from Kemi (on the Gulf of Bothnia) via Rovaniemi to Kemijaervi was the least efficient of the Finnish railroads.

The efficiency of the Murmansk railroad during the last war was estimated as follows: The railroad bed was not good and repairs were often necessary. But the Russians had the required personnel and matériel ready at numerous points for rapid repairs. The average speed of the trains was twenty to twenty-five miles per hour. The Leninigrad–Petrosavodsk line was double-tracked. At the time of the Finnish surrender (1944) the intended double-tracking of the rest of the line had not yet been carried out. The average daily traffic on the Soroka–Kandalaksha line in the summer of 1942 amounted to ten to fifteen trains in two sections in both directions. An increase up to forty trains in two sections daily is alleged to have been possible. Bituminous coal was the fuel generally used for the locomotives. In 1939 the line was electrified from Kandalaksha to Murmansk. The average speed on this stretch is said to have been forty miles per hour.

By the laying of a new single-track railroad in 1938–41 from Soroka via the region south of the White Sea to Oboserskaya (on the Archangelsk–Moscow railroad), the Murmansk railroad was connected with the Archangelsk railroad and thereby to the railroad net of inner Russia, greatly increasing its strategic possibilities. When enemy action impeded railroad traffic at any point along the Leningrad–Soroka line, the front in the Far North up to the arctic coast could always be supplied by making use of the new Oboserskaya–Soroka railroad. That was the case, for example, in the summer of 1941, after the Finns had first cut the Murmansk railroad at the Svir River, and later had taken possession of the entire line from the Svir via Petrosavodsk to Medvezhegorsk and beyond. The supply of the Soviet front in the Far North as well as Anglo-American lend-lease shipments to Russia remained completely undisturbed by the loss of the southern portion of the Murmansk railroad.

As far as is known the Finnish-German offensive of 1941 at no point reached its objective—the vital northern stretch of the Murmansk railroad. Soviet resistance could not be broken despite repeated attempts; but the Red Army, which eventually passed to the offensive, did not fare much better. In stubborn and costly fighting the most that could be gained was small improvements of position, but at no point was a decisive success achieved.

After the Germans and Finns had failed to gain possession of the Murmansk railway in 1941, and after Operation LACHSFANG[5] (Salmon Catch) of 1942 had to be abandoned as too ambitious, other means were tried to reach the same objective. All the expedients which were employed, namely, bombing of railroad bridges and viaducts by the Luftwaffe, frequent air attacks on Murmansk and other railroad stations, and demolitions by combat patrols or by parachuted commando troops, led to no lasting result. Only slight damage was ever inflicted. This the Russians were able to repair after a few hours' work. The strategic problem—the destruction of the railroad either completely or for a long time—was never solved.

V. The Finnish Transportation Network

The transportation situation of the Finns was quite critical during the war. The Finnish Chief of Transportation, Colonel (later

General) Roos, was an outstanding specialist in the field of transportation. He did what was possible; nevertheless, serious crises arose, especially at the end of 1941.

All personnel and the bulk of the freight transported to and from Finland moved over the Baltic Sea. The German army in Lapland was supplied for the most part by water via Kirkenes and Liinahamari. Lesser quantities went via the Baltic Sea, the Finnish railroad, and then overland by the Arctic Highway. A small portion of supplies to the front, evacuation to the rear, and small numbers of replacements went via Sweden.

Transport by water via the Baltic was seriously curtailed and delayed by Russian U-boats, mines, the necessity of convoys, shortage of tonnage, lack of buoys, inadequate storage facilities in the Finnish harbors, and shortage of unloading personnel. From the middle of January the Baltic Sea freezes for a rather long period, so that shipping stops altogether at this time of the year.

Railroad transportation in Finland suffered not only from shortage of rolling stock (a result of the expansion of the railroad system and of the increasing demands made by the war) but also from the low and differing capacities of lines and stations, the lack of shunting yards and of sufficient Finnish railroad personnel, as well as from delays in the unloading of cars, the effects of the cold upon woodburning engines, and partisan activity.

The German Army command was able to deliver some serviceable broad-gauge rolling stock captured from the Russians. On the other hand, Finnish requests for the construction of new railroad equipment in Germany could not be met.

The northern line from Rovaniemi to the front was a special headache to the Finnish and German railroad authorities. The line was originally intended to handle the traffic of the primitive economy of a thinly populated and self-sufficient region. The Finns worked on this line continually during the entire duration of the war to increase its capacity. The section from Oulu via Kemi to Rovaniemi had been improved. To relieve pressure on the northern line, the Twentieth Mountain Army with its own labor force and matériel built the

Hyrynsalmi–Kuusamo field railroad, about 200 miles long.
The work, which was to facilitate the supply of the right flank
corps of the Twentieth Mountain Army (at first the Finnish III
Corps, later the German XVIII Corps), was considerably delayed because of the lack of skilled labor and because the difficulties of building the railroad had been underestimated.

The German and Finnish troop trains always moved over
Finnish railroads quickly and smoothly. The Finnish railroad
personnel showed itself resourceful and very skillful in impro-
vising. German soldiers on furlough went through Turku in the
summer and via Hanko in winter. The bottleneck was not in
railroad transportation but in sea transport. Russian U-boats,
mines, lack of shipping, and other things caused this bottleneck. A monthly average of about 25,000 Germans on furlough
was carried to and from the Reich.

Despite all improvements and expedients, the capacity of
the Finnish railroads imposed a limit on any large-scale increase in the number of German troops located in Lapland, a
limit which could not be exceeded because of the problems in-
cidental to supplying the troops. To be sure, under favorable
weather conditions and during the long days of the arctic summer the Finnish railroad authorities were able to get more out
of the low-capacity northern line for an operation of brief duration. An increase in the number of troops and especially
horses would have led to reductions in the level of supplies
on the German front in Lapland. Railroad construction troops
and material would have to be assembled in advance of any
extensive and lengthy operation in order to first build the
lines that would be required. Only with considerable German help would this have been possible.

Oversea transportation to and from Finland was considerably interfered with by enemy action during the war. Besides a
total loss of Finnish and German shipping sunk in the Baltic,
ships repeatedly ran aground because there were no buoys.
These ships were then laid up for lengthy periods. Ships had to
be used as escort vessels for convoys because of the presence
of Russian naval vessels based at Kronshtadt and Leningrad.
This resulted in loss of their services as transport or supply

ships. It was unfortunate that the German-Finnish offensive of 1941 did not succeed in permanently knocking out the Soviet naval bases.

Notes

1. The Winter War began 30 November 1939 and ended 13 March 1940.
2. Finland declared war on Russia on 26 June 1941 and sued for peace on 19 September 1944.
3. The designation was derived mostly from the main locality in the German-Finnish zone, sometimes also from the objective on the Murmansk railroad (designated in parentheses).
4. Detachments composed of border population familiar with conditions in the wilderness.
5. LACHSFANG was an elaborate plan for a junction of the Finns and German Army Group North in the area southeast of Lake Ladoga.

CHAPTER 46

Organization and Tactics

The course of the fighting for the Murmansk railroad confirmed the lessons of the Winter War and seemed to justify the following conclusions:

1. Warfare in primeval wilderness and in the tundra is tied to the few available roads. This is especially true in the summer. When the situation required an encircling movement off the road in the border area, time-consuming road construction work became a prerequisite, requiring not days but weeks. Decisions once made could not be reconsidered. Once troops had started advancing through the wilderness or once the order had been given committing them, nothing could be changed. The movement had to run to its completion. Everything required endless time to bring results.

2. The most favorable season of the year for a war of movement in high latitudes is the winter. The attempt to reach the Murmansk railroad would perhaps have been successful if it had been undertaken, as Mannerheim had suggested, at the beginning of March and with sufficient forces. In the Far North the winter roads play an important role. Running over the ice of lakes and moors, they are the nature-given traffic communications in the long winter. The winter road over the ice of Lake Ladoga played an especially important role during the war; over it went the supplies for besieged Leningrad and the evacuation of a considerable portion of the Leningrad population. Neither the Germans nor the Finns were able to interfere with these movements. Overland communication in Finland for seven to eight months of the year takes place by sleigh, the method preferred for use in winter on the snow-covered ice. The ice covering usually does not melt until June, which is later than the snow thaws on land roads.

I. Ski Troops

During early and late winter, troops equipped with skis and akjas can operate off the roads and bring along all that is really needed for existence and for combat; but they must leave behind everything that cannot be carried easily through primeval forest or rocky wilderness. The superior skill of the Finnish troops in covering long distances gave them a high mobility and consequently a decided ascendency over troops of the Red Army in the Winter War. The Soviet command recognized the great importance of using skis in fighting in the Far North. According to Finnish accounts, the Russians formed and trained special elite ski units in Siberia and concentrated them before World War II on the eastern border of Finland. These Soviet troops soon acquired great skill and during the war became almost as good as the Finnish ski units, whose marching speed is surprisingly great even in especially difficult terrain. Combat operations, even in trackless regions, are executed much faster on skis in winter than on foot in summer. The open flanks of the Finnish-German sectors between Lake Onega and the Arctic

Ocean could only be effectively protected by mobile Finnish ski patrol detachments. The fight against the Soviet partisans was carried on by the Finns with the passion of skilled and experienced hunters. It was most successful in winter when the enemy's tracks could be followed in the snow, and he could be brought to bay.

The strength of the Finnish soldier lies in individual combat. The Finns possess an infallible instinct for finding their way in the dense growth of the pathless wilds. They are accurate trail readers and move noiselessly in the woods. Nothing is heard or seen of Finnish troops whether resting or marching, even from the closest proximity. Terrain training is of a very high order. A special technique for movement through woods has been developed and practiced so that the troops advance quickly, in the right direction and without losing contact. A Finnish company moves in the primeval forest just as smoothly and unerringly as a German company in the open landscape of central Europe. All Finns are enthusiastic hunters and sport lovers and fighting wakens in them all their hunting instincts. The aggressiveness of the troops is very keen. Their achievements in long-range combat patrolling cannot be surpassed.

II. Organization of Finnish Troop Units

The Finnish infantry is equipped with skis in winter. Accustomed from earliest infancy to move on skis during over half of the year, the Finn accomplishes marvels in covering long distances. The use of the simple Finnish toe-binding enables the soldier to put on and take off his skis quickly. The enemy is approached on skis in small, well-separated groups echeloned in depth. The crouching skiers, camouflaged in snow shirts, rapidly approach the enemy in short bounds. Just before the final rush they quickly kick off their skis. Often the men drag their skis along, or else a member of the group gathers all the skis and brings them forward.

The Finnish cavalry in general has the mission of mounted infantry. The guiding principle in its training stresses encirclement and attack deep in the enemy flank. It is able to carry out this task because the Finnish horse is used to traveling even over difficult wooded terrain covered with rocky debris. In the winter the cavalry troops are also equipped with skis.

Training and organization of the Finnish artillery is primarily designed for combat in woods and achieved a high level of efficiency during the last war, despite the fact that the armament was to some extent old-fashioned and lacked uniformity. Since opportunities for observation were limited in the wilderness each battery, as a rule, needed several observation posts. Therefore, every battery had at least two forward observers. By means of a signal-communication net specially organized for this purpose, every forward observer was able to deliver fire with all batteries of the regiment. In the defense it was even possible to deliver fire with all medium and heavy mortars. The forward observers of the mortars in turn were able to do the same. The forward observers were connected with the firing positions by wire and radio. Great stress was laid on surprise fires. Survey was well perfected and very rapid when the aiming circle was employed.

In tank combat the Finns lacked practical experience. Not until World War II did the Finns undertake to organize an armored division. The matériel consisted of captured Russian equipment, to which a few German tanks were added in the last year of the war. Training was based on German regulations. The Karelian Isthmus is especially favorable for armored operations. The Russians employed numerous tank units there in the Winter War and in the summer of 1944. But tanks were also used in the Red Army's offensive on the Svir in April 1942.

On the long Finnish east front no tanks were used up to the time of the Finnish capitulation. When the Russians advanced against the Petsamo region in October 1944, the Red Army reportedly used only a few tanks against the German front. These weapons moved on the roads; undoubtedly tanks would encounter great difficulties on the rocky slopes of the tundra. In the Kandalaksha sector a Soviet tank unit advanced through the trackless wilderness and participated in the attack on the hilly country in the Salla area.

Finnish training of antitank units was hampered by lack of practical experience. Sufficient quantities of modern matériel were available by the end of the war.

The technical and tactical aspects of Finnish signal communications were still in the first stages of development. The use of bare wire, occasioned by special conditions of combat in woods and the critical situation in the manufacture of field signal cable, was remarkable. For this purpose a galvanized iron wire 2-mm. thick was strung overhead. In winter, if the situation was urgent, it was also possible to utilize the insulating property of completely dry snow by laying wire in the snow as a metallic circuit. Messenger dogs and carrier pigeons were not used in the Finnish Army.

III. Finnish Training Doctrine

The Finnish troops had been trained according to German principles and were in possession of the German training regulations. A comparatively large number of the senior Finnish officers had served with the 27th Prussian Light Infantry Battalion in their youth and had fought against Russia in the First World War. They were thoroughly familiar with the ideology of the German soldier. However, in a number of Finnish officers of high rank the influence of French principles of command was unmistakable. Some of the Finnish generals who held the highest posts in the last war had been detailed to the École de Guerre from World War I, and thus became acquainted with French doctrine. Perhaps this influence is responsible for the fact that many of the Finnish higher commanders remained farther behind their troops than the German commanders did in the last war. However, it is also possible that this difference in concept as to the place of the commander in battle resulted from the fact that the Finnish Army had been trained mainly for defensive warfare. It is evident that there was no one in Finland before the summer of 1941 who gave any thought to the possibility of a large-scale Finnish offensive against the Red Army.

IV. Marshal Mannerheim as a Commander

Marshal Mannerheim received his training as a soldier in the Imperial Russian Army and attained a high rank in it. He studied warfare under the most varied circumstances (in the Russo-Japanese War, World War I, the Finnish War for Freedom, the Winter War, and World War II) on the side of the Russians as well as on the side of their opponents. His wealth of experience, extensive intellectual culture, and outstanding traits of character destined him to find an undisputed place among the great military leaders of history. Characteristic of his art of strategy was his caution, based on the realization of his great responsibility. "I must be cautious," the Marshal once said to the German general in his headquarters, "because the Finnish Army is so small, the theater of war so gigantic, and the losses suffered thus far are so high." In typically Finnish fashion he loved to study things out and to deliberate before deciding on a course of action. But once he had made a decision, he carried it out energetically and unwaveringly. His authority in the Finnish Armed Forces was unlimited.

V. Peculiarities of Finnish Tactics

For the first time in its existence the Finnish Army had the opportunity to prove its mettle in an offensive on a large scale during the summer of 1941. It performed its mission with the highest honor, at first east of Lake Ladoga, then on the Karelian Isthmus. On the long eastern boundary of Finland the offensive of the year 1941 soon lost the momentum and character of a large-scale battle and broke up into local actions fought by isolated combat groups. In this type of warfare the Finnish soldier felt at home and did excellent work. As the Winter War and World War II have shown, fighting in the lonely and trackless wilderness of eastern Finland must necessarily assume the character of guerilla warfare, in which the Finns are unsurpassed. Submachine guns, hand grenades, and the Finnish dagger *(puukko)* here played the chief roles.

Finnish tactics aim to penetrate the front of the enemy, to separate the enemy's strong points from each other, to cut off these strong points completely from all arteries of supply, and to encircle them. In this manner the famous *mottis* (a Finnish word with no English equivalent, which means an encircled enemy center of resistance) were formed in the Winter War. Here the fighting completely demonstrated the great superiority of the Finnish soldier over the Red Army man. In the Winter War the fighting for the *mottis* clearly represented an attempt to starve the enemy into surrender. This was so because the Finns had little heavy artillery with which to break the Russian resistance. During World War II, when the Finns were well equipped with German artillery and ammunition, the resistance of surrounded strong points was crushed much more quickly. The struggle for the *mottis* was always a very stubborn one and demanded the utmost in bravery. It ended either in victory or annihilation because the Russian soldier continued his stubborn resistance even if there was little prospect of success. He fought courageously until his destiny was fulfilled.

VI. Russian Tactics in the Far North

The events of the Winter War created in many of the nations not participating in the struggle the impression that the Red Army with its crushing superiority in numbers and modern armament had accomplished much less than might have been expected. After a 100-day war characterized by bitter fighting, the situation of the Finns had become critical only on the Karelian Isthmus. On the entire eastern boundary of Finland the Soviet attack had been checked and repulsed with great losses for the Russians. To the Red Army man the Finnish soldier, insufficiently armed and lacking ammunition, had proved himself to be a superior fighter.

The achievements of the Red Army in the Winter War lagged far behind expectations. This resulted in an erroneous opinion even in Germany concerning the military worth of the Russians. It was a surprise when the Red Army in World War II accomplished so much more in Russia proper and showed a strength and hardiness not expected by the Germans. How can this disparity in the achievements of the Russians in the two wars in Finland be explained? On 4 March 1943 Mannerheim

made the following remarks on this subject to the German
general assigned to Finnish Headquarters:

> The Russians have learned a lot from you. Timoshenko himself
> said precisely that to our commissioners after the Winter War. This
> means that the Soviet generals are apt pupils and very quickly put
> into practice what they have learned. Today the commanders of the
> Red Army attack boldly and aggressively, and employ envelop-
> ment tactics just as the German generals do. In the Winter War of
> 1939–40 the poor showing of the Russians was not camouflage; it
> was the true picture.[1] Since that time they have learned a great deal
> and made tremendous progress.

There can be no doubt today that the Red Army evaluated
the experiences gained in the Winter War in a surprisingly short
time. Another surprising thing is the fact that the Red Army did
not lose its vigor during World War II, as so often happens in
the course of a long conflict. Despite serious crises and enormous losses, the Red Army maintained its power of resistance
and attack and even improved in quality in several respects.
This was due to its rapid adaptation of the technical developments of the period. Whatever the Soviet infantry lost in combat value was more than counterbalanced by the rapid increase
of the tank arm. The magnitude of this admirable achievement
is without parallel in the history of wars and present day
armies. However, because of the peculiar character of the north
country, the Red Army was unable to assert its superiority over
the Finns in the Winter War. After the Red Army had beaten off
the Finnish-German offensive of the year 1941, it tried in the
spring of 1942 to throw the enemy back by counterattacking on
the Svir front, in the Kestenga sector, and on the coast of the
Arctic Ocean. These attempts, based on the old methods, were
just as unsuccessful and costly as the Soviet offensive of the
Winter War against the eastern frontier of Finland and the attacks against the Murmansk railroad executed by the Germans
and Finns in 1941. The experiences gained by both sides in
these wars warrant the conclusion that the Karelian wilderness
is not suitable for decisive operations on any large scale. The
offensive attempts were not repeated by either side until the

summer of 1944. In the long interim uneventful position warfare prevailed on the extensive front between the Gulf of Finland and the Arctic Ocean.

Then, on 10 June 1944 the offensive on the Karelian Isthmus, prepared by the Red Army on a large scale, began as a complete surprise to the Finns. The Russian attack was carried out according to the latest principles which had been developed in technical science and in the tactics of war. The Russian method of attack, so successfully applied against the German east front since the fall of 1942, namely, smashing a limited portion of a position by the combined attack of an immensely superior air force and massed artillery and then driving through the resulting gap with numerous tanks, led to rapid and complete success on the Karelian Isthmus. The Russian penetration widened with destructive speed to a breakthrough. The Finnish High Command quickly realized that it was impossible to regain the old positions by the committing of reserves. The only thing to be done was to withdraw the troops, while they were still able to fight, from the attacked sector to a secondary defense line where Finnish reinforcements brought up from sectors not under attack, and supporting troops and weapons provided by the German High Command, could join the withdrawing Finnish troops. This covering position was established in the Viipuri–Vuoksi area, where the Finnish Army previously had brought the assault of the Red Army to a halt during the Winter War. This position, which was only very hastily organized, had the advantage of being located in terrain which allowed the Russians to make only limited use of their offensive weapons. The main portion of the position lay in extensive wooded terrain which denied observation to the Red Air Force. Numerous lakes and the broad Vuoksi River assured comparative safety from tank attacks. The Soviet offensive came to a standstill at this Viipuri–Vuoksi position and never got started again.

After about a month the Russians definitely discontinued their offensive against the Finns and moved strong forces from the Karelian Isthmus to the region south of Leningrad, where the offensive of the Red Army against German Army Group North was making good progress. This decision of the Russians to shift their main effort may have been prompted by the consideration that it would be easier to gain successes opposite the German front, which had already been shaken, than opposite the Finnish front, which had become stabilized. The Soviet Army High Command may have also been influenced in their decision to break off the offensive against the Finns by the very costly experience they had had in this area during the Winter War.

VII. Lessons from the Russian Summer Offensive

The course of the Soviet offensive north of Leningrad in the summer of 1944 led to the following conclusions:

1. The Karelian Isthmus is the most suitable area on the Finnish–Russian frontier for decisive operations of large-sized units. Here the road and railroad nets permit the quick concentration of large forces for a large-scale attack in the territory between Lake Ladoga and the Gulf of Finland. (This confirms experiences of the Winter War.)

2. The Red Army's method of attack brought into play the great superiority of the Russians in numbers and modern means of combat. The Finnish positions, which had been well organized during a period of two and a half years, were quickly penetrated and rolled up in a violent assault. (Experiences from the Soviet offensives against the German east front confirm this.)

3. The large-scale Soviet attack in the summer of 1944 was, however, only initially successful. The Finns were able to bring it to a standstill on the Viipuri–Vuoksi line and to drive it back eventually. This Finnish victory was gained because of:

   a. Mannerheim's early decision not to fight for the position when it was penetrated but to reorganize his forces on a secondary line.

   b. The solidity of the Finnish soldier and the preservation of his inherent steadiness and fighting qualities despite reverses.

   c. The timely German assistance with troops, planes, armor-piercing weapons, and ammunition.

   d. The natural strength of the Viipuri–Vuoksi line.

   e. The season of the year was favorable for defensive operations. It is probable that in winter the Viipuri–Vuoksi line would not have been able to check the enemy for any length of time.

Note

1. In this connection Marshal Mannerheim had reference to a speech of *Reichsmarschall* Goering delivered a short time before, in which Goering had described the Russian fighting in the Winter War as the greatest bluff in history. This speech stirred up great resentment in Finland.

CHAPTER 47

Prospects

The capitulation formula dictated by the Soviet Government and accepted by the Finns in September 1944 again confirmed the cessions of territory which had been stipulated by the Peace of Moscow of 1940. The cession of the Karelian Isthmus, the country northeast and north of Lake Ladoga, and the hilly region of Salla was confirmed and, in addition, the region of Petsamo had to be ceded to the Russians. The leasehold of Hanko was given back to the Finns. On the other hand, Porkkala, which is located directly in front of the gates of Helsinki, became a Soviet strong point for the next fifty years.

These territorial changes alter the basis of all staff planning for warfare on the Finnish–Russian frontier and demand entirely new points of view on economic, military, and political matters. The axiom of Heraclitus that "war is the father of all things" has again proved its validity in the fighting in high latitudes. The last Finnish war introduced a new chapter in the history of the earth. From now on the Arctic region is accessible to man in both war and peace. The events of the wars in the Far North proved that even large numbers of men are able to live, work, and fight in the desolate regions north of the Arctic Circle. Modern technical science has provided the means for overcoming difficulties of climate and terrain in the frigid zone and has even made life tolerable there. The man of the twentieth century has the means of pushing into the Arctic region in rather large numbers, establishing healthy homes and places to work, and preserving the creative impulses and the joy of life of the pioneers in the Far North. Airmail and radio establish communication with the outer world. It was shown during the war that suitable organization can provide all the necessities for spending the winter in high latitudes. Today no real obstacles exist to opening up the arctic region. If strong incentives and a prospect of good returns exist, courageous and enterprising men will be attracted by the land of the midnight sun. The rich mineral treasures which lie buried in the earth at the northern cap of the globe will act as powerful incentives for penetrating the polar region. On the Kola Peninsula, in the Petsamo region, in northern Sweden, great treasures lie in the earth which are needed by the modern man of industry and will be exploited by him. Navigation is possible in the Arctic Ocean throughout the year. In order to avoid air and submarine attacks, most of the convoys from England and America to Murmansk and Archangelsk traveled during the dark winter months. When the Far North of Europe develops into an industrial region, the harbors on the Arctic Ocean (Murmansk, Liinahamari, Kirkenes, Narvik) will flourish. The shortest air route between the Old and the New World is via the North Pole. Therefore this will be an area of intense activity in the future, both in peace and in war. In this connection problems which arose during World War II in the fields of radio navigation and radar instruments still remain to be solved. The disturbances and deflections caused by the proximity of the magnetic pole will require exhaustive research. To this must be added the difficulties occasioned by the tremendous size and emptiness of the region which increase the difficulty of installing a sufficiently dense net of radio stations and radar instruments. It is in these fields that future development will present complicated problems, the solution of which, however, is already indicated.

The new boundary between the Soviet Union and Finland—Norway too has now become an immediate neighbor of the Soviet Union—creates a new strategic situation in the Far North. Karelia with its numerous waterways and lakes and its trackless wilderness no longer lies as a protective zone in front of Finland proper but has become a Russian troop concentration area. If there should be another armed settlement of differences in the European Arctic region, the Soviet armies will stand immediately in front of the land regions most important to the defense of Finnish independence. This fact also makes Sweden's position much less secure than formerly. There is no doubt that the Russians, having the energy and flair for doing things in the big way characteristic of the Soviet Union, will immediately organize Karelia into a powerful base from which all Scandinavia could be held in subjection. Soon new branch railroads and military roads will be built from the Murmansk railroad through the Karelian wilderness in the direction of the new Finnish boundary. The chief objectives toward which Soviet endeavors point extend from Viipuri to Turku and the Aaland Islands, from Salla to Kemi and Oulu, and from Murmansk and Petsamo to Kirkenes. New forces have appeared in the Arctic region. These territories are no longer at the end of the world far removed from human contacts. Who can say what the future has in store for the land of the midnight sun? Indications increasingly point to the growing importance of the polar regions for the future of mankind.

PART FOUR

Combat in Russian Forests and Swamps

By General der Infanterie
Hans von Greiffenberg
Chief of Staff to Army
Groups Center and A

Preface

Combat in Russian Forests and Swamps, prepared for the Historical Division, EUCOM, by a committee of former German generals and general staff officers, deals with the principles of combat in the vast woodlands and swamps of European Russia. The main author and all other contributors have drawn upon their own extensive experience on the Eastern Front and that of their allies, especially the Finns, to present the actual lessons learned from the events of the war. When the study was translated and prepared for publication, every effort was made to retain the point of view, the expressions, and even the prejudices of the original authors.

The reader is reminded that publications in the GERMAN REPORT SERIES were written by Germans from the German point of view. Throughout this pamphlet, any mention of "normal methods" or standard infantry tactics refers to German combat doctrines, and applies to units organized and equipped in accordance with German regulations. Similarly, the recommendations contained in the final section are made against the background of German methods of individual and unit training before and during World War II.

Department of the Army
July 1951

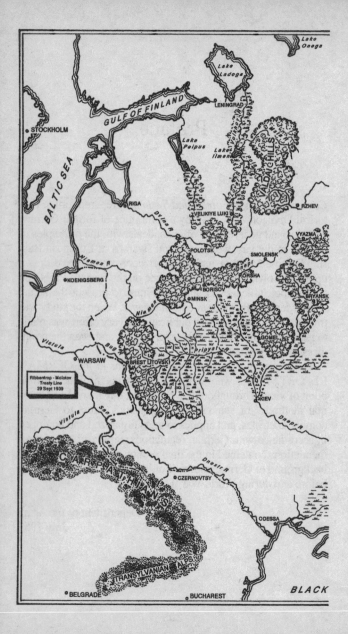

Map 16

REFERENCE MAP

COMBAT in RUSSIAN
FORESTS and SWAMPS

Foreword

In conformance with the assignment, this study had to be confined to a discussion of tactical principles. The author's lucid and methodical presentation fully corresponds with the experiences reported to me by our combat forces during the Russian campaign.

Apart from tactical principles, however, another problem calls for serious consideration: the problem of education and training, of teaching self-confidence to young men of military age and of training them in the art of improvisation. The need for this training is pointed out in the final section of this study.

Furthermore the presence of vast forest and swamp regions, as encountered in eastern Europe, must be taken into consideration in the planning of military operations. Future planners will have to make certain that extensive areas of woodlands and swamps are not permitted to assume more than tactical importance. The German command in Russia was not always successful in this respect, partly because it did not see clearly all the elements involved and partly because it did not succeed in driving the enemy away from the large wooded and swampy areas. On the contrary, there were numerous occasions when we deliberately drove the Russians into the swamp, assuming that this would prevent them from interfering with the further course of operations. That proved to be a fatal error.

When the enemy has been maneuvered into a large forest and swamp region, the area cannot be sealed off by the same methods as a beleaguered fortress. Even a force with great numerical superiority will never have enough men available for such a task. It was also our experience that Russian forces, once they were driven into wooded and swampy areas, were extremely difficult to attack by normal means and could hardly ever be completely destroyed. On countless occasions, we were confronted with the fact that the Russian was able to move about in these impenetrable forests and treacherous swamps with the certain instinct and sense of security of an animal, whereas any soldier reared and trained in a civilized country of the West was severely restricted in his movements and thereby placed at a disadvantage. There are no effective tactical remedies to compensate for this disadvantage. Even the most thorough training applied to troops from the West cannot replace the natural instinct peculiar to eastern Europeans who were born and raised in a region of forests and swamps. In the course of several generations the Soviet policy of concentrating masses of workers in large industrial areas will certainly have the effect of eliminating these natural instincts, even among people of the eastern type, but this is still far in the future. Until that time arrives, I am convinced that there is only one really effective method to use against the dangers of Russian forests and swamps, namely, to plan and conduct operations in a manner which will drive the Soviet forces from those areas where—for the time being—they enjoy a natural advantage, and force them to give battle in open terrain where western soldiers have an even chance in the tactical sense and superiority in terms of matériel. It is entirely conceivable that even the most modern weapon, the atom bomb, might serve as an effective instrument in support of such a strategy.

General Franz Halder
Chief of the General Staff of the German Army 1938–1942

CHAPTER 48

Military Aspects of Russian Forests and Swamps

Aside from their tremendous expanse, the forests and swamps of European Russia are of military significance because of their almost impassable and practically featureless terrain. Vast areas are left entirely in their primeval state and differ distinctly from the cultivated regions of western and central Europe. By far the greatest part of the extensive woodlands in European Russia is the result of undisturbed natural growth. Modern forestry methods, such as selective cutting and systematic reforestation, are virtually unknown to the Russians. As a result, very little progress has been made, even in recent years, in exploiting these forests or in making them more accessible, except in the immediate vicinity of major highways.

Inhabited places are few and far between; they are located in man-made forest clearings and particularly along the river courses. Since most Russian rivers flow from north to south or vice versa, the natural road network also developed in these directions. Lines of communication running east and west are extremely rare.

During any season of the year the small number and the doubtful condition of traffic arteries in Russia was the chief source of anxiety to all German field commanders. By far the majority of roads and trails proved to have no more than local significance as connections between villages, as logging roads, or simply as cleared lanes through the forest. They were built accordingly. In critical periods, particularly during the muddy season, they proved completely useless. They were replaced, once the ground was solidly frozen, by so-called winter roads. Wherever bridges had to be crossed, their load capacity and their strength against floods or drifting ice had to be estimated with extreme caution.

In view of the fact that the Russian river systems are rarely regulated, inland water transportation, except on lakes, played only a minor role. The so-called *Rollbahnen* (highways reserved for motor vehicles), which were built and maintained on a large scale by German construction units using as a foundation such stretches of hard-surfaced roads as were already available, proved invaluable. Wherever they existed, they provided the starting points for tactical operations and served as the lifelines of the German supply system.

The great wooded areas of European Russia actually begin in Poland and grow denser as one advances east. The forest of Byalovizh, forty miles north of Brest Litovsk, at one time the game preserve of the czars and later of the Polish Government, does not quite fit into the general picture because, to serve its specific purpose, it has been better provided with roads. East of Brest Litovsk, however, extend the broad marshes and forests of the Pripyat region. Adjoining them, the huge tracts of forest around Gomel, Minsk, Bryansk, Borisov, Orsha, and Vyazma dominate the landscape. They are continued north of the low ridge of Orsha in the forests of Polotsk and Velikiye Luki and in the marshy lowlands along the course of the Lovat and the Volkhov, all of which were scenes of bloody fighting during World War II.

It is typical of the large Russian forest areas that nearly all of them harbor extensive swamps. Whatever general rules are applied in this study to combat in forests or in swamps are therefore interrelated in many respects.

Southern Russia, especially the Ukraine, is nearly devoid of woodlands; some parts are highly cultivated, others consist of steppes. Since ancient times Southern Russia has been the favorite scene for the operations of large armies.

Except for the rolling terrain of the Valdai Hills, all wooded areas of western Russia extend over flat land. The only mountain forests are in the extreme south: in the Yaila mountains on the Crimea, in the Carpathians, and in the Caucasus where, in addition, treacherous swamps are found in the western foothills.

Toward the extreme north the woods become thinner and are gradually replaced by underbrush and swamp vegetation. The landscape appears more and more desolate the farther one advances in the direction of the White Sea. Economic and military objectives, of necessity, take second place to bare survival in the face of the bleakness of nature. Here some fishermen, hunters, and lumbermen eke out their precarious existence in a constant struggle against the rigors of nature. North of the Arctic Circle only Lapp nomads and their herds of reindeer are to be found. Farther to the east, beyond the Ural Mountains, tundra and taiga (northern coniferous forests) extend over the vast expanse of northern Asia.

The swampy forest areas of European Russia defy any uniform description. Conditions vary too greatly, depending on weather, season, and geographic location. The woods and marshes of the Pripyat, the only large river which flows from west to east and clearly divides western Russia in reality as well as on the map into two parts, offer a typical example of the great variety of terrain that may be encountered. Even this region has sandy plains with high forests, cultivated farm land and pastures, localities with a comparatively dense population, river branches that have been converted into canals, and paved roads on causeways. But its predominant features are extensive swamp areas with luxuriant weed-covered moors, countless ponds and lakes full of sedge islands and bordered by treacherous, meadow-like ground, a type of terrain which is definitely impassable except during winter. There are birch and alder forests which, according to the season of the year, may have a dry and firm ground surface or may turn out to be a bottomless morass. A constantly changing maze of floodwater streams and tributaries makes any troop movement off the paved roads a dangerous undertaking.

Despite all these difficulties the Pripyat marshes, taken as a whole, are considerably more accessible and better adapted to military use than other Russian forest areas. During World War II, therefore, even this region, which had been viewed with apprehension by many military men, became the scene of tactical movements and engagements in which the principal role, to be sure, fell to the infantry and the horse cavalry.

In southern Russia there are no large and continuous swamp regions like that of the Pripyat river system. The only swampy areas that might be of tactical importance are the marshy tracts in the partly wooded lowlands along the Dnepr River and the treeless lagoons near the mouths of the Kuban, the Don, the Terek, and in the lower course of the Volga.

Finally, in considering the military peculiarities of Russian forests and swamps, one must refer to the great variations in climate that are encountered in the vast expanse between the Black Sea and the Arctic Ocean. Over any extended period of time the physical constitution of the average European is unable to stand the humid, sultry weather in the marshy regions of the south, the icy dampness of the ground in the forests of central and northern Russia, or the sudden storms and rapid changes in temperature in all parts of the country. Contaminated drinking water, mosquitoes and other harmful insects, extremely cold weather, and other unusual natural phenomena caused sicknesses of many kinds. The casualties resulting from frostbite, rheumatic fever, intestinal disease, malaria, and swamp fever equalled, in many instances, the number of men killed or wounded in combat.

CHAPTER 49

General Tactical Principles

I. Command

Combat in forests and swamps requires firm, farsighted, energetic leadership by commanders who are able to cope with the peculiarities of this type of warfare and avoid unnecessary crises and reverses. During initial engagements uncertainty about the enemy and terrain is far greater than in the open. Unpleasant surprises may occur at any moment—in dense forests because of lack of observation and in swampy areas because of the difficulty in obtaining an accurate terrain estimate. In such situations, ignorance on the part of the staffs, defective organization, or lack of advance planning will have an immediate effect on the physical condition and the morale of the troops and may cause a loss of human lives which could have been avoided.

In forest fighting, commanders easily lose control over their troops. In the forward area their direct influence is confined to the men in their immediate vicinity. Limited observation, the intensified noise of combat, and the excitement created by fighting at close quarters make it difficult to distinguish between friend and foe, increase the danger of overestimating purely local events, and the danger of panic is thereby aggravated. Combat of this type will always prove to be a heavy strain on troops. Units which have been engaged in serious forest fighting frequently are unfit for action for a considerable time thereafter. Any unit that no longer is able to provide adequate reserves for its combat missions should be temporarily relieved or rehabilitated before it is completely battle-worn.

The general principles of tactics in open terrain—the teamwork of mutually supporting arms and services, culminating in a main effort at the decisive point or points—also apply to combat in large forest and swamp areas. Only the outward forms are changed insofar as they must be adapted to the conditions created by nature, specifically to the lack of observation and the absence of suitable roads. The objectives remain the same.

The place of the small unit commander is within view or earshot of his men, where he is able to exercise direct control and take charge of critical situations. Command posts of larger units are protected by the forest and rarely exposed to enemy reconnaissance. Their locations, therefore, are selected less for reasons of concealment than for good communications with friendly troops. Approaches must be marked by unmistakable day and night road signs to aid messengers and subordinate commanders in finding their way.

Large wooded areas provide an abundance of concealment for movement and troop concentrations, even against an enemy with superior air forces. Furthermore, they offer distinct advantages in the conduct of delaying actions, blocking maneuvers, and diversionary attacks. They are not, however, suitable as a battleground for major decisions. This is true not only for large forests but also applies in even greater degree to extensive swamp areas. The attacker, if at all possible, must therefore seek to avoid large, continuous forests and swamps by passing them at both flanks, particularly with mechanized and motorized units. Only if the enemy is firmly entrenched in such areas and appears determined to fight, despite the danger of being outflanked and enveloped, must he be attacked or at least effectively contained. Otherwise, the successful conduct of subsequent operations might be jeopardized.

In the defense, on the other hand, or for the purpose of blocking the enemy's maneuver, it may be advisable to exploit extensive forest and swamp areas, even by occupying them with one's own forces. This will seriously interfere with the adversary's plans, force him to use his troops on time-consuming missions, slow down his movements, and hamper his supply operations. Moreover, forests and swamps often provide favorable opportunities for raids and attacks on the aggressor's flanks and rear.

The inhabitants of the eastern European forest and swamp areas are generally agreed—and this is borne out by the German experiences of World War II—that midwinter is the most suitable season for offensive operations in that type of terrain. When the streams, lakes, and marshes are frozen, so that wide stretches off the roads become passable, the so-called winter roads are established. Running across the frozen surface of open moors and swampy tracts of woodland, such winter roads constitute the natural lines of communication during the long Russian winter and thus make it possible to utilize the terrain for military purposes. The proper equipment must, of course, be available to operate under such circumstances.

Since the many items of technical equipment necessary for living and fighting in almost inaccessible forest and swamp areas cannot be available everywhere at the right time and in sufficient quantity, commanders of all echelons must apply themselves to the art of improvisation. The Russians proved to be past masters of that art and obtained amazing results by using the most primitive expedients, particularly by the ruthless employment of civilians present in such areas.

As a means of orientation in the interior of extensive Russian forests and swamps, maps alone are inadequate and unreliable. The picture presented by the landscape is subject to constant change brought about by natural growth and the varying effects of water in every form, and every commander should use his maps only with the greatest caution. Any map information must be supplemented by aerial photographs and by interrogation of local inhabitants, as well as by the evaluation of captured documents. Foreign place names may have to be overprinted in one's own alphabet. A uniform map with a standard grid system is an indispensable prerequisite for the proper coordination of all arms.

In such areas, more than in any other type of terrain, commanders must be seriously concerned about providing adequate medical and sanitary facilities and individual equipment in order to make life bearable under the most adverse conditions.

The conduct of operations in forests and swamps requires the most meticulous preparation in every respect. This is true not only for reconnaissance and security but also for the composition and commitment of units, their equipment, the organization of communication and command channels, the training of the various arms, and last but not least for the utilization of local resources.

Operations in forests and swamps are further characterized by the methodical execution of all measures. This, of necessity, involves a loss of time and requires an increased number of service troops. In many respects it constitutes a departure from the conventional German principles of combat in open terrain, which emphasize initiative and independent action on the part of all command echelons.

II. Arms and Services

The task of conducting a successful campaign against a tough and primitive opponent who is able to take advantage of the peculiar conditions of forests and swamps calls for well-trained troops of high morale and unusual physical endurance. It is in that type of terrain that the infantry regains its time-honored reputation as the "Queen of Battle." Here the individual fighting man assumes even greater importance than during combat in open terrain. Fighting at close quarters plays a major role and numerical superiority is less significant than personal courage. Light and heavy infantry weapons, submachine guns, machine pistols, hand grenades, bayonets, the long hunting knife, and flame throwers are the most suitable weapons for this type of combat.

The Russian campaign demonstrated that the cavalry, regarded as obsolete in central and western Europe, still had many tasks to perform. It was successfully employed in envelopments and flank attacks, pursuits and long-range missions—admittedly not in the sense of the cavalry of former times but rather as a highly mobile mounted infantry with great powers of endurance. Also, the man on horseback was often indispensable in maintaining liaison and carrying messages.

Composition and employment of the artillery must be adapted to the peculiarities of woods and swamps. Lack of observation, especially from the flanks, and unusual difficulties in selecting suitable positions are the main handicaps of artillery commitment in this type of terrain. In the dense forests of Russia it was never easy to identify even the foremost enemy line. Unobserved fire on rear area targets proved even more uncertain. Finally, the artillery faced a downright impossible task whenever the front line fluctuated in attacks and counterattacks and when observation, even at close range, failed to provide a reliable picture.

In forest fighting the psychological effect of artillery fire is greatly amplified while that of small arms is generally reduced.

Prepared concentrations, if laid down to block the enemy's main route of approach, can be highly effective. Only in exceptional cases, however, is mass employment of artillery possible in direct support of attacking or defending forces. The most suitable solution, in the German experience, was to attach one artillery battalion to one infantry regiment. Frequently a further subdivision was necessary and individual batteries were attached to infantry battalions. Thus, during combat in woods and swamps the artillery found its main function in the close support of front-line infantry.

The number of forward observers equipped with voice-radio sets can never be too large; several are necessary to direct the fire of each battery.

Massed fire on important targets must be planned with extraordinary care. Systematic area fire from map data has little promise of success and, in most instances, merely constitutes a waste of ammunition. In swamp areas, furthermore, a considerable part of the fragmentation effect is lost unless time fuses are available.

The artillery must use high angle fire in direct support, especially in tall forests, once the advancing infantry is separated from the enemy by only a few hand grenade throws. The use of infantry heavy weapons, particularly mortars, is subject to similar principles.

In densely overgrown terrain, rocket launchers have a considerable effect on morale, particularly at night. Even if little accuracy can be achieved, the enemy frequently is forced to evacuate because of grass and brush fires started in the impact area.

Engineer troops are called upon for a great variety of tasks in swampy and wooded terrain. A large number of well-equipped engineer detachments must be available not only for combat missions and construction of obstacles but also for mine laying and mine detecting, clearing roads and fire lanes, constructing bridges, corduroy roads, and fascine mats, and for building observation towers and abatis. Particularly great during the entire German campaign in Russia was the need for bridge and road construction units. Native labor proved to be valuable because the Russian peasant and inhabitant of forest regions has considerable experience in wood construction and is not dependent on the use of iron and steel.

German experiences demonstrated that even armored units can be employed in the forests of Eastern Europe, particularly in those areas that have a fairly adequate road net and are not too densely overgrown. Despite all technical advances, however, the difficulties imposed by the peculiarities of terrain remain enormous. They are further aggravated by greater density of tree growth and deep snow and, during the muddy season or after extensive rainfall, become insurmountable in swamp areas. In continuous forests and swamps, therefore, the employment of entire mechanized or motorized divisions should be avoided. If this is impossible, the tanks should be held in reserve and only motorized infantry and combat engineers should be committed at first. Utilizing the existing road net and considerably echeloned in depth, the armor should then move up on a narrow frontage. Much greater opportunities present themselves for the employment of individual tanks, sometimes in small groups up to platoon strength, and of assault guns and tank destroyers. Of course, they too are hampered by difficulties of terrain and lack of observation. So long as the ground is reasonably firm, however, their commitment appears justified since the infantry cannot expect too much support from any of the other arms.

In signal communications the greatest emphasis must be placed on the use of radio. The wild, uncultivated forces of European Russia present unusual obstacles to the construction and maintenance of telephone lines. Radio, therefore, is the proper means of communication not only for higher echelons but particularly for front-line units. Blinker communications are suitable in the more open marshes but not in dense forests. Other visual signals, as well as messenger dogs, may be used over short distances and, at times, it may be necessary to resort to relay systems of mounted messengers and runners.

Tactical air support in forest areas is subject to restrictions similar to those present in the employment of artillery. Lack of observation and the absence of distinct features in the terrain such as crossroads, railroad tracks, and inhabited places, often lead to serious errors in the commitment of planes. Dive bomber attacks in forest areas have a strong psychological effect. The screaming of diving planes, the detonation of bombs, and the crashing of falling trees wreak havoc on the nerves of all but the most seasoned troops. On the other hand, the employment of dive bombers requires the most methodical coordination, perfect timing, and the greatest possible accuracy in the designation of targets, all of which can be achieved only under the most favorable conditions. Although less effective in close support of forest fighting than under ordinary circumstances, the air force can render invaluable assistance to ground forces engaged in that type of combat. It is capable of keeping vast combat areas under constant surveillance and of providing through aerial photography a prompt and reliable supplement to ground reconnaissance.

In support of an advance over terrain that offers practically no ground observation, air reconnaissance has the additional task of reporting the location of forward elements and of indicating points where major road congestions have occurred. Equipped with infrared devices, air observers are able to produce usable photographs at any time of the day or night, in fog, or in rain.

Heavy supply vehicles, whether motorized or horse-drawn, are a cumbersome hindrance in any operation in woods and swamps. The troops must be forced to limit themselves to the few items absolutely essential for combat and to leave behind everything that is not of vital importance. At the outbreak of the Russian campaign in 1941 the German divisions were equipped with native horse carts, the so-called *Panje* wagons, drawn by small but extremely hardy native horses. Another organizational expedient typical of the campaign in Russia was the formation of light infantry divisions after the Germans discovered that their mountain divisions were the most effective type of unit for sustained combat in forests and swamps.

CHAPTER 50

Combat Intelligence, Reconnaissance, and Observation

When an attacking force approaches a large forest and swamp area it is usually provided with intelligence estimates indicating whether or not the area is occupied by strong enemy forces. But since intelligence estimates furnished by higher headquarters cannot always provide conclusive data, it is the responsibility of every commander to obtain more specific information about the enemy and terrain in his zone of advance. This is accomplished by distant, close, and battle reconnaissance through the combined efforts of all arms. If distant reconnaissance missions fail to obtain adequate results, improper employment of forces can hardly be avoided. Failure to carry out adequate close and battle reconnaissance may involve the danger of falling into an ambush or encountering unexpected enemy resistance. This applies in an immeasurably higher degree to wooded and marshy areas than to any other type of terrain.

All items of information concerning the road net in the area of advance must be entered on road maps which are distributed before going into action. Numbers or names must be assigned to all roads and prominent terrain features that are not so marked on the maps. Such designations proved invaluable in simplifying orientation and communications in the Eastern Campaign.

At the beginning of the Russian Campaign German panzer divisions still had air squadrons attached for close support and observation. Because of excellent Russian camouflage, however, air reconnaissance over vast forest regions was at first not too effective. Somewhat better results were achieved over large swamp areas. In time and after experience German air observers realized that the most inconspicuous signs were likely to offer valuable information. For example, the presence of horses at rest, stacks of straw and hay that should long have been stored, or fresh tracks in the mud led to important conclusions. These air reconnaissance activities were mainly concentrated on the route of advance with special emphasis on detecting enemy battery positions and tank movements. In addition, each squadron had to protect the advancing columns of the panzer division to which it was attached. The planes were also used for artillery observation and at times were the only means of directing effective counter-battery fire. Flight for reconnaissance was usually carried out at low altitude, a most suitable technique over dense forests and overgrown swamps since the enemy caught no more than a glimpse of the aircraft as it passed overhead.

Apart from air reconnaissance and aerial photography, strong combat patrols are still the primary means of obtaining vital information. Wherever the terrain is suitable and affords adequate observation, single tanks or armored reconnaissance cars may be employed, provided they can be accompanied by security and mine-detecting squads.

In conjunction with continuous reconnaissance to the front the security of both flanks must be assured. Any commander who neglects to provide for all around security, particularly in forests and swamps, has but himself to blame if his troops sustain heavy casualties from enemy surprise attacks or are caught in a prepared ambush which was not recognized in time. The more difficult the terrain, the greater is the need for continuous and intensive reconnaissance. In contrast to operations in open terrain, reconnaissance and security patrols must be held close to the main force. Advancing by bounds, they must work their way through forest and swamp and must never lose contact with their units. Prearranged signals, such as rockets, signal flares, warning shots, and colored smoke, are suitable means of communication even in woods with dense underbrush. Wherever possible, observation posts should be established on high ground, in treetops, hunting lookouts, and observation towers.

Climbing irons and rope are indispensable items of equipment in terrain of this type.

Similar principles apply to a defensive situation in forests and swamps. Forward of the main line of resistance the defender must attempt to establish a closely knit security and reconnaissance network, a task that is greatly facilitated since the forces are familiar with the terrain. Reconnaissance units in contact with the enemy have the additional mission of deceiving the attacker as long as possible as to the actual location of the main line of resistance.

In exceptional cases, for instance when contact with the enemy has been frequently broken or lost altogether, the employment of so-called raiding detachments may become necessary. These are long-range combat patrols with the mission of collecting specific information, harassing the enemy rear area, and creating unrest behind the enemy lines. Their success will depend entirely on the proper selection of personnel, notably the leader, and on the suitability of their equipment. They must be led by a man of unusual abilities who combines the best qualities of a trained soldier with the natural instincts of an experienced hunter. Every man in the patrol should carry his own rations, weapons, protection against inclement weather, and any items that might be needed to care for the wounded.

On missions of this type vehicles are likely to be a hindrance rather than a help. During the Russian winter, however, small boat-type Finnish sleds, called *akjas*, proved very useful for transporting weapons, ammunition, equipment, and occasionally for evacuating casualties. These sleds could be drawn by one man and, in the far northern regions, were pulled through the most difficult terrain by reindeer. Whenever the ground was fairly solid, the raiding detachments used small two-wheeled carts drawn by hand or by native horses.

CHAPTER 51

Troop Movements

An advance through a large forest region traversed by several hard-surfaced roads will generally follow the same principles that are observed in any other type of terrain, except that the units involved are echeloned in greater depth than usual. Strong advance guards must push well ahead of the main body. Moving along the roads, they should advance through the forest and swamp areas as quickly as possible with the primary objective of gaining open terrain and securing it for succeeding elements. These advance guards must be strong enough to overcome the resistance of small enemy forces in the woods and, in cooperation with friendly air units, must be able to hold newly gained open terrain until reinforcements arrive.

During the German campaign in Russia road conditions permitting such an advance proved to be the exception rather than the rule. Road nets, or what appeared as such on the map, consisted mainly of unimproved, sandy, or swampy country roads, frequently no more than beaten tracks through the wilderness. In these circumstances the advance of large units had to be carefully planned and organized in every detail. For example, with no more than one through road available, as was often the case, the movement of a division would be carried out as follows:

Each element of the advancing column was, as a rule, preceded by its own advance guard. This unit, in addition to its usual tactical functions, had to report the presence of mines and roadblocks along the route of advance and to indicate the time required for their removal. It was also responsible for reconnoitering all possible detours around obstructed or impassable stretches of the road.

The order of march, especially with respect to forward components of the column, had to be so prescribed as to eliminate any need for subsequent changes. On narrow roads it proved virtually impossible to move any unit from the rear of the column to the front without causing considerable difficulties.

All advance detachments were accompanied by engineer details which repaired the worst stretches of the road and placed road and terrain markers to aid in the orientation of previously issued road maps. At an early stage of the movement, construction units were put to work along the entire route of advance. When movement was interrupted by rest periods or at night, these units performed road maintenance, constructed bypasses, and built bridges and corduroy roads. In addition, a highly mobile engineer unit was held in reserve to cope with special emergencies.

Traffic control also required careful organization and more personnel than in other types of terrain. The traffic control officer was responsible for the even and uninterrupted flow of the movement. In order to enforce strict traffic discipline and to prevent any column or single vehicle from moving in the opposite direction, he was necessarily given special authority within the scope of his assignment. Even officers of higher rank had to follow his instructions.

On many occasions the poor condition of the only available route of advance made it necessary to provide towing facilities at particularly difficult points along the road. The regulation of supply operations so as to keep them from interfering with troop movements had to be planned in every detail. One item of major importance in moving through Russian forests and swamps was the procurement and transportation of safe drinking water.

Along the route of advance effective antiaircraft protection and adequate telephone communications had to be provided, the latter connected with branch lines, traffic control, and towing details.

Immediate local security measures had to be taken by every

unit during rest periods or extended halts in the forest. At night it was found advisable to provide for all around defense by forming concentric security and defense belts around individual elements of the column.

In any advancing column the location of the commander is of great importance. This is particularly true of movements through forests and swamps which, far from being mere road marches, might at any time turn into meeting engagements. In the German experience the best location for the division commander in a movement through wooded and swampy terrain was with the reconnaissance battalion or, when such a battalion was not organic, with the foremost elements of the combat team. In the case of two combat teams the commander placed himself with the one that, according to the situation, was of greater importance. He had his own radio with him and was usually accompanied by the combat team commander. The forward echelon of the division staff was under the command of the operations officer. It did not move with the column but was established in a suitable location along the route of march. It included the divisional radio communications center, where all radio messages were received, including those from aircraft reporting on the progress of the column. The operations officer transmitted all important information to the division commander on a radio frequency reserved for that purpose. Thus, the division commander had the complete picture not only of the situation at the head of the column where he himself was located, but also of anything that occurred behind him.

Even the most careful regulation and supervision of movements through difficult terrain cannot altogether prevent traffic congestions if the troops fail to observe proper march discipline. Since strict central control is an absolute necessity, all movements through forests and swamps follow a more rigid pattern than those in open terrain and are generally executed at a lower rate of speed. Whenever German units attempted to penetrate large, continuous forest and swamp areas recklessly and without adequate preparations they were doomed to failure. The proper procedure, whenever contact with strong enemy elements in forests appeared probable, proved to be an advance by bounds. This procedure assured firm control of the troops at all times. Even in approaching a large forest area the Germans often used the flame procedure, depending, of course, on what information had been obtained about the enemy situation.

When the leading echelons of the column were about to enter the woods, the commander had to decide whether his force should deploy or continue to advance in column. His dispositions for this phase depended to a high degree on the adaptability of his troops to the difficulties of the terrain.

Densely overgrown and swampy areas always present considerable problems of orientation. Under the conditions existing in Russian forests and swamps it was found to be most important that every officer and man be able to orient himself on the terrain. Otherwise, any action was likely to end in confusion with the troops losing their bearings, deviating from their march objective, and eventually firing on friendly forces. In many situations the compass proved the only means of orientation, but it was always difficult to determine the exact distance from the starting point because of the many detours involved in an advance through terrain of that type. Serious mistakes could be prevented only after considerable experience had been gained by officers and men alike.

To aid succeeding units in finding their way, directions were indicated by the use of marking tape, luminous paint, and tree and road markers. To provide orientation at night, vertical searchlight beams and the firing of tracer ammunition proved satisfactory.

Undoubtedly, the average European does not possess a well-developed sense of direction. Nor is he capable of moving swiftly and noiselessly through the compact wilderness of primeval forests. The inhabitants of the Russian and Finnish forest regions, on the other hand, have a native instinct for the lay of the land and an astounding ability for self-orientation. Therefore, the German forces in Russia often found it advisable to use intelligent local inhabitants under close supervision as guides for marching columns and even for leading elements in the attack.

Columns equipped with horse-drawn vehicles had to be instructed to leave behind all baggage, equipment, and supplies that were not absolutely essential. For this purpose, vehicle collection points were established, and the horse teams which thereby became available could then be employed as pack animals, for the transportation of fascine mats, or as additional teams for vehicles that had to be taken along. If suitable pack saddles had not been procured beforehand, they had to be improvised. Any vehicle that broke down and obstructed the road was blasted out of the way without hesitation.

Marches of armored or motorized columns through forests and swamps called for the most careful preparation. All elements, not only the divisional units, had to proceed in close formation under strict observance of road space and rate of march. Thus, as a rule, corps headquarters did not order its non-divisional units to move forward until the last elements of the division had cleared a certain phase line. Constant air observation of such movements was of the greatest importance. Air observers reported the location of traffic congestions or unusually prolonged halts, as well as the phase lines crossed by the various units and the overall progress of the movement.

In any daylight advance of armored or motorized columns through the Russian forests and swamps, effective air cover was an absolute necessity. Under attack from the air, armored or motorized units were unable to disperse, or even to move one inch off the narrow roads, and were therefore infinitely more vulnerable than in any other terrain under similar tactical conditions. To carry out any large-scale movement of such units at night, however, proved to be impossible.

As the Russian roads deteriorated, wheeled motor vehicles were the first to become useless, especially the personnel carriers of armored and motorized units. Unaccustomed to long foot marches, the armored infantry, laboring through swamps, mud, and snow with its heavy weapons and all its abundant equipment, could not stand up under the considerable strain. Foot ailments and similar causes were soon responsible for a large number of casualties.

As a result of these experiences wheeled vehicles were

eventually dispensed with and each company of armored infantry was issued two or three track-laying vehicles for the transportation of heavy weapons, ammunition, and rations. Where such a changeover was impossible, as in the case of radio cars, track-laying prime movers were employed to tow several wheeled vehicles at a time. As a rule this was done at the expense of units normally equipped with track-laying vehicles, such as artillery, antitank, and Flak.

CHAPTER 52

Development and Deployment

Generally, the development of a column in wooded terrain in Russia became necessary as the troops approached close contact with the enemy. Individual units continued to advance in a broad formation behind a screen of strong reconnaissance forces and with adequate flank protection. Frontage and depth of the formation depended largely on the type of terrain to be crossed, but the primary consideration was always the possibility of exercising effective control over all elements of the command. Furthermore, every unit had to be ready to meet the enemy at any moment and therefore had to adopt the formation most suitable for close combat under the prevailing terrain conditions.

Equipped with close combat weapons, automatic rifles, and hand axes, the advance guard followed the reconnaissance force. Several heavy weapons were held ready for action. The rifle companies, in wedge formation and advancing by bounds, followed the advance guard at a distance. Battalion reserves and additional heavy weapons were brought up close behind the main body.

If the terrain was densely overgrown or if darkness or fog

made it difficult to maintain contact, the advance of each separate column was controlled by so-called center guide lines and phase lines. A center guide line is a prescribed line along which the center of a unit is ordered to advance. In the absence of visible reference points in the terrain, the compass is usually the only reliable means of maintaining direction. Phase lines run perpendicular to the direction of march and divide the zone of advance into several parts. Conspicuous terrain features, such as fire breaks, trails, clearings, streams, peat banks, and villages or several individual houses, were usually designated as phase lines. They were entered on maps or aerial photographs and announced to the troops either verbally or by the distribution of sketches. Each advancing unit had instructions to halt as soon as its leading elements reached the next phase line and to establish contact with the units on its left and right. This procedure enabled the leading elements of all units to keep abreast and assured the maintenance of order and contact in the advance, even over difficult terrain. If there were no conspicuous features that could be indicated on the map or identified in the terrain, the halts were arranged according to a time schedule. During darkness it was sometimes possible to establish contact with adjacent units by the use of blinker lights shielded from the enemy.

Of course, this method of advance, interrupted as it is by scheduled halts, will slow down the forward movement of the entire force. But even at the risk of losing time, it is far better to maintain full control and to conserve the strength of the troops than to expose entire units to the danger of losing contact and straying from their route of advance with all the serious consequences involved.

In many situations during the German campaign in Russia, the very nature of the forests and swamps precluded the possibility of deployment and development prior to close contact with the enemy. As far back as the old Russian border no more than one route was usually available for the approach march of any German unit. On a few occasions the unusual width of the zone of advance assigned to a division offered some opportunity for deployment, although that was hardly deployment in the ordinary sense of the term. It took the form merely of another march unit, normally organized as a combat team, following an alternate route, far separated from and at best in loose contact with the main force. But even that form of deployment was largely an involuntary measure adopted to counter an enemy attack from an unexpected direction.

Contact with the enemy was often established under the following circumstances: The Russians were dug in around a village, at the edge of a forest, in a large clearing, or in any other strip of solid ground. Their position was hastily fortified and usually protected by mines. Well deployed in width, they were able to concentrate considerable fire power on the narrow exits through which the Germans were expected to emerge. The attacker, after trying by reconnaissance and observation to obtain a clear picture of the enemy situation, usually had to fight his way from the narrow approaches into the open spaces where he could develop his forces. Facing the enemy on a narrow road, the German commander could apply but a small portion of his fire power and was unable to make effective use of his heavy weapons. He had to develop his forces toward both flanks in a desperate struggle through the swampy terrain, trying to form a small bridgehead on firm ground and to gain sufficient space for the employment of his heavy weapons, tanks, and rocket launchers. Rocket launchers particularly proved to be most suitable for this type of combat. Frequently, the defender also had no more than one narrow route to the rear through the woods and swamps. If that road could be taken under effective artillery fire, it was sometimes possible to block the route of withdrawal and to capture the entire enemy force.

On many occasions, however, when the Germans faced a strong Russian force supported by accurate artillery fire, any development from the narrow route of advance proved to be impossible. Then the German commander had to resort to the time-consuming procedure of rerouting his entire unit in order to launch an attack from a different direction. Even without interference from the enemy, reversing an entire column on a narrow, swampy road or on a corduroy road, where the slightest departure from the right-of-way would mean sinking into the mud, was certain to involve tremendous difficulties.

CHAPTER 53

Attack

The attacker usually seeks to capture small woods by enveloping action, making certain that any protruding salients are attacked and occupied in the course of the envelopment. The artillery blinds the enemy's observation by smoke and neutralizes the hostile weapons capable of delivering flanking fire against the attack.

If wooded areas of moderate depth are to be crossed, special care must be taken to prevent any substantial body of troops from advancing beyond the far edge of the woods without adequate fire support. In such situations there is always the danger of running into a counterattack by enemy tanks.

Any offensive action in large forest regions or in swamp areas without adequate observation calls for a considerable expenditure of time and the most painstaking preparations. This seemingly obvious requirement cannot be overemphasized and should be fully understood by all officers and noncommissioned officers. Swift and bold action and close-range assaults are indicated only in the case of a meeting engagement or for the elimination of minor enemy pockets. In all other instances the attack must be carefully planned and developed. Much time and effort will be saved if the troops are deployed in proper formation and have gained the necessary width and depth during the advance. All such preparations must be made in strict conformity with the general plan of attack, and the expected location of main efforts must be taken into consideration. Maps alone are of limited value for this purpose, and every commander will first have to conduct a thorough reconnaissance on the ground.

Quick success may sometimes be achieved by an advance and breakthrough off the main road, but only if the enemy has committed the obvious error of neglecting to secure the intermediate terrain.

Under the conditions peculiar to combat in forests and swamps the selection of objectives is always one of the most difficult tasks. As a rule, commanders have a tendency to assign objectives as distant as possible. German experience has shown, however, that units engaged in prolonged forest fighting soon become intermingled, are then extremely difficult to control, and lose much of their striking power. Assigning too distant an objective may have the effect of jeopardizing, if not completely precluding, any chance of success. Flank threats and the disruption of communications between the attacking elements and their supporting heavy weapons and artillery are some of the immediate consequences. Assigning too close an objective, on the other hand, prevents the full exploitation of gains made in the attack.

It is clear that this problem cannot be solved by any rule of uniform applicability. In view of the difficulties of observation and orientation in large forest and swamp areas, the troops need distinct terrain features which are easily recognizable as objectives, such as rivers and streams, ridges, clearings, crosscuts, trails, or the edge of swamps. Generally, if only for reasons of proper control and cohesion within the units, major objectives in forests and swamps will be selected at closer range than in open terrain. Intermediate objectives in the form of successive phase lines are required particularly in dense woods.

The attack itself will not be carried out by a single assault wave of great width and density, but rather by separate assault detachments and assault columns which must be properly organized and equipped. Success will be assured not by the number of men but by the combined effect of all arms and by the constantly renewed cooperation of all elements participating in the attack. The composition of these assault detachments cannot be determined by any standard rule. Decisive factors, apart from the enemy situation, will be the density of trees and undergrowth and the general passability of the terrain.

The Germans established special antitank teams composed of infantry, antitank, and combat engineer units attached to the leading elements. They were used for close-range antitank combat and proved extremely valuable in the Russian forests where the dense vegetation facilitated their unobserved approach. Generally, these teams advanced on foot with the infantry, carried their antitank weapons, such as Molotov cocktails, demolition charges, or antitank rocket launchers, and were equal to any tank attacking without infantry support.

Even in forests and swamps commanders should strive to use artillery and air support under principles similar to those for combat in open terrain. Since observed fire in densely overgrown areas is often impossible, it follows that such support cannot always be obtained. It should also be noted that according to German experience the actual damage inflicted by artillery and air bombardment on enemy positions in the woods is not as great as the psychological effect on enemy personnel. Dropping incendiary bombs on identified or suspected centers of resistance many facilitate the mission of the attacking infantry. Because of the danger to friendly troops from resulting forest fires, the wind direction must be carefully observed. Since all traffic is of necessity channelized, harassing fire on bivouac areas, frequently used roads, and defilades has a considerable effect on the enemy's dispositions.

If the enemy has established himself in a continuous line through a wooded and swampy area, each individual strong point must be reduced separately, either by envelopment or by frontal attacks.

For any advance in this type of terrain squad columns are better suited than skirmish lines. Also, the troops must not be permitted to bunch up in the immediate vicinity of roads and trails, where they are more likely to encounter strong enemy ambush parties.

Local reserves are held close by. They are immediately used

to exploit any break in the enemy line or to restore the situation in case of unexpected reverses. Larger reserves follow at the usual distance. Prior to an attack, artillery observers should be attached not only to forward elements but also to the reserves, because under conditions peculiar to forests and swamps it may not be possible to do so later on.

Enemy counterattacks or flare-ups of enemy resistance behind the front must be expected at all times. Particularly in such situations it is the foremost duty of junior and noncommissioned officers to maintain strict control within their sectors, since the means available in the field cannot assure the clear identification of front lines in that type of terrain.

The terrain features usually designated as objectives in swamp fighting are stretches of road over high ground, railroad embankments, dikes, or islands in the swamps. Whereas the protection and support of heavy weapons and low-flying aircraft are here more easily obtained, the attacking infantry finds its greatest difficulties in approaching such objectives over the surrounding swampy and open areas. Even without effective enemy interference the infantry may have to resort to various expedients in order to accomplish its mission over soft ground. On many occasions the Germans used so-called swamp bridges for closing in on the enemy. They were constructed in the rear areas and brought forward in sections under the cover of fire. Swamps that were not too soft often could be crossed with the aid of planks or fascines. In overgrown swamp areas where the surface vegetation was densely intertwined and formed small, firm islands, it usually was sufficient to take along duckboards and snowshoes. Furthermore, some of the brush was cut down and used to cover the soft ground between these islands.

The vast forest and swamp regions of European Russia offer little opportunity for the employment of airborne forces. Small paratroop units might perhaps be dropped over clearings or some of the few open stretches of firm ground, but even then it is imperative that these airborne units operate in close coordination with forward elements because they will not be able to hold out on their own behind the enemy lines for any length of time.

In the Russian forests and swamps even the successful breakthrough of an enemy position usually did not mean that the struggle for that position was over. Only on rare occasions did the enemy withdraw his forces completely from such areas. As a rule he reestablished himself quickly and forced the attacker to dislodge him again from his new hideouts and strong points. Even a victorious force must therefore take full precautions in the form of reconnaissance and security measures and continue to patrol the area for dispersed enemy units. For days and even weeks remnants of Russian units and individual Red soldiers held out behind the German lines in completely hopeless situations, harassing and disrupting German rear communications.

CHAPTER 54

Defense

In wooded and swampy areas, where the attacker is usually less familiar with the terrain, the defending force will make every effort to increase this natural element of uncertainty and to keep the enemy in the dark about the situation. This may be accomplished by outpost action, raids and ambushes, aggressive patrol activity, effective camouflage, mines and booby traps planted on the enemy's natural avenues of approach, and the construction of tank traps.

In forests of moderate depth the location of the main line of resistance will depend upon the possibilities of observation available to the supporting artillery. The edge of the forest must be avoided because it serves as a reference for hostile artillery observation. Even if the defender withdraws into the forest for only a short distance, he will hardly eliminate this disadvantage. Therefore, the most advanced defenses are preferably located either far outside or at a safe distance inside the woods. In the latter case, combat outposts must be placed at the edge of the forest where some rifles and automatic weapons can be very effectively employed from trees.

Positions located outside the woods have the advantage of better command and control facilities and are also more easily provided with effective fire support. Their main disadvantage lies in the difficulty of obtaining proper cover and concealment.

In large forest areas the main line of resistance runs across woods and swamps far from the edge of the forest. It is irregular in trace and well concealed from ground and air observation. Many principles otherwise applied to the defense, such as the use of flanking fire and the need for good artillery observation, are of secondary importance here. The primary requirement is to keep the attacker from discovering whether he has actually hit the main line of resistance, an outpost line, or a strong point, or what relation the resistance encountered locally may have to the general plan of defense.

It was one of the characteristics of combat in Russian forest regions that, upon transition from mobile to static warfare, defense positions established during an engagement did not form a continuous line. Furthermore, lakes and moors, impenetrable stretches of forest wilderness, and other natural obstacles in many places prevented the usual close contact between the opposing forces.

In the forest an effective battle position capable of meeting any form of attack should be a fortified zone comprising all types of defensive installations. Its main strength lies in a well-prepared fire plan for all weapons and in the extensive but inconspicuous use of tactical wire and mines in the outpost area. The Russians preferred mass employment of mines ahead of their main line of resistance and planted antipersonnel, antitank, and wooden mines in their main battle area.

A cleverly devised system of obstacles, in addition to holding up the enemy, should also have the effect of leading him into false directions and of exposing the attacking troops to flanking fire. All obstacles must be in sight of well-concealed outguards or sniper positions. Abatis may increase the value of obstacles but should not be permitted to obstruct the field of fire. Dug-in tanks may be used to form key points of the defense. In many situations decisive results can be obtained by weapons which hold their fire until the last moment and then hit the enemy with devastating effect. All these defensive measures call for time-consuming preparations made in conformity with a carefully devised plan and executed in proper order of priority. The location of mines must be entered on maps to prevent accidents to friendly troops.

Obviously, the greatest possible concentration of artillery should be used to meet an attack. But the number and employment of artillery units will depend chiefly on the nature of the terrain. Furthermore, every battery position must be organized as a strong point capable of all around defense.

Numerous small reserve units are placed throughout and closely behind the main battle position to repulse by prompt local counterthrusts any hostile forces that may succeed in passing through the defensive line. Individual tanks are of great value for that purpose if the possibilities for their commitment have been carefully reconnoitered and prepared. Not too much reliance, however, should be placed on organized counterattacks. German experience has shown that they are never executed in time.

The question whether a position is safe from armored attack requires careful examination. This can never be determined on the basis of map information alone but must be thoroughly checked by ground reconnaissance. The Russian proved to be a past master of infiltration over the most difficult type of terrain and was capable of stubbornly pursuing his objective under almost incredibly adverse conditions.

Clearing of fire lanes is usually a difficult task and may involve the risk of disclosing the location of positions. In many cases, the careful removal of underbrush will suffice to assure defensive fires at effective range. For this purpose large clearings, often the result of forest fires, should be integrated into the defensive system. Large open areas behind the front, which might be used by the enemy for the landing of airborne troops, should be carefully guarded and adequately protected.

The efficient exercise of command in a defensive situation, as in the offense, requires the establishment and maintenance of a well-functioning messenger and signal communication system. In an area of forests and swamps not much can be expected for this purpose from aircraft alone. In addition to radio the most primitive means of sending messages, such as runners, mounted messengers, and visual signals, might prove to be the most reliable. Listening-in stations for the purpose of intercepting enemy wire communications are more easily established in forests than in open terrain. With adequate concealment provided by dense vegetation, it is often possible to place ground rods close to the enemy and, under particularly favorable conditions, even behind the enemy lines. Deeply rooted, hardwood trees in wet ground often can be used to pick up currents from enemy ground return circuits.

In heavily forested mountains the main defensive effort is directed toward the blocking of passes and roads. The selection of defensive positions should be made on the basis of a thorough terrain reconnaissance, and special consideration should be given to the danger of being outflanked by the enemy. Particularly in dense woods, this possibility is all too frequently overlooked. Obstacles can be constructed quickly with the use of tactical wire, mines, and felled trees. They are of value only if they can be covered by fire to hinder their removal by the enemy.

Lateral communications behind the front must be reconnoitered and improved to permit the shifting of counterattacking forces and other reserves at any time even through dense and pathless woods. When corduroy roads are constructed for that purpose, the fact should not be overlooked that through continuous use they will gradually sink into the swamp.

Should the enemy succeed in penetrating a position in forests and swamps, those units that have not been dislodged must protect their flanks and stand their ground. Individual strong points must provide for all around defense and hold out until counterattacks by reserves have restored the situation. On principle, groups of buildings present in the area should be organized into strong points. The Germans found that Russian blockhouses, usually of very low construction, were well suited for that purpose. As a rule, these buildings commanded the few routes of communication and had facilities for drinking water.

In swamps and marshes the defending force clings to islands, dunes, farmhouses, clumps of trees, and any natural elevations in the terrain. Digging-in is frequently impossible because of the high groundwater level. In areas of this type a small but well-trained unit, familiar with the terrain and determined to take every possible advantage of impassable stretches, ponds, fallen trees, or peat pits, is often able to delay a far superior enemy for a long time. This was amply demonstrated by the effective resistance of the Finnish Army against the onslaught of the many times superior Russian forces during the winter campaign of 1941.

A system of defenses in the swamp may also include artificial islands, such as anchored rafts, stacks of wooden planks, or peat piles, provided they are adequately camouflaged. In the lagoons and reed flats of the Taman Peninsula, which separates the Black Sea from the Sea of Azov, German and Russian lines faced each other for weeks with observation and fields of fire reduced to very short distances. Their positions were mainly artificial islands constructed of reeds and logs and connected by narrow channels. In such areas, where the nature of the terrain severely restricted the usefulness of all types of vehicles including tractors, the problem of supplying the German frontline troops could only be solved with the aid of various expedients. All vehicles and self-propelled guns carried short fascine mats about four feet wider than their tracks. In most instances, however, supplies were moved by pack animals, pack bearer columns, on swamp sleds, or even in improvised boats; sometimes supply operations on the ground had to be supplemented by air drops.

CHAPTER 55

Retrograde Movements

In retrograde movements through forests and swamps there is always the danger that the enemy, by concentrating against a few selected places, might break through or overtake the withdrawing force. The defender who wants to break contact with the enemy and withdraw his troops takes advantage of the vastness of woods and swamps to obscure the movement of the main body, to cause successive delays to the pursuing forces, and inflict the greatest possible losses on them. For this purpose covering forces must maintain contact with the enemy and prevent him from conducting a rapid pursuit. All elements that are no longer needed for actual combat, especially supply trains and units of limited mobility, must be withdrawn at an early stage, at the cost of whatever comforts these units normally provide to the troops.

Especially at night and during the extended periods of morning and evening fog that are characteristic of damp forests and swamps, the evacuation of a position cannot be observed from the air or ground. Information on such a withdrawal can be obtained only through the continuous activity of combat patrols and from the statements of captured enemy personnel. Units engaged in rapid pursuit, on the other hand, must not permit themselves to be lured into a trap, which the enemy had ample opportunity to prepare, and thus be cut off entirely from their main force.

In the execution of German retrograde movements in Russian forests, proper timing was of paramount importance. As a rule, a body of troops was not withdrawn alone but in connection with similar movements on adjacent fronts. Higher headquarters would prescribe the time for the beginning and completion of the movement and designate intermediate lines of resistance as well as the ultimate defense positions. Pertinent orders were issued as early as possible to lower echelon commanders who then proceeded to make the necessary preparations for the withdrawal.

Subordinate unit commanders were first briefed about the mission, the disposition of forces, and the time available for the entire operation. Unit boundaries were announced in accordance with the existing road net. Successive lines of resistance based on natural compartments in the woods and swamps were designated on the map. The requirement that the enemy, after taking one line of resistance, should be forced to displace his artillery before attacking the next line determined the proper distance between successive lines.

Construction units were attached to the forward elements of the command according to the importance of their tactical missions. The Germans did not find it advisable to have higher headquarters direct the fortification of lines, much as it may seem desirable to take this burden from subordinate units who are still engaged in combat. Experience proved beyond doubt that a unit which planned and fortified its own line defended it with greater obstinacy. Therefore, the preparation of lines of resistance in a retrograde movement was the definite responsibility of lower echelons (division, brigade, combat team) within their respective sectors.

Whenever sufficient time and adequate construction forces are available, the fortification of several successive lines of resistance should be started simultaneously. Viewed in the perspective of subsequent withdrawal actions, it is a tactical error to waste time and labor on the line of resistance closest to the enemy. As a result positions farther to the rear will be inadequately prepared or not prepared at all. Particularly in the closeness of woods and swamps a unit engaged in a retrograde movement for any length of time must be able to fall back on prepared positions. If such positions do not exist, the battle will assume the characteristics of a war of movement in which the advantage is clearly on the side of the stronger attacking force.

When any retrograde movement is begun, demolition measures acquire increased importance. Such measures include burning or blowing up all bridges, demolishing roadbeds, destroying wells, flooding fords, and mining all narrow passages. A detailed demolition plan—depending on the time and the number of engineer troops available—must be prepared for every sector. Much more effective than a large number of demolitions can be a few large scale demolitions at points of tactical importance where repair work is difficult and few bypasses, if any, exist. (Such places may later be turned into permanent obstacles to the enemy by subjecting his repair efforts to constant interference from the air.) All bypasses, of course, must be heavily mined.

The Russians invariably planted time bombs and booby traps by the thousands in areas they were forced to evacuate. They also used demolitions on the largest scale, often carried out in chains of great density, to tear up the few available hard-surfaced roads.

Retrograde movements are not necessarily damaging to the morale of the soldier. If the commander succeeds in maintaining proper control and achieves some striking successes in the conduct of the defense and if he does everything possible to care for the combat troops, their fighting spirit will remain unimpaired.

CHAPTER 56

Combat under Special Conditions

At night or in fog most of the difficulties normally encountered in forests and swamps are greatly intensified. In terrain of that type, therefore, large-scale engagements at night should be avoided. The attack bogs down in most cases, friendly troops fire on each other, the danger of confusion and panic increases, and the result is failure.

Activities during night and in fog will be restricted, as a rule, to reconnaissance and raids on well-defined, nearby objectives. Even after a successful breakthrough, a night advance through the woods will usually fail to produce the desired results. It is far better to let the troops rest, reorganize, and not continue the advance over wooded and swampy terrain until daybreak.

If the situation is such that a tactical movement at night cannot be avoided or if conditions appear unusually favorable, only small task forces should carry out the advance during darkness, the remainder of the main force following at daybreak. It is clear that at night any movement through woods and swamps will take much longer than during the day. Bright moonlight may reduce many difficulties, but it will at the same time aid the enemy in his defense.

Heavy frosts create favorable conditions for movements and offensive action in wet forests and particularly in swamps, because the hardened surface of the ground permits far better utilization of the terrain for tactical purposes. On the other hand, the rapid construction of earthworks in deeply frozen soil of high moisture content will be extremely difficult.

In cold weather the numerous lakes and ponds characteristic of northern European Russia, Karelia, and the Pripyat River basin lose their value as military obstacles. At the same time they offer excellent opportunities for the take-off of aircraft equipped with sledge runners.

Snow, particularly large snowdrifts, will constitute a considerable hindrance to all movements. It may require extensive snow clearing operations and the construction of special winter roads. Furthermore, a single heavy snowfall can neutralize the effect of all minefields in the area. But it will also create favorable conditions for the employment of properly equipped ski troops, which are ideally suited for the rapid execution of long-range reconnaissance and combat missions in forests and swamps. For such purposes a supply of sleds, protective winter clothing, snow goggles, and white camouflage suits must be held in readiness. In an area blanketed by snow effective concealment is very difficult to obtain. Footprints and ski tracks in the forest are easily detected by the enemy.

Thaw and masses of melting snow will slow military operations in every type of terrain. In forests and swamps such conditions can have the effect of virtually immobilizing a substantial force for some time. All maneuvers are limited to the movement of foot troops, cavalry, and the lightest type of vehicles. Small unit actions take the place of large-scale operations.

Twice each year, during the spring and fall muddy seasons, the terrain difficulties normally encountered in Russian forests and swamps become insurmountable, and large areas turn into formidable natural obstacles in the path of any military advance. Heavy floods are not infrequent and impose serious restrictions on all military operations. On such occasions the construction and maintenance of even the smallest airfield or landing strip will be a difficult problem.

Entire sections of tall forests are sometimes knocked down overnight by violent windstorms, with the effect of blocking any passage. Also, the occurrence of extensive forest fires, often the result of long periods of drought, may force the military command to alter its plans of operation.

In World War II the large forest and swamp regions of European Russia were the natural sanctuaries for growing partisan cells and provided ideal conditions for their purposes. Remnants of Red Army units, having escaped capture or annihilation in earlier engagements, were able to hide in almost inaccessible places and often formed the nuclei around which the partisans rallied. Bands of hardy individuals, well acquainted with the terrain and controlled by fanatical leaders, were combined into a substantial fighting organization and conducted ruthless guerrilla warfare against the German forces in the woods and swamps within and behind the combat zone.

It should be pointed out, however, that while things are going well the effect of partisan activities on the course of major military operations is not quite so serious as one might believe or anticipate on the basis of some reports. The danger grows considerably as soon as an advance is halted, the occupying forces suffer reverses, or the attackers fail to take effective countermeasures at an early stage. Then the partisans will rapidly increase their efforts against railroads, highways, and communication lines which, in woods and swamps, are as scarce as they are vulnerable.

During World War II Russian partisan raids on German rear installations eventually assumed serious proportions and forced the occupation troops to resort to complicated protective measures and police actions. Toward the end of the war the vast Russian forest areas were becoming so insecure that a special warning radio channel had to be included in the signal operation instructions of higher headquarters, to be used exclusively for urgent calls for assistance in case a unit or strong point was attacked or threatened by partisans.

Ordinary combat units are not particularly well suited for partisan warfare. As a rule, they lack the necessary flexibility and thus are not equal to the combat methods of a tough and ruthless enemy who is usually invisible, difficult to apprehend, and who attacks without warning. Partisan combat calls for special units which are properly equipped and thoroughly trained in forest fighting. Local inhabitants may be used as valuable reinforcements, but only if their loyalty has been assured beyond doubt.

The key to success against partisans operating in wooded and swampy areas where ordinary means of intelligence fail is a smoothly functioning network of agents and informants. This alone will make it possible to identify and apprehend the more important leaders and to locate and seize main supply bases. Following the pattern of large-scale police raids, such anti-partisan actions must converge on a definite objective, achieve complete surprise, and be executed with the utmost thoroughness. Merely combing through a vast forest and swamp area for partisans or trying to seal it off will require the use of inordinately large forces and may have the effect of pacifying the area temporarily. But the result in the long run will hardly justify the means employed.

Under German occupation in World War II the villages in the Russian forests and swamps required constant surveillance.

Their inhabitants—some voluntarily, some under pressure— cooperated with the partisans and gave them valuable support, not so much as combatants but, at the least, as agents and informers. The use of force on the part of the German occupation troops (evacuation, taking of hostages, punitive expeditions) fell far short of producing the desired results. Since the Russian partisans hardly adhered to the rules of civilized warfare, such measures were most likely to provoke reprisals against German troops and against the friendly elements among the local population.

Railroads and highways leading through partisan-infested areas had to be protected in two ways. First, it was necessary to establish an effective network of strong points and fortified blockhouses, and then highly mobile patrols had to operate at irregular intervals along the threatened routes. Through many areas vehicles could only move in convoy and, on numerous occasions, the Germans had to use tanks, armored cars, or armored railroad trains to avoid heavy casualties from partisan attacks.

As the war progressed, the Russians employed aircraft in the logistical support of their partisan forces. To an ever-increasing degree, leaders, specialists, weapons, rations, and equipment were flown to the partisan centers. Shielded by large forests and virtually impassable swamp areas, such operations could hardly be prevented by German measures taken on the ground. Only through intensive aerial reconnaissance by day and night and by intercepting enemy radio communications was it at all possible for the Germans to identify the location of probable landing areas. Since even the Russian fliers had great difficulty in orienting themselves at night over large wooded areas, the Germans occasionally, through the use of deceptive devices, succeeded in inducing enemy pilots to drop their loads or land their planes on German-held air strips.

Conclusions

Combat in woods and swamps calls for great endurance and unusual resourcefulness. The German soldier fighting in Russia would have been in a much better position to stand the physical and psychological strain involved if he had been previously subjected to a thorough training program in that specialized type of warfare. The following is a list of subjects that should be included in such a program:

1. Instruction in the peculiarities of forest and swamp fighting.
   a. Training in endurance of hardships imposed by unusual climatic conditions such as excessive humidity, subzero temperatures, extended periods of darkness, and violent storms.
   b. Effect of these peculiarities on the individual and the unit.
2. Adjustment to the natural conditions encountered during a lengthy stay in wooded and swampy regions.
   a. Training the eye and ear for the sights and sounds characteristic of forests and swamps; recognition of tracks; woodcraft.
   b. Practice in pathfinding and orientation in densely overgrown terrain by day and night and during all seasons of the year, with or without the help of technical aids.
   c. Practice in moving swiftly and noiselessly through high forests, second growth, thickets, and morass, with particular emphasis on continuous observation, effective use of cover and concealment, and constant readiness for action.
3. Special instruction in close combat, using the most suitable weapons and techniques.

    a. Practice in rapid fire on close targets; training as tree-snipers, using telescopic sights.

    b. Preparing ambushes and organizing raids.

    c. Close cooperation of separate assault detachments with each other and with special antitank detachments.

    d. Construction and defense of blockhouses, strong points, and artificial islands in swamps.

    e. Ski training and the use of winter camouflage.

4. Preparation of earthworks and other defense installations.

    a. Use of whatever materials may be available such as felled trees, bushes, and reeds, with emphasis on proper concealment to blend with the surrounding foliage.

    b. Construction of cover and foxholes in spite of high ground-water levels.

5. Promotion of personal resourcefulness in case of separation from the unit.

    a. Construction of primitive shelters made of logs, brushwood, reed, or snow.

    b. Building of fires with wind protection for heating or cooking.

    c. Training in first aid in case of accidents or snakebite; protection against vermin.

    d. Recognition of edible fruits, berries, or mushrooms.

    e. Observation from trees; use of pole climbers.

    f. Instruction in the most important phrases and written characters of the enemy's language.

Unit training also must be adjusted to the unusual requirements of combat in forests and swamps. Such a program, which would presuppose the completion of individual training, would have to include the following:

1. Exercises for troop commanders with the use of maps and sand tables for the solution of difficult problems of movement, particularly designed to promote efficiency in the assembly and movement of supplies as required for combat in wooded terrain.

2. Command post exercises extending over several days, for

the purpose of training staffs and communications personnel in guiding columns through woods and swamps with the aid of maps, compasses, stars, and other references.

3. Exercises in the assembly and movement of entire units, including their rear echelons.
    a. Movement at night and under other conditions of poor visibility.
    b. Rapid construction of short stretches of corduroy road.
    c. Training entire march units in turning around on corduroy roads and on narrow, swampy forest trails.
    d. Preparation by each unit of all around defense at halts in forests and swamps.
    e. Training suitable officers and noncommissioned officers as leaders of raiding parties.

4. Thorough preparation of the various arms and services for their special missions in woods and swamps.
    a. Training engineers in repair of swampy roads and in the technique of removing mines and obstacles.
    b. Training tank commanders in the tactics and techniques of armored combat in woods.
    c. Training the artillery in observation and fire direction in densely overgrown terrain.
    d. Training service troops in the use of pack animals when moving through underbrush, ravines, and swampy areas.
    e. Training air observers in recognition and photographic reconnaissance over dense forests.

5. Checking conditions and loading plans of all vehicles with a view toward their increased use.

6. Training in service and maintenance of motor vehicles exposed to excessive wear and tear in difficult terrain.

7. Special sanitation courses in the prevention of epidemics, frostbite, and disease likely to occur as a result of living on damp ground.

The experienced instructor will find many additional possibilities to prepare his unit technically and tactically for commitment in forests and swamps. (Under expert guidance even premilitary training and Boy Scout exercises can bring out—in the form of play—many of the important attributes required for combat in wooded and swampy terrain.) Never should this type of training be permitted to lose its close relation to actual combat. The techniques of war are subject to change. Therefore, every new experience must become the knowledge of each person concerned, and that as rapidly as possible.

During World War II, in adherence to this principle, it was part of the mission of the Training Branch of the German Army High Command to evaluate and disseminate new combat experiences in the shortest time possible. Combat-experienced officers and specialists were assigned as temporary observers to critical combat areas, and field commanders were required to submit brief reports on combat experiences after each major engagement. The knowledge gained in this manner was then made available to the service school, sometimes even to the smallest units, in the form of circulars, training manuals, booklets, and pamphlets.

All these measures, however, will solve only part of the problem. To assure maximum performance, not only the instruction and training of individuals and entire units but also clothing and rations, equipment of men and horses, weapons and vehicles must be adjusted according to climate and geography to the varying requirements of combat in forests and swamps. Still, even the best and most complete preparations will not rule out the possibility that some units or individuals might find themselves in situations in which all available means are inadequate. In addition to thorough training and the best type of equipment, therefore, the soldier will need self-confidence and the ability to make use of improvisations and field expedients.